Home

A Personal Geography of Sheffield

Carl Lee

Fou Fou Publishing

Published by

Fou Fou Publishing

185 Sandford Grove Road,
Sheffield S7 1RS

ISBN: 978-0-9561957-0-8

Printed in Sheffield by

Front cover: Sheffield from Brown Edge, Ringinglow.

Acknowledgements: So many people have willingly given of their time to help me write this book, most didn't know me from Adam. But particular thanks to Peter Birtles, David Blunkett, Mary Byrd, Gian Bohan, Alan Capes, Paul Cocker, John Cornwall, Danny Dorling, Neil Fitzmaurice, Richard Hawley, Johnnie Higginbottam, Sally James, John Killion, Ian Lee, Donald McLean, John Mitchell, Joe Mhlongo, John Palmer, Jan Wilson, and finally generations of Geography students who have endured my ramblings.

In memory of Martin Jackson

"Sic transit gloria mundi"

Carl Lee was born and raised in Bedfordshire. He came to study at Sheffield City Polytechnic in 1982 and has strived to become a local ever since. He has been a lecturer in Geography at Sheffield College since 1995.

His is co-author (with Graham Drake) of 'The Urban Challenge' (2000) Hodder and Stoughton.

Contents

Preface

Why bother? Normally there has to be a reason. Sometimes it is a broken down rural retreat to renovate, a new language to master, strange foreign cultures and customs to negotiate, perhaps even a desire to discover the inner me among the cicadas of a Mediterranean garrigue.

How about because it is there and so am I.

This book is about living in Sheffield, over a year, 2008. For me this is nothing new. I've done it loads of times. In fact I've clocked up 25 years, on and off, since arriving in Sheffield in October 1982 to take up a not very highly coveted place at Sheffield City Polytechnic.

It wasn't exactly love at first sight. I initially spent days tramping the streets of this alien city, with just my passing acquaintance of London and an upbringing in a southern shire county market town as reference points.

In my first term I was sent, Marsmatic pen in hand, to map the land use of the Lower Don Valley, Sheffield's steel-making heart. I discovered an awe inspiring conglomeration of blackened and mostly derelict hulks, with occasional hints of what used to be until a matter of years before. A thumping drop forge, the glow of a furnace through the holes in ill-repaired steel walls. Eerie streets of cobblestones criss-crossing rubble strewn wastelands cut through by a dank, hemmed in River Don. It got much worse a few years later.

When, in 1985, I graduated with an improbable degree in Geography, I should have done what all that learning had suggested to me, and what any sane and vaguely ambitious graduate would of have done, flee back south. But it was too late. I was smitten. I was a Sheffielder; it's just nobody local would believe me for another couple of decades.

This isn't really a love letter to a city. If it was I would have to admit I have been unfaithful. Over the years, Barcelona, Montpellier, Delhi, Nottingham, Bangalore and Amsterdam have all had a good tug at my heartstrings in one way or another. I've even flirted with the countryside. Of course the Peak District, that goes without saying. What middle class teacher in Sheffield hasn't entertained a fantasy of a rural retreat in Andalucía/Provence/Tuscany/Greece (delete as appropriate) at some point as they wrestle with a bottom set year 9 on a Friday afternoon?

It was the seemingly remorseless exhortation of the delights of everything beyond our shores that drew me into looking at Sheffield anew. It wasn't just the plethora of reality relocation TV shows; “This week we visit the bijou Stalinist flats of Moldavia to show you where the sensible investment money is now going”. Nor the acres of newsprint devoted to the charms of the Cape Verde Islands and other far-flung outposts of the 'equity investment possibility'. It was a BBC News website which invited ex-patriots to e-mail in why they had left Britain that really did it for me.

Now don't get me wrong. I'm all for broadening your horizons; I spent a year tramping around India, I have backpacked through China and even lived in Nottingham for a couple of years. However I quite like this little island. But casting my eyes over the pages of posts in response to the posed question I started to think about why I hadn't fled to sunnier, less taxed climes? See for yourself.

'Home' Preface

Published: Monday, 11 December, 2006, 08:54 GMT UK BBC News: Have Your Say

> **"Almost one in 10 British citizens lives overseas, according to new research.**
>
> The study, carried out by the Institute of Public Policy Research, and published on the BBC News website, suggested that at least 5.5 million Britons are living abroad and that this number is likely to grow.
>
> Researchers found that 75% of expat Britons are based in 10 countries. These are Australia, France, Spain, Germany, Canada, Ireland, Cyprus, the US, New Zealand and South Africa.
>
> **Have you moved away from the UK? What do you think of the report's findings? If you live abroad, why did you leave your native country? Send us your comments."**

Three of the most popular choices were as follows. First with 246 recommendations was David Horton.

> **"Many have gone because they are frustrated by astonishingly corrupt, overtaxing and incompetent government, a feeling exacerbated by a multicultural society where it is a crime to be English.**
>
> **As more of the country [*sic*] wealth creators leave, we will increasingly be living in a melting pot of internationality.**
>
> **This Sceptred Isle is truly becoming a Septic Isle."**

Or how about second placed David from Newport;

> **"Given the state this country is in, with rampant crime, a huge influx of mainly the wrong kind of immigrant (i.e. unproductive and hostile to western values) over the last ten years, and the simpering egalitarian, socialist nonsense peddled by our excuse for a government, is anyone really surprised that so many native British people are leaving?"**

But I think Peter from Middlesbrough really tipped it for me.

> **"Why do I want to leave? Political correctness, multiculturalism, ghettos, violence, racism (I am called honky & whitey in London), declining social values, high cost of living, skewed legal system, high taxes & freeloaders living off my taxes, my house is a magnet for welfare thieves, we pay the highest taxes in Europe & get the worst services, & a hundred more reasons. I am leaving while I can still afford to, but before I go I am going to cast my vote for the BNP to show my utter disgust."**

If you are nodding to yourself thinking "umm yes I can see what Peter is getting at" this probably isn't the book for you. You could probably run a competition to see who could spot the most factual inaccuracies in Peter's rant but there is no doubt that it is heartfelt and vitriolic. Mind you stuff a balanced critique, fuck off to where ever you are going and hand your passport in as you leave if you wouldn't mind Peter. We don't want your sort around this way again.

Even allegedly respectable politicians, such as Conservative George

Walden, were getting in on the act by publishing a book entitled 'Time to Emigrate'. If only he would.

The idea that Britain was going to 'hell in a handcart' was clearly gaining currency, yet I couldn't see it, couldn't quite grasp it. This was despite the fact that I fed myself a daily diet of The Guardian (hardly a happy bunny) and The Independent (The left-wing Daily Mail). I had the relentless cynicism of the Today Programme on BBC Radio 4 to negotiate before work and if I was really unfortunate I might catch Melanie Philips on the Moral Maze in the evening. This normally resulted in me destroying the radio in moral indignation that at least suggested I'd made my way out of the maze.

I had just witnessed, and been a part of, a quite remarkable transformation, in fact a transformation that had appeared to be increasing in pace as the first decade of the 21st century started to slip away. Was society crumbling before me? My taxes just used to give handouts to freeloading asylum seekers or endless nanny state bureaucrats or even worse, subsidies for French farmers.

It seemed that so many people who wanted to leave, or had left the country, felt that this transformed Britain had somehow lost its sense of itself. The longest period of continuous economic growth that Britain had ever experienced in modern times was as nothing. By any quantitative measure it could be demonstrated that never had the average Britain been wealthier, consumed more of the world's scarce resources and been as healthy and long lived. It might be stretching it a bit to call it a golden age but it wasn't 1984, when de-industrialisation, mass unemployment, the miner's strike and the Russian nuclear arsenal hung above our heads in our day-to-day lives.

Whatever Britain had become it wasn't what millions of my fellow citizens wanted it to become. They had voted with their feet but so had I. I'd stayed put. This was home.

Of course everybody's experience of living in Britain is shaped by the place they live in. This to some extent is what is known as psychogeography. The study and engagement with the specific effects that the environment in which we live shapes our emotions and behaviour, how our sense of ourselves grows out of where we live and how we live.

This minor offshoot of mainstream Geography has tended to pride itself on its radical roots which lie with French intellectual and founder of the Situationist International, Guy Debord. 'The extraordinary' is what most of Debord's intellectual heirs search for in the city, however it is the banality of every day life punctuated with moments of sensory thrill that really shapes our relationship with space. This book is interested in the ordinary, the everyday, and even the mundane. All of it possibly extraordinary if only we place it in the right context.

Perhaps the most recognisable contemporary expression of psychogeography is Peter Ackroyd's “London a Biography”, a masterly and magical book about the nooks and crannies, places, spaces and people of the world's greatest city. The magic realism of local history. Suketa Mehta has delved deep into the soul of Mumbai in his book 'Maximum City' and Delhi has been revealed by William Dalrymple as a 'City of Djinns'. There are many other chroniclers of living cities I have yet to read.

The fascination with place and space abounds as we become more spatially cosmopolitan. Budget airlines have brought us stag nights in Tallin, gigs in Barcelona, art in Florence and the riads of Marrakech. We are increasingly aware of the emotional power of place. We are also more aware of alternatives and I guess it is those alternatives that so many of the migratory critics of Britain were exploring as they rejected a place that no longer 'filled up their senses'.

Sheffield is on very few peoples list of city breaks but its charms can often be heard about in various parts of Britain, hollered by travelling bands of Sheffield United supporters whose hymn to their home is rendered to the tune of John Denver's 'Annie's Song'.

"You fill up my senses
Like a gallon of Magnet
Like a packet of Woodbines
Like a good pinch of snuff
Like a night out in Sheffield
Like a greasy chip butty
Like Sheffield United
Come thrill me again."

What this song is about is an affinity to place realised through our senses. This could be the jagged but paradoxically smooth mosaics that adorn Gaudi's seats in Parc Gruell in Barcelona, the view of ordered chaos that lurches at you as you leave New Delhi's main railway station, the taste of a pint of Fullers in a London pub, the smell of grilled fish on the Gallata Bridge crossing the Golden Horn in Istanbul or the hum of the city and the rushing of the London bound train that is the soundtrack to long hot summer evenings in my back garden.

I would like to get a grip of the sensory architecture of Sheffield. I'm not sure exactly what that means in reality but I suspect it will help me to understand what made me call this place home. After all I could of chosen anywhere in this hyper-migratory world to live. I could still but it is going to take one hell of a pull or an almighty push now that Sheffield has seeped into my bones. This isn't about, as is sometimes uttered in Germany, "blut und boden"(blood and soil) it is more like that other German idea, that of an landscape and cultural idyll, "landschaften", except an urban rather than rural idyll.

In fact it is far from an idyll. Sheffield, so George Orwell observed in 'The Road to Wigan Pier' Sheffield could;

> **"justly claim to be called the ugliest town in the Old World: its inhabitants, who want it to be pre-eminent in everything, very likely, do make that claim for it".**

What leaves the greatest impression on Orwell is the stench of the city.

This stench is something I can only imagine, as Sheffield when I arrived in 1982 was a grubby, decaying city but also one that had greatly benefited from the clean acts of the 1950s. Yet the sulphurous stench of Sheffield is as significant factor on its layout as any other. The prevailing winds in Sheffield, some 45% across a year, come from the southwest, normally as part of a depression rolling into Britain off the Atlantic Ocean. A fact not lost on Sheffield's Victorian industrialists who choose to live in the southwest of the city to escape the worst of the outpourings of their wealth creating dark satanic mills. So much money was made that its expression in stone and mortar was a collection of suburbs that is beyond compare in England. Don't take my word for it consider the view of Sir John Betjeman, a man deeply attuned to the multifarious nuances of Britain. In 1961 he described the Sheffield suburb of Broomhill lyrically.

> **"Greek, Italian, Gothic, they stand in winding tree-shaded roads, these handsome mansions of the Victorian industrialists who made their pile from steel and cutlery in**

> **the crowded mills below. They lived in what is still the prettiest suburb in England."**

Personally I think if he had wondered a further mile west he would have had to reappraise this view as he would have been in Ranmoor, a suburb cloaked in a forest of trees punctuated by the precipitous spire of St John, a church described by Pevsner, Britain's greatest architectural historian, as "opulent outside and inside". Here the ultimate expression of solid Yorkshire wealth extracted from the labour of the masses found its pinnacle, Endcliffe Hall. Built for the steel magnate John Brown in the early 1860s, a time when Sheffield's bulk steel production was constructing an empire and forging the railway tracks that opened up America, Endcliffe Hall was the most sumptuous of all Sheffield's Victorian piles. It is relatively unloved and unseen today, a Territorial Army base, 212 RAMC (V) Yorkshire Field Hospital, its grand gardens broken up for new developments. Most people in Sheffield probably don't know it exists. But it is there shielded by its cloak of trees. If it were in London Roman Abramovich would probably live in it.

So whose view best fits Sheffield today, Orwell or Betjeman? Neither.

This book was initially meant to be a snapshot of life in Britain's fifth largest city in 2007, a Britain that both Orwell and Betjeman would only occasionally recognise from their post-war gaze, and a city whose realities that they, in their brief sojourns, could only guess at. However I got bogged down. Self-imposed deadlines were missed and events went uncharted. Life rattled on at breakneck speed.

However this midwinter evening, December 21st 2007, my resolve is anew. The days are getting longer. Term has ended. Santa's grotto has been visited and a bottle of Louis Latour Corton Chateau Grancy is winking suggestively at me. Sheffield 2008. Who needs to flee for sunny climes? Actually a persistent hill fog enveloped the city all day, so the thought did idle across my mind.

If you are still reading by April you can obviously assume that I've managed to get a bit better organised than last year. Alternatively my benevolent employer, The Sheffield College, has offered me redundancy and my life is reduced to kicking my heels in front of a word-processor. Either way a year in Sheffield, who knows what the future will hold? I've planned barely anything about this book. A blank page and circumstance awaits every month. Bring it on: but be warned I am a Geography lecturer and this is a book about Geography. I even used to own a tweed jacket with leather elbow patches.

Settle down at the back, we're about to begin.

January

Recent years have seen some very bright New Year's Day mornings. Cold, crisp, with a sharpness to the light that eludes you on even the very best of a summer's day. It's a good to be alive air, another year survived clarity and it is best taken in up high.

Fifteen minutes driving up Brincliffe Edge towards Bents Green and the Ringinglow Road beyond takes us to a pull off just beyond the forestry plantation, a stile, five minutes of treacherous boggy path and there stands a white gate, attached to nothing but a view.

And what a view. Spread out beneath me sits Sheffield, reached via a rapidly descending valley of wooded copses, stonewalled defined fields and a constrained suburbia. Four miles east the clustered city centre sits a few hundred metres below us.

Beyond the city the River Don valley and a collection of extremely large industrial buildings stretch towards the sentinels of 'Salt and Pepper', two defunct cooling towers that mark not only the site of the M1 flyover and the border with Rotherham but that cathedral to consumerism, Meadowhall Shopping Centre.

And beyond that Yorkshire and Humberside revealed. On a crisp, clear winter's morning the plumes of condensing air rise miles into the sky from a line of Trent Valley power stations. Furthest north is the big daddy of them all, Drax, just outside Pontefract, at least 40 miles away. Its plume the biggest contribution a single place in the UK makes to atmospheric carbon dioxide. These engines of climate change are just a benign addition to a huge, breathtaking view on a morning like this.

'Home' Chapter 1: January

Turn around and unbroken moorland, with no sign of human habitation, stretches off to the far horizon. In the summer meadow pipits flit through the heather and skylarks swoop across the huge sky endlessly proclaiming their affinity with this bucolic landscape. On this January morning only a biting westerly wind welcomed us.

I remind myself why I live in Sheffield.

It is not just the city, it is this. The ability to rise above it all. The green frame to a dirty picture, as it used to be said in Sheffield's glory days of big steel.

A few years ago I spent almost the entire month of July in an enclosed windowless edit suite with a colleague. We were piecing together a student made video about the economic history of Sheffield. The student's camera work was at an embryonic stage and we couldn't find any acceptable footage to end the film with. On a peerless summer morning we grabbed a camera and drove up to this spot and shot a long focus sweep across the city, panning into the cooling towers. The city hummed in unison with the insects around us. Like this January day not a cloud crossed the sky. The heat haze obscured the horizon. It was perfect.

On that summer's day we pushed on for a couple of miles across Hallam Moor until we came to Burbage Brook Bridge. Here the Hathersage country road clips the edge of widening cragged valley that wraps itself around the tor and Iron Age fort of Carl Wark before dropping down into the Derwent Valley. We were cheating a little as we clambered onto the rocks below the bridge where, even in a hot dry July, the water draining off the moor vigorously plunged down. We shot a sequence of water tumbling over rocks, it was the gravity, the potential energy we wanted to show. The voiceover for this section said;

> **"From as early as the 14th century artisans harnessed the power of these rivers to power the forges that started to produce what would eventually become known as one of the World's first global brands; metalwork stamped 'Made in Sheffield'.**

In reality this stream would end up looping southwards where the River Derwent would meet up with the River Trent which would then bisect Nottingham, before increasingly meandering northwards providing the coolant for that series of power stations that are the backbone of Britain's electricity supply. Some of this water, utilised as a coolant, would no doubt evaporate into the air from these energy generating turbines, as if part of a huge cloud making enterprise. An idea I really believed below the age of six, but solely on the advice of my father.

The stream was important to us to get our point across. Like so many places around the world Sheffield's fortunes to some extent were based on water. It was the ability to harness the fast flowing streams tumbling out of the Pennine Hills that led to the development of Sheffield as a place that basically clouted, crushed and belted metals into a myriad of shapes and forms.

The streams tumbling eastwards out of the Pennines all congregated in the River Don and it was at the confluence of The River Sheaf and The River Don that an aspirational immigrant, the improbably named William de Lovetot, decided that this is where he would plant his French/Danish roots way back in the late 11th century.

No doubt locals already existed. One of my old Geography lecturers at Sheffield City Polytechnic, Melvyn Jones, is a mine of information on the historical geography of place-names in South Yorkshire. The Viking 'thorps' of Hackenthorpe, Upperthorpe and Grimesthorpe. The Anglo-Saxon Loxley, Walkley and Heeley. All serve notice that those Norman usurpers, the Lovetot's, were muscling into an established turf.

The Iron Age hill fort of Wincobank, which still affords the finest view of Sheffield's post-industrial lower Don Valley, is tangible proof that the Normans were only following a well established path of conquest and subjugation; The Iron-Age Celts who laboured to create the ramparts of a fort on this dominating hill were also migrants from the east. New DNA research suggests Bulgaria; or rather what was Bulgaria 2500 years ago.

The impression they left is still visible, remnants of a now grassy rampart can be found amongst the scrubland that has now become the domain of dog walkers and daredevil teenage motorcyclists. This hogsback hill is on the horizon of the view I glance up at from the computer monitor in my office at home. Its prominence indicates why it was chosen as such effective defensible space. However it was not that defensible as the Celts era of dominance was ended by the Romans, who had very little interest in the area, and who left the locals to evolve slowly with changing times. It's hard to escape the fact that from the very beginning Sheffield was a place shaped by migration.

Regardless of all this pre Norman push and shove, the award for the founding father of Sheffield must go to the man with a name like an Acid House DJ, Lovetot. No statue of him exists, I suspect he had long hair and flowing robes and liked his madrigals at 180 BPM. What we do know is he built a castle. The remains of this lie under a 1960s homage to concrete, Castle Markets.

The redevelopment of this part of the city centre has provided archaeologists with the opportunity to excavate this site and talk is of some sort of display of its buried heritage being put on display within whatever replaces the soon to be demolished markets. Whatever is created to 'showcase' the physical roots of Sheffield it will not draw crowds from far and wide. Further down the River Don valley as it approaches Doncaster is the towering Norman keep of Conisborough Castle and westwards in the Peak District are the impossibly romantic ruins of Perevil Castle precipitously perched above Castleton. The competition when it comes to castles in Britain is stiff, although France could give us a run for our money.

But as the mantra of estate agents goes, location, location, location are the three most important things about where you live and Lovetot clearly was an 11th century Sarah Beeny. A bluff of land at the meeting of two rivers, clear views and a rich hunting forest made this prime Norman real estate. Add one bridge to traverse the widening River Don and you have all the ingredients for a small but thriving medieval town. None of it exists today and the castle, like so many across Britain, was torn apart by the republican forces of Oliver Cromwell in the late 1640's. Names remain; Waingate, Haymarket and Snig Hill still vie for acknowledgement in the A to Z.

Sheffield provides only a tantalising glimpse of its medieval heritage, if you want old York is really the place to go. However this could be seen as unfair competition, York really is swamped by its history. Further afield sites that are heralded as major tourist attractions can clock up but a fraction of the history of some Sheffield's surviving buildings. I recall a guided tour of the 'ancient' Siam city of Sukthai, north of Bangkok, where upon the proud description of a decaying pile of stone as a temple 250 years old I casually recalled that I knew people who lived in houses older than that; was that the best they could do? Mind you the ravenges of a tropical climate probably would have reduced most of Sheffield's early architecture to an indistinct pile of stone in double quick time as well.

If I had stood and pondered all of this on the windswept edge of Hallam Moor I would have frozen to death by the time you got to the part about pre Norman push and shove. That was last year. This year, 2008, it's a different meteorological mix. The cold crisp New Year's Day's has been supplanted by the sort of dank grey that leaves the horizon a theoretical place obscured by a mist that merges land and air into an indistinct amorphous mass. This is the sort of day when hungover aspirations are likely to be tinged with a sunny hue. Perhaps that new life in a finca in Portuguese Dao country growing olives and harvesting tourists in some converted barns.

Rather than admire the non-existent Yorkshire panorama afforded by a mist strewn Hallam Moor I choose to consider the possibility of a nicotine free life wondering through the forest of cranes that have sprouted in Sheffield city centre over the past year. 'Skyscappercity' the internet portal for those interested in all buildings tall has a community of building aficionados from Sheffield who keep an eye on cranes. At the beginning of December 2007 the figure was 31 across Sheffield. Of those, five are tightly clustered in the heart of Sheffield city centre putting together the last element of the geographically accurately named 'Heart of the City' project, Sheffield's flagship regeneration of it's once decaying city centre. These cranes are a good, tangible symbol of Sheffield's transformation. From them will rise a 32 storey residential block that will act as both economic phallus and marker point for a city reborn from a time, not so long ago, when some muttered about Sheffield becoming the first 'ghost city' of the post-industrial age.

However on this grey day, grey thoughts about such enthusiasm for the future abound. After a dozen years of unprecedented economic growth, a generation without appreciation of recession may be about to comprehend something of the dark days of Thatcherism that had laid much of Sheffield to waste.

A global 'credit crunch', born out of what was labelled a 'sub-prime default crisis' in the USA, had given ample demonstration to the notion of a globalised world economy when the first 'run' on a British bank for over one hundred years nearly bought a major high street bank to its knees. How this would all translate into the wider economy in 2008 had been speculated over in acres of newsprint, weeks of debate on TV and radio and the conclusion, “we're not sure” seemed to be the dominant view.

Could it be that 2008 would signal the end of what Gordon Brown boasted was the longest run of unbroken economic growth in modern British history? Would this result in the 'whitest of white elephants' littering Sheffield City Centre as testament to a speculative bubble on a par with the 1630 Dutch tulip boom? Was this idle speculation a reflection of the dreary drizzle that was starting to permeate my sieve like cagoule as I stared up at the vertiginous cranes? Maybe it was time to flee to a land where cagoules were a novel concept, only paraded on a few occasions a year, tropical downpours that sort of thing.

It came as no surprise that four days into the new year that the front page story of The Sheffield Telegraph was an exploration of this concern by Peter Kay, the leading journalist of Sheffield's best, well only, serious weekly newspaper He started off by stating;

> **"Sheffield city centre is facing a big challenge in 2008 as its revival is tested by the predicted economic downturn. Cranes have soared above much of the city centre over the past year-and more are due to rise above redevelopment sites. Council and business leaders believe the momentum is too strong to be knocked off course immediately, but the credit crunch and dip in the housing market have introduced elements of uncertainty."**

Peter probably only took advice from clear vested interests in putting together his piece. A bit more digging might have made for a more pessimistic assessment. Buoyant commercial markets had seen insurers Standard Life splash out £26million on the unfinished No2 St Paul's Place in the Heart of the City development in September 2007 but within a month British Land, owners of £1.7 billion Meadowhall were already hesitant about selling on a stake of its monolithic shopping centre due to the impending credit crunch. Morgan Stanley Bank suggested at the end of 2007 that British Land's share price was over valued by up to 33%. A similar situation applies to Hammerson developer of the proposed 'New Retail Quarter' in Sheffield. Norwich Union, who have a considerable presence within Sheffield, recently lost 50% of the liquidity of its property portfolio fund. In fact at the start of the year an estimate of £110 billion of potential defaults on commercial property globally paints a less than rosy picture.

However, whatever the economic prognosis for 2008 and beyond is for both the global economy and Sheffield, the city is now a long way from where it was twenty years ago. A crane count then would have been a quick and simple affair. And I was as optimistic about the future as anybody who had exchanged one of his best friends of the past 25 years with nicotine chewing gum could be. The city had travelled a long way. If it was about to crash and burn now, as a cursory glance of the media would have suggested, a quick fag would hardly make me feel any better. Things were not looking up, cranes accepted. The weather was Yorkshire grey and a new term was about to start.

The Thursday afternoon of the first week of term was spent discussing with a group of students what they understood about the concept of 'development'. Inevitably to begin with most of the ideas were concerned with 'having more'. Bigger houses, cars, more bling, money, wealth and luxury. This was the point of life and for some students the least work put into achieving this the better. When I suggested that 'love', friends, family, community and identity might be worth considering we started to move towards that bit of Geography where Philosophy is as important as space. What is the point of life?

If I had left my mobile on I might have had some help addressing that most perplexing of questions. My friend Mary had been trying to ring me to tell me that Jack, her life partner, my oldest friend from my polytechnic daze, had died in his sleep from a massive heart attack. He was 46. He was very interested in questions about development; he had a degree in Environmental Studies. These were ideas we had discussed hundreds of times without ever reaching a definitive answer. No number 42 for us. For Jack a dismally short 46 instead.

Jack was a southern man, not in the 'Lynard Skynard' sense, but in that he was born in Muswell Hill in London and raised facing France in Hythe just outside Folkestone. Like so many people he came to Sheffield to study and never left. I had first met him on the top deck of the 76 bus to Pitsmoor in January 1983; he looked my kind of hippie, a bit punky around the edges. It was the early 80s after all. He came round to my slum of a house on Page Hall Road the next evening and disparaged my record collection and left laughing. We became friends literally for life.

This was a time of dereliction and decay for the city but a time of growth and discovery for a gaggle of young, idealistic and hedonistic students studying Geography and Environmental Studies. And now we were going to meet up again, chastened by age, idealism honed into pragmatism, hedonism blunted by reality, to remember a life. An ordinary life not punctuated by great achievements or swept up in a dazzling career. A life that revelled in the everyday, the understatement, the mundane even. A life, which like the city in which it was lived, was the sum of a multitude of small parts. As the tears washed my face on that starlight dappled Thursday night, the slate roofs of thousands of city houses shone with the rainwater of the day's earlier storm, Sheffield always had the power to look melancholic with its hues of grey.

One of the first practical things that that I discussed with Jack's partner, Mary, was where he was going to be buried. His last resting place. The geography of memory.

No one knew whether Jack had ever expressed a preference to be buried or burned. And if buried where? It had certainly never been a topic of conversation around the dinner table. However he had always loved gardening and composting and it was felt that a return to the soil in a beautiful place certainly wouldn't have been against his wishes.

After a day or two of traversing the city, deflecting grief in a frenzy of activity, Mary settled on the council run green burial cemetery at Wisewood. This spot ticks all the boxes for somebody who loved

Sheffield, as Jack did. It was nestled down in the bottom of the Loxley Valley with the river burbling away beside it. Located on the outer edge of the city the dark horizon of The Peak District, perched behind Bradfield village at the end of the Loxley Valley, is a humbling backdrop to this saddest of sites. Mary and Jack had walked this valley in the early days of their romance. From the riverside stroll through woods and industrial archaeology, to the lowland heath atop Wadsley Hill north of the cemetery, this was as good a home as any within a world of infinite possibilities. In death as in life.

I wondered how many of those 5.5 million Briton's living abroad feel that way about where they live? That innate pull of soil or rock, of culture and history. All overlaid with the future lived out around your memory by your continuing kith and kin rooted in the local. I had once wandered through the derelict graveyards of colonial Calcutta, marvelling over the short brutality of the lives of so many laid to rest there. Malaria, childbirth even tigers had prematurely pruned the pioneers of Anglo-Saxon globalisation. How much did it matter that their immortality was reduced to a crumbling headstone alighted on by so few and even less who could comprehend their lives. Very little. In the general temporal scheme of things humanity, agriculture, society and cities are such a small fraction of our planets history. Undoubtedly all this will be but a foot note in galactic history. But that's the genius of life, it makes us feel that this is all here just for us, right here, right now, and then we delude ourselves we can have something so wonderful for ever.

Graveyards reflect the growth and development of a city and connect it with the people who shaped it. They fundamentally link both the city and its citizens to their personal and public past. In pre-industrial times burial was an act that was controlled to a large extent by the established church. They could deny burial to those ıot conform to its predefined ritual. The rapid expansion of ..d set in train by the industrial revolution brought with it ..a plenty. Life expectancy in the slums in the 1830s barely rea..ıed 30. That there was a need for more graveyards in the town was indisputable. An account in 1845 described a church in the middle of town as "very much crowded with bodies...the exudation of putrid liquid from the soil is visible to the eye and offensive to the smell". Sheffield's heavy clay soils clearly slowing down decomposition.

The industrial revolution through up a new class of citizenry, a dissenting class, whose wealth and development owed everything to manufacture, trade and commerce. Often this evolving middle class was drawn to ideas of non-conformism in both politics and religion. With the existing city church cemeteries full literally to bursting in 1834 a group 24 local industrialists set out a commercial burial ground on what was then the edge of the city, the River Porter valley beyond Sharrow. The Sheffield Central Cemetery was built to accommodate the expanding city and allowed citizens to escape the intellectual tyranny of established religion. This was one of the first cemeteries to encompass the Victorian principle of landscape, borrowed from the great English gardens and new urban graveyards, such as the famous Cimitiere Pere Lachaise that opened in Paris in 1804 - which served as a model for much of the Egyptian influenced architecture that was added to this new Sheffield cemetery.

A walk through the now full, remodelled and increasingly well looked after Sheffield General Cemetery is a walk through the lives of those who shaped Sheffield's past and present, some 87,000 in all.

The Cole Brothers, John, Thomas and Skelton, whose name will still adorn the largest department store in the 'New Retail Quarter' planned for the city centre. George Bassett of Liquorice Allsorts fame whose imprint in the city today remains the sweet smell of confectionary that wafts over Hillsborough. Industrialist Mark Firth, one of Sheffield's most notable Victorian philanthropists, (whose monument is fittingly surrounded by freshly painted cast iron railings) and Samuel Holberry, Chartist leader and potential revolutionary who, if he had not been grassed up and jailed as he prepared to seize control of Sheffield for the radicals, may have changed the political direction of Britain beyond imagination. All lie in close proximity to each other.

All of these eternal incumbents of the General Cemetery shaped Sheffield's consciousness and all chose to lay their mortal remains within its boundaries. For them a sense of place remains beyond life but one that was forged through life. I have walked the same streets as them, commanded the same views across the city's hills and breathed in the same air of belonging. Although our lives bare little comparison, the city in which they are played out in has underlying familiarities.

Only two months previously Jack and I had gorged ourselves on our familiar and shared city by completing the 'Sheffield Round Walk' 14 miles of rivers, goyts, blue bell saturated woodlands and open parkland. Conveniently its path goes right past my front door with its clear view across the heart of the city centre. Jack had breezily called around at 8.30am and within 90 minutes we stood perched on the edge of moorland staring down at the jumble of cranes that clearly marked the city centre. We talked about the new city developing before our eyes, we talked about the future and we talked about getting married, not to each other but to our respective partners who, for both of us, was a relationship of over twenty years.

'Home' Chapter 1: January

We ambled across the cricket pitches in Whirlow Park reminiscing about games we had played there. When we reached the sharp climb up Chancet Wood, a cut staircase through, what in April would become a hillside of blue, nodding bells, Jack waited for me, perched on the seat at the summit of the climb as I puffed my way up in his wake.

Nothing links us so finally to a place more than our grave or where our ashes are scattered. There was no hesitation in saying Jack would have wanted to be buried or burnt in Sheffield. We had never really talked about it, we were not that old, or so we thought. However, one of the few things that we could assert with utmost confidence was that Hawkwind's Silver Machine and the Orb's Fluffy White Clouds would have been his chosen music to enter his hippie Valhalla.

And so it was. When the doors of the northern memoriam room at Skew Hill Crematorium opened up the space rock chords of the once mighty Hawkwind welcomed the pallbearers. The entry was also a respite from the wind that shook the building perched, as it is, on the very ridge atop of the fore-mentioned hill. The panorama afforded by the magnificent windows that framed the rested wicker coffin was of scudding clouds across a pale blue January sky. Zephyrs of swirling leaves in the foreground gave the eye a pattern of randomness across a constant but dynamic backdrop.

Departing to the Orb's 'Fluffy White Clouds' the funeral party formed up a procession of 30 or so cars and slipping past the Birley Stone, which is perched on the summit of the hill, headed down into the upper Don Valley to Oughtibridge and the Wisewood Cemetery in the Loxley Valley.

This cemetery, although not that old, is filling up nicely with people who shaped Sheffield through the 20th century. It vies for space within Sheffield's hotly contested western greenbelt, which forms a development barrier between the city and the Peak District. This area of the urban fringe wasn't incorporated into the city of Sheffield until 1921. Today developers covetously eye up the old industrial sites for housing but essentially the valley retains the same character it has held since Victorian times. The Loxley was one of the river valleys upon which Sheffield's early industry was driven by the water wheel. It was along this valley that the waters released from The Dale Dyke Reservoir collapse on the 11th of March 1864 rushed, precipitating 'The Great Sheffield Flood'. The deaths of 240 people and monumental havoc the consequence. Today the cemetery was raked by a persistent wind aspiring to be a gale.

The cemetery slopes down the south-facing hillside until a copse of trees, through which the River Loxley flows, halts its descent. Nestled down at the bottom is Sheffield City Council's woodland burial ground, which although a relatively recent addition to the bereavement portfolio of the council, is already showing signs of the potential of what this site might evolve into. Young native trees are bedding down into the nutrient rich clay, and often saturated soil. A tangle of dense rough grass is interspersed with the rising leaves of the spring bulbs. Small, discreet memorials give account to the dead.

In 100 years time it will have started to blend into the semi-ancient woodland of Little Matlock Wood that cloaks the north-facing flank of the Loxley valley. The memorials will be distant memories to future distant relatives, forgotten to all but the keenest of amateur historian. I hope badgers will still roam the woods, dippers will still scud the river and the daffodils will still bloom. This is a good place to compost your carcass, a beautiful place for the living to reconnect with their loss. The ceremony was Humanist, brief but heartfelt. People stood around in the piercing wind trying to avoid stepping on the bulbs.

The funeral party retired to a spread at the Wisewood Tavern and people reconnected after families, careers, triumphs and tragedies. An old friend, Joe Cocker, from the Cockers the scissor makers, not Cockers the musicians, mused on the fact that his father, the last in a line of Sheffield master craftsmen, was also buried at Wisewood. In fact he'd grown up in Loxley village; “Nothing has changed” reflected Joe wistfully, “the pub, the old houses, the valley”.

Later a wake was held in another unchanging place, a series of vaulted Victorian cellars that had once housed one of Sheffield's first music clubs in the 1960s. Now a rehearsal space for bands, an increasingly rare commodity as the old industrial buildings that ringed the city centre are either demolished, or more likely to be redeveloped into 'characterful urban flats”.

In the early to mid 1990s the city throbbed to uplifting bass of rave culture in all its permutations. An underground counter culture scene developed that many of the people at Jack's funeral had whole-heartedly embraced. In the 60s they would have called them bohemian. Personally I was reasonably restrained at this time in counter culture history, on occasion being the only person propping the bar up. Yet dropping down into that Shalesmoor cellar, the sort of place families of Irish immigrants occupied in the fetid slums that dominated this part of town in the 1880s, the memory of 'Garden Street' was rekindled.

They didn't happen often, they were never advertised, strictly word of mouth and it felt like you were at the coolest club on the planet when you were there. 'Garden Street' was a little meisters from the mid 1800s, situated on the edge of the city centre. A rabbit warren of blackened workshops around a courtyard. Two basic outdoor lavatories, a hulking great arched entrance gate and the ghosts of industry past. In it was slotted, three dance floors from nose bleed techno to funky house, a tea room, bar (until the local plod politely advised against this one early Sunday morning), assorted object d'art, performance, sound and light. All free! Jack loved those evenings. JK on visuals, all sorts on the decks, Hairy Tim and Dan propping the dance floor up with acroprops, Dave on the door, Mandy making tea. Your own private Glastonbury deep in the heart of the city's decay.

After an evening of partial re-enactment of the Garden Street vibe clearing heads was the order of the day on the Saturday morning and a midday rendezvous at the Rockingham Arms in Wentworth was surprisingly well adhered to.

Wentworth was where it all began for so many of those friends gathered at Jack's funeral. In 1977 the newly created Sheffield City Polytechnic set up a base in what was one Britain's grandest country homes Wentworth Woodhouse.

Stretched out along a valley that culminates in the highest point between The Pennines and the North Sea lies the grand park of the Wentworth Estate. The house, Wentworth Woodhouse, which was the seat of power for the extensive estates collected first by the Rockinghams who on the death of the childless Lord Rockingham passed onto his heir, a nephew, William, the 4th Earl of Fitzwilliam in 1892.

Now this was a piece of real estate worthy of the grandest of Earls.

'Home' Chapter 1: January

Grouse moors on the distant Pennine Hills, acres of farmland, woods and a deer park scattered with monumental follies. And the house itself, well it is really two houses, a west facing one dating from the early 18th century and the small matter of a 600-foot extension facing east. This 'extension' was built in a fit a pique over the extension being put up at Wentworth Castle, in which the Stainborough branch of the Wentworth family lived, some ten miles north of the Wentworths of Wentworth. Now clearly the longest frontage of any country house in England is a concerted piece of one up-manship perhaps metaphorically represented by the collection of follies constructed at the same time. These people where as rich as Croesus, were lords of all they surveyed and clearly as vaingloriously bonkers as they come.

On a lesser scale of bonkers was the decision to give students the run of the eastern half of this manorial pile whilst educating them up the drive at the house's stables, which had been built in 1768 in a style that made them probably the best kept nags in the nation. The students were a little less well looked after. A 70s extension was unwisely added to introduce new fangled ideas like proper classrooms and science labs to the 18th century grandeur.

On returning to Wentworth Woodhouse I was struck how the ambivalence of youth had blinded me to quite what a startling experience studying at Wentworth Woodhouse was. On arrival as a 'fresher' I was housed in some functional 70s built residential blocks built just inside the park's entrance. Improbably for something so architecturally inept they still exist. I lasted eight weeks, tormented by rugby playing PE trainee teachers and their threats of baths of cold baked beans, disturbed by the banshee lovemaking of my over athletic neighbour through the gossamer walls, (who I intriguingly met at a job interview 10 years on), but mainly lured by the bright lights and the hustle and bustle of the big city that I knew nestled tantalisingly over the far ridgeline. I moved to a £6 a week slum on Page Hall Road, Firvale, in northern Sheffield and commuted out to the bucolic baronial splendour of the Geography and Environmental Studies department every day, often via Rotherham bus station.

We did however explore the Wentworth Estate far more than would be allowed today. We marvelled over the almost perfect lawn that faced the west house, an experience occasionally aided by the magic mushrooms that grew on it. We wandered through the deer park, sometimes being berated by estate gamekeepers and visited the now out of bounds Mausoleum. This dramatic memorial to the late Lord Rockingham by the rather chuffed recipient of his largesse, The Earl of Fitzwilliam, does reflect the required magnitude of thanks for his benefactor for being given something that was the equivalent of winning the lottery, the Euro one, with the hundreds of millions. This was 'fuck off' wealth or rather if you were an estate worker, 'yes m'lord' wealth. The mining villages that surround the Wentworth Estate, one of the closest being Brampton Bierlow where the 1984 miners strike was set in motion, became hotbeds of socialism. With this pile as a mirror to their lives it was hardly surprising.

However Catherine Bailey in her book 'Black Diamonds', an account of the Fitzwilliam 'dynasty' and Wentworth House, spins a tale of benevolence and patrician respect in the family's relationship with the miners who dug up so much wealth for them. The fall of the house from housing one of the richest families in Britain to housing some of the more feckless of Sheffield Polytechnic's students is a tale of disputed paternity, wild house parties, an affair with a 'Kennedy' named Kick and of course as in the run of things with that most influential of American families, a tragic accident. It ended up being a teacher training college named after the 'red' sheep of the

Fitzwilliam clan, Lady Mabel Smith who always thought the place far too privileged. Strangely today, with the estate and house back in private hands, public rights of way are the only access to this startling slice of munificence and might.

On this January afternoon we revisited a treasurer trove of memories as we strolled with our children down to the monumental lakes, keeping assiduously to a way-signed path. I wanted to crunch down the gravel drive to the small door underneath the main stairwell, which via a simple Yale lock had led into an ante-hall set out with 'mockney' Greek statuary, just for old time's sake. We walked by. The red deer watched our passage, pheasants rustled in the rhododendron undergrowth within the artfully located wooded copses. The sky was a steely grey. The view down the valley was as I remembered; a tangle of chimneys that rose above the Rotherham steel mills and the limestone ridge that lay beyond. This was one of my first impressions of Sheffield and it wasn't even Sheffield.

February

The month that it is most likely to snow in Sheffield is February. In February 1986 I nearly lost my life in a 'whiteout', a blizzard so intense it was barely possible to see more than a few metres ahead. This wouldn't have been hugely problematic if I had been on my way to the corner shop but at the time I was somewhere up near Derwent Edge. In the summer Derwent Moor is a reasonably benign grouse moor, albeit fairly expansive, with a selection of sculptural tors atop its highest points. It is about nine miles west of the city centre.

On that winter's day it could have passed for Antarctica. I recall thinking that I was going to die of hypothermia a mere few miles from my warm, toasty living room, at that time in the western suburb of Malin Bridge. The snow, on the gale-strewn edge, an interesting mix of 2 inches of solid ice atop about 2 foot of powder snow, would eventually drain under the bridge that gave that suburb of Sheffield its name. It felt like my future was also about to drain away.

After a brief argument with my increasingly panicky companions about which way was down, or north, south, east or west, I grudgingly consented to have my judgement over-ruled and we followed my friend, and more competent Antarctic explorer, Martin Jackson, down the moor, crashing through cornices hung over rushing streams, until we reached The Strines Inn, which all things considered at 2 o'clock, a midweek afternoon, in a blizzard, was surprisingly open. We were the only customers. If my companions had followed my advice they wouldn't have had any customers at all. This is a hard thing for a Geographer to confess, getting lost, but the snow! Well it was mountainous, that's my excuse.

Now you tell kids a story like that today and they don't believe you!

Snow? Deep? In Sheffield? Getaway.

It was with some surprise and a little excitement that snow was forecast to herald in February. It is fast becoming the exception rather than the rule. Weston Park Museum in Sheffield are curators of one of the World's oldest sets of continuous weather data gathered from its measuring equipment within the park; 126 years of records. Gaynor Boon, Curator of Earth Sciences at the museum is currently the person with the data at her fingertips and the Royal Meteorological Society clearly state that

> **"Sheffield is almost unique in having the foresight to maintain a climatological station in the long term, thus providing the greatest and clearest evidence for the study of climate change".**

A quick trawl of this data reveals that between 1998 and 2007 an average of 6.7 days a year saw snow lying across Weston Park's green swathe. That decade also saw the wettest month, (July 2007, when floods in the city centre made the front pages of the national press), the hottest and sunniest month (July 2006) and a remorseless rise in average long-term temperatures for the city. From 1988 to 1997 an average of 12.5 days of lying snow could be expected in Sheffield, a decade earlier, 1978 to 1987, saw this average at 29 days. That is to say a 300%+ higher chance of snow than the current decade in less than 40 years. Back in the winter of 1962-1963 snow lay on the ground for over two months; the last two years have mustered just a single day. Although 1996 provided a brief window to what was in the past when 40 days of snow, and deep snow at that, smothered the city. I recall walking into the city centre after one particular large fall without a single car passing me, the silence was un-nerving.

Saturday morning is announced by the loud arrival of my children at an hour only rivalled by Christmas Day morning. It had snowed! An uncertain inch of dry powder snow lay across the city. The road outside the house, down which a clear panorama of the city centre is spread, was barely touched by the early morning traffic. This thin veneer of snow temporarily soundproofed the city and the first rays of a bright winter sun were striking the metal cranes in the city centre, illuminating them to such an extent that they appeared much closer than they were.

Whilst the family went sledging on the meagre rations of snow to be found in Chelsea Park, dodging the copious mounds of dog shit scattered about by the pedigrees of this park's upmarket neighbours, I found myself dropping down towards the city centre. Initially it was to pay my first ever visit to a private dentist, a painful experience, physically and politically, and then onto a selection meeting for the new Labour Party candidate for the re-configured constituency of Sheffield Central, potentially a painful experience politically but not physically, unlike the time I walked the gauntlet of radical venom once encountered on entering a Labour Party meeting in the 1990s. Some pushing, shoving and a dose of spit to try and persuade me to vote against; a war? Privatisation of the NHS? Decreasing taxation for the wealthy? Nope, the closure of an old persons' home that couldn't meet new health and safety specifications without a budget-busting load of cash being spent on it. Such is the passion aroused occasionally in the world of local politics.

I must unashamedly confess a long-standing membership of the Labour Party. My parents were activists, my grandparents members. In April, as a child, my father disappeared for a month of canvassing only returning home to hand me what were called 'redding pads'. These were to be attached to large pieces of ply wood for checking off the Labour vote on polling day. On the day of the poll itself my job was to get on my bike and go and collect the completed sheets from the checkers standing outside the polling stations collecting electoral numbers from voters going into vote. It was the 1970s so virtually everybody obliged. Furthermore as a child it meant staying up late to hear the latest thumping your father had got at the hands of the hated Tories; I grew up in South Bedfordshire so defeat came with the territory. Not so in Sheffield.

The Labour Party is a significant part of what has shaped Sheffield over the past 100 years. Sheffield returned its first Labour council in November 1926, led by the redoubtable Ernest George Rowlinson, a legend who later had a whole council estate named after him as well as a school. What greater honour could there be for a municipal socialist? Six months before this victory the General Strike had galvanised the Labour movement and Sheffield became its first major political victory nationally. From its first weeks of power the Labour controlled City Council launched into a public house building programme the like of which had never before been seen in Britain. Its legacy was sprawling suburban council estates of brick built semis with mile after mile of privet hedge; the creation of some of the first decent housing in Britain for the working class.

Initially this housing was targeted at the 'deserving' poor; or rather those who could afford to pay slightly higher rents due to regular work, the artisans of the metal trades. But the scale of ambition shown by these early Labour councils was transformative, 22,648 houses were built between 1926 and 1940 creating the estates of Wisewood, Parson Cross and Longley. The area that the city covered grew disproportionately as these were homes with gardens, most were semi-detached; population density fell. Between 1921 and 1951 the area of Sheffield expanded by 59% whilst its population only rose by 4.5%.

The Labour Party's ambitions were not restricted to housing, it rolled out a programme of civic engagement in society that had never before been seen in Britain and thus became the role model for aspirational democratic socialists across the country. Maternity and child welfare centres, improvements to waste management, building a series of public baths (a very important consideration in a city that at that time, in the 1930s, had baths in only a fifth of the city's homes), extending the publicly owned tram system, taking over the water board, building new reservoirs and developing a level of municipal benelovance that allowed the Labour Party to build a base of political support within the city that was almost unshakeable until the arrival of a re-invigorated Liberal Democrat party in the 1990s who rode a populist wave at the same time as the complete collapse of the Conservative Party within Sheffield.

It was that Liberal Democrat 'threat' that made this selection meeting so interesting. Boundaries had been changed and Richard Caborn's 7,055 majority looked a realistic target for the ambitious leader of Sheffield's Liberal Democrats, Paul Scriven. They had already chipped away successfully at Caborn's 16,906 majority in the 1997 election and now Walkley and Broomhill, two west Sheffield Liberal Democrat held areas had been added and Burngreave, a rock solid inner-urban Labour area, had been lost. Furthermore a feeling of impending loss of power of the city council in May's city council elections hung all around the Labour Party, fuelled by a range of simplistic but successful opportunistic attacks upon the city council by a clearly confident Cllr Scriven and the stumbling performance from the man from the manse at Westminister, Gordon Brown.

The Trades and Labour Club on Duke Street nestles behind Park Hill Flats, Britain's largest listed edifice, building would be too strong a word. A highly functional 1970s building, The Trades and Labour Club has played host to generations of Labour Party activists. I first crossed its threshold when I became a delegate to the District

Labour Party meeting from my ward branch, Heeley, in the early 1990s. I was impressed by the cut and thrust of these meetings, passions ran high amongst comrades, contentious decisions often left metaphorical blood on the walls. Enmities were made quite clear, factions existed and all of this was presided over by Paul Bloomfield, 'Mr Sheffield Labour Party', and Chair of the D.L.P. He was an impressively calm and organised meeting chair, always businesslike. He was also Chair of Sheffield City Trust and his fingerprints were all over a host of major developments within the city over the past decade and beyond. He was at those 1990s meetings aided in his scrupulousness to the rule book by his steadfast minutes secretary Patricia Wray, whose calmness probably came from the fact that she was a special needs teacher at one of Sheffield's more challenging schools, Myrtle Springs. A job my partner also held at that time.

I had fallen out of political activism when I moved house out of the Heeley Ward and into the Nether Edge Ward. I also was getting to grips with having my first child. This was 1999. Later in 2003 the Iraq war was a strong barrier to getting back into the campaigning saddle, although ironically that abomination apart I had been broadly supportive of Blairism and could argue a cogent case in its support domestically. As a Blairite in my trade union I was viewed a little to the right of Genghis Khan.

It was with the intention of supporting Paul in his attempt to secure the nomination for the soon to be hotly contested Sheffield Central constituency that I gave up that gloriously sunny and snow dusted first Saturday in February. I needn't have bothered; Paul got 78% of the vote, romping home against a field that all bar local activist Jane Thomas was surprisingly lacklustre.

The meeting was not a smoke filled room. The average age of its participants was in excess of 50, predominantly white, well educated and almost gentle and deferential in its treatment of the candidates. It was heartingly packed. I spent much of the gaps between speeches and questions jousting with my neighbour, an unknown comrade and Christian socialist, about the inequity of the state funding of religious schools. His friend produced a box of Marks and Spencer chocolate biscuits to poor balm on any fractious political differences of opinion. He was a very nice man, calm, considered, with a clear argument; I just significantly disagreed with him on this issue. It was a reminder of what I had been missing after my retreat from political activism. Would it be enough to get me out on the stump again?

One of the fundamental issues facing the development of society, and that is a predominantly urban society, is that for a participatory democratic system to exist people must participate. A culture of relentless cynicism now pervades a media saturated perspective on the political process. “They are only in it for themselves” is the oft-heard cry. This is along way from my experience. In most cases local politics is a rather thankless task. It is about dog shit, broken paving stones, holes in the road, old people's services and the like. Few of the pillars of municipal socialism remain; Thatcherism put pay to council house building, public transport on the rates and the city council's direct works department. Water, waste management, gas and electricity, the utilities of life, were in the hands of often foreign owned private companies. The Liberal Democrats understood this well, their main campaigning tool, 'Focus', their household 'newsletter', was inevitably adorned with a concerned councillor pointing at a broken street light or peering into a hole in the road as if Hades was to be found at its bottom.

I had always had more than a little bit of fellow feeling for my political opponents; they could be bothered, they cared about where they wanted to represent, they were prepared to forgo a normal family life in exchange for some of the dullest and most procedure laden meetings Britain's innate capacity for bureaucracy could dredge up. This I admired, I certainly couldn't be bothered to commit myself to that, yet, if ever. I'm glad somebody did.

One of the advantages of political campaigning is the intimate view it gives you of an area. I wouldn't think it an unreasonable claim that at some time or other I have stuck a leaflet through the door of every home on the Gleadless Estate and knocked on a fair few as well. You get to see estate life in all its facets; the graffiti strewn lift stairwells blessed with the mingling odours of piss and 'skunk', the lonely old widows who invite you in to chat about the old days, reminiscing about Sir Ron Ironmonger's halcyon Labour Party of the 1960s and their lost cat, the harassed young mother who “hasn't the time” and the hardworking aspirational families who dream of getting on a housing ladder that is rapidly being drawn up out of their reach.

To explain the relationship between the political canvasser and the canvassed I have often recounted to students this story of a Sunday afternoon's canvassing on the Gleadless Estate. At one house I was assailed by an irate barrage of criticism of the incompetence's of the city council that culminated in the dressing-gown clad woman,(it was a sunny spring mid-afternoon), pointing at some weeds growing out of the pavement by her front door. “I've rung those bastards to do something about these weeds, but do they ever come and do it?” she declaimed.

“Madam”, I said, “consider it done”. I turned heel, pulling up the weeds as I went and putting them in her bin. “Oi, who said you could put them in my bin” resounded in my ears as I moved onto the next barrage of insults. I hoped my Liberal Democrat rivals would be forced into a little light tidying up around her garden when they knocked on her door.

'Home' Chapter 2: February

Ten days after Paul Bloomfield fulfilled his ambition to perhaps forlornly tramp every inch of pavement in Sheffield Central I found myself sitting opposite a man who been there, seen it all, and had known political success and abject ridicule. Except he had only metaphorically seen it all as David Blunkett was the most successful blind politician who had graced both Sheffield's council chambers and the red leather seats and ministerial boxes of Westminister. Surprisingly politics was pretty much off the agenda.

Between us lay a table assiduously set with a potentially bountiful range of cutlery and glass wear. Underneath David's dog, Sadie, dozed.

What was on the agenda was wine and the comments that David had made two months previously in Sheffield's pre-eminent, well only weekly newspaper, 'The Sheffield Telegraph'. He had spoken out about the paucity of quality service in those local restaurants that harboured aspirations to be considered a classy establishment. This was not a conversation I could have imagined holding with David when I first arrived in Sheffield and he held the post of leader of the City Council.

Then David was the leading light of the 'Brightside mafia' who argued for "a radical socialist approach to solving the problems of those in greatest need in the city" and sought this through raising the money to provide a quality of services "second to none" through assertive revenue raising, mainly using the rates system.

Tonight we started the meal with a bottle of 'Moet and Chandon Cuvee Dom Perignon 1983'. Except I think it is only fair to recount that David did not take a single sip as he drinks no fizzy drinks at all, from Pepsi to vintage champagne. No accusations of being a champagne socialist can be made against David. Me yes, I'll accept that label if only I could afford champagne more often. David is more of a Burgundy bureaucrat, just like that other Labour Party ex Home Secretary, Roy Jenkins. Instead I poured David a glass of Lengs and Cooter Riesling from the Clare Valley in South Australia. This was a vague attempt at political irony as Leng was the name of the editor of the Sheffield Telegraph in the late 19th century.

I had organised the dinner to generate some debate about David's comments in the paper. I had found myself springing to his defence through the occasional wine column I had been writing in the Sheffield Telegraph over the previous two years.

The political grip on Sheffield in the late 19th century by the Conservative Party, it has been argued by Sheffield historian Helen Mathers, was very much down to Leng and "the electorally helpful connection between Conservatism and the drink interest". In 1901 they were swept away by the temperance dominated Liberals and have never regained power apart from a single year, 1968, when a surge in the Communist Party vote temporarily led to a minority Conservative administration. New housing areas built in Sheffield around the turn of the century time of that 'dry' Liberal administration, such as Meersbrook, are often without any pubs, being replaced on street corners by non-conformist chapels

Our fellow diners upstairs at West One restaurant on Fulwood Road were owner and host Johnnie Higginbottam, his good friend and business partner John Mitchell, who through his family wine merchants is worthy of the accolade of 'Mr Wine' of Sheffield. Johnnie and John were long standing friends who had recently gone into business opening an up market champagne and wine bar in the city centre. Finally there was Gian Bohan, co-owner of Nonna's, a culinary chunk of Italy on Eccelsall Road, the 'Golden Mile' of Sheffield, covering an enoteca, cucina, gelateria, restaurant, café and bar. All except me were born and bred in Sheffield and loved wine almost as much as the city, or is that the other way round?

It occurred to me that Ranmoor Church, a hundred metres further down Fulwood Road from West Ten, had been the birthplace of a forum, set up in 1986, to try and bridge the gap between Labour politicians led by David and local businessmen. It was perhaps from this root that the mold-breaking public-private partnerships that have characterised much of the decision making in Sheffield in the 1990s and early 21st century grew.

There was clearly a tension between the opinions of David on Sheffield's restaurant trade and restaurateurs in the city. As David stated in his argument 'Surely our city can do better';

> **"How is it that a city of half a million people, with at least one corner being the second wealthiest in the north of England, still struggles to have a decent, reliable and consistent restaurant? Of course, the chippies remain as good as ever and there is nothing wrong with popping in for a quick bite to eat in the many fast food outlets that exist. But I am talking about equalling Leeds, Manchester, Nottingham and, these days, Newcastle and Glasgow. We seem to struggle on two fronts: whilst the food that is produced in many of our "better" (read for that expensive) restaurants is, on the whole, pretty good, front of house service remains problematic."**

The following week The Sheffield Telegraph had to set aside two pages to cover the feedback from readers and restaurateurs alike. Leading the attack was Malcolm Schooling, the avuncular owner of Platillos, a new tapas bar that had been built into the converted 19th century Sheffield School Board offices;

"I would expect that many colleagues were amazed, disappointed and angered by Mr Blunkett's outdated comments that were perhaps based on years of privilege while serving taxpayers, when he was guest at some of the world's higher-end restaurants. Service and knowledge of food and wine is important but the restaurants now gaining Michelin stars are the ones stripping away 'old school' snobbishness.

Having availed myself of Malcolm's tapas in 'Barca chic' it is true nobody could accuse him of snobbishness with the wine arriving in 'authentic' glass tumblers. Good as the food is neither will he be securing Sheffield's first Michelin star. Although in reality, even though Sheffield, as George Orwell observed on a visit in the 1940s, "wanted to be pre-eminent in everything', this probably didn't extend to haute cuisine and if such a star ever arrived it would be as likely to engender suspicion as much as admiration. As writer Richard Burns suggested Sheffield is "a city that mistrusts celebrity but prizes graft and craft".

My favourite response in the paper came from Dave Sissons, who continued a fine line of satire within the city by observing;

From all of Sheffield's restaurants
'The Good Food Guide' lists two
it recommends for patronage
from gourmets just like you.
So Sheffielders must get out more
and get more posh on nosh,
especially those Hallamites
with wallets stuffed with dosh.

Brightside's bright on chipped potatoes,

not so bright on vino,
and not a place New Labourites
would choose to have a beano.

In Sheffield you snap your fingers,
shout, "The wine list, Charlie!"
A youth, half-trained, comes up and says,
"There's red, there's white, there's Barley."
Sheffield's haute cuisine will serve you
fish knives for the meat,
white wine in a red wine glass
and soup spoons for the sweet!

The amount of glass wear that we swilled our carefully selected wines in could have stocked a small shop. Jonty, West Ten's chef, who like so many young chefs in the city was ambitious and skilled, did himself proud. The conversation rollicked around.

John Mitchell, somewhat unfairly, attracted the label as the Bernard Manning of wine from David as he unleashed a small part of his endless store of wine anecdotes. His is a life in wine; born as he was above his father Dennis's wine and butchers store on Meadowhead on the southern edge of the city. Dennis himself was born in the Wagon and Horses Pub that now nestles in the middle of Millhouses Park but back at the start of the century was in rural Derbyshire. He went on to be publican at the George IV on Infirmary Road where he played 'mine host' to the Moony gang, one of the infamous 1920s Sheffield street gangs. In a working class city hard drinking and rough and tumble was nothing new; Alan Sillitoe told the same story for Nottingham. It could be argued that less violent crime occurred today in the city than at any time since its industrial enlargement, certainly there were a lot less pubs and less boozing. Or was it all hidden by middle-class home wine drinking today?

Underpinning the interconnectivity of so many Sheffield lives, a trait that has led to Sheffielders describing their city as the world's largest village, it transpired that Johnnie's mum had taught David at a school for the blind some 50 years hence, however Jonnie still hadn't forgiven David for his 'assault on the rates'. Johnnie commented on David eating with a 'Tory' like him to which David sharply replied that he had eaten with people far more right wing that Johnnie. It was an eclectic evening.

Gian Bohan upstaged us all by digging deep into his cellar and producing a clutch of Italian wines that brought out the anoraky oenophile in us all which transcended politics on a night like this. A pair of beautifully aged Barolo's and a 1992 Sassacia, the original 'Super Tuscan'. For an amateur wine writer, writing what the doyen of English Wine writers, Michael Broadbent described as 'odd wine journalism' on 'obscure regional papers', who normally supped at the supermarket level, this was a bit like a Sheffield United playing host to AC Milan.

I drank too much and my fevered note taking ground to a halt, I forgot to take any photographs, but boy was it great wine, I'd have drank it happily out of a plastic tumbler.

David certainly didn't recant his comments in the paper, if anything the consensus was more like it was broadly fair comment, Sheffield could raise its game, should raise its game if it was to be a 'European city of quality', something its current leaders and urban managers constantly exhorted. However there was clearly a tension between Sheffield's continuing evolution built upon hundreds of millions of pounds of inward investment and those local entrepreneurs who still wanted to create something that was rooted in a sense of locality.

In Italian, Spanish and French cities small retailers, restaurants and bars abound, often proudly selling regional produce. This is declining in those European countries but nowhere near as fast as it is in Britain with the endless march of the Tesco/Sainsbury/Asda axis of supermarket retailing.

In the new residential areas being carved out of Sheffield's inner-city industrial heartland it is the arrival of a Tesco's Metro that conveys the areas anointment as a 'neighbourhood'. In the 'St Vincent Quarter', once a jumble of work-less industrial decay hanging down the northern bluff of the city centre and now a transitional and embryonic new 'city living' area, the blue neon of Tesco is the only service in sight. Newsagent, off licence, deli, grocer, butcher, baker, all together in one shop, no need for any other business to chance their arm against the hegemonic power of the 'super' supermarkets. The Tesco Metro or Jackson's 'Sainsburys' is normally snuggled up against a range of unlet retail units that is almost becoming a feature of new build city centre apartments.

A little closer to the River Don than 'The St Vincent's Quarter' a similar story is being played out in Kelham Island, albeit with a collection of Britain's best independent pubs scattered about to encourage a sense of local identity. As Andrew Simms, Policy director of The New Economics Foundation, has put it.

> **"Clone stores have a triple whammy on communities: they bleed the local economy of money, destroy the social glue provided by real local shops that holds communities together, and they steal the identity of our towns and cities. Then we are left with soulless clone towns. The argument that big retail is good because it provides consumers with choice is ironic, because in the end it leaves us with no choice at all"**

In Sheffield so many of the new restaurants that were arriving on the redeveloped 'high street', are multiple chains found in 'every city'. Café Rouge, La Vina and Wokmania for example. The same is true of wine. Blossom Hill, Hardy's and Kumula, all marketed by the huge US multi-national Constellation, have colonised the taste buds of millions of burgeoning wine drinkers, led by supermarket discounting and brand familiarity.

Successful Sheffield businesses like Nonnas, Malcolm Schooling's Platillios, Mitchell's Wines and Johnnie Higginbottam's West Ten are part of the fabric of the city. People don't visit Barcelona to visit shopping centres but to go to the Boquira Market, sip Cava on the Ramblas and eat at tapas in Placa Reil. This is local culture and this is at the heart of David Blunkett's argument, Sheffield should not aspire to be a clone town.

Food and drink is a significant part of any local culture, whether it is at my local café, Café #9, sipping espresso whilst Captain Beefheart warbles in the background, the heart-attack inducing cakes of Millhouses Park Café, the 'dabba' authenticity of The Kashmir on Spital Hill or The Blue Moon Café's vegetarian smorgasbord within it's mid Victorian auction hall splendour across from the city cathedral's main entrance.

London Road reflects the newly emerging global culture that was fast becoming as integral to Sheffield's sense of itself as piquant Henderson's Relish or Kelham Island's Pale Rider.

This had always been my favourite road in Sheffield. It had evoked a sense of multi-cultural dynamism for decades. Arterially feeding traffic southwards from the city centre, the road was the centre of an area that reflected what E. W. Burgess, the 1920s Chicago Sociologist and founding father of theoretical urban geography, called "the zone of transition". These inner urban areas have been evolving ever since they became a jumble of industry and working class housing in the opening decades of the industrial revolution, marking the city's first major expansion. It was over one hundred years on, in the uncertain decade of the 1960s, when slum clearance peppered the inner city with high-density social housing cheek by jowl with industrial Victoriana, that these areas became synonymous with deprivation and decline.

It was that decline that gave inner-city areas like Sharrow, which is bisected by London Road, so much potential. I moved into the area to occupy a cheap terraced house in the second year of my degree course, students rubbed shoulders with those in society who lacked the means and aspiration to flee towards suburbia. Recent immigrants were drawn in setting up disparate diasporas in supportive competition with each other. Chinese take aways, Jamaican record shops and Pakistani grocers. It was down at heel, it was edgy and vibrant, it was place of endless social animation.

More than twenty years on from my introduction to London Road it remains Sheffield's global artery and the best in the city to eat without unduly concerning yourself with the quality of the wine waiter (they don't have one), or the wine for that matter, (decidedly not premier cru but where else could you get the industrial taints and sweet fruits of Thailand's Monsoon Valley red?). Turks vie with Kurds for your pound. Chinese, Japanese, Thai and Vietnamese cuisine tempt the taste buds. Greek, Italian, Bangladeshi, and Pakistani migrants have all set out their kitchens along the road. A clutch of small, often aspirational businesses intersperse the restaurants looking up towards long term survivors like Ted Williams, the self styled bespoke tailor of Sheffield. This is a road that is the antithesis of a clone town.

A regular Friday evening ritual is to park up midway along London Road, avoiding the 'glaze' of the congregating methadone users who are semi-detached to the 24-hour chemist and trawl the menus. The penultimate Friday of February we parked up at the city centre end of London Road and met up with the student son of old Nottingham friends at the Ban Thai Restaurant. This restaurant acts as a sort of post-modern indicator of what to expect the length of London Road. This solid, neo-classical old bank has had a Siamese makeover. Buddhas instead of bank tellers. Next-door another ex bank is home to 'The Chinese Fireworks Company'. Half a mile of global eating, cheap hard drives, 'continental food shops' and quirky publicans await the enquiring stroller.

Our 19 year old dinner companion had not been that enquiring so far. We compared notes about where this generation of students hangs out between lectures and sleep compared with our own. Clearly life has moved on.

Back in the early 1980s pubs called last orders during the week at 10.30pm. It was a real challenge finding a drink beyond 11. Today Monday night, student night, was awash with cheap drink offers in bars that had embraced the concept of extended licensing with gusto. Organised binge drinking events trading under names like 'Oblivion' or 'Trashed' cut straight to the inebriated chase. Only chains with their huge buying power could squeeze their margins so thinly; students really didn't do local pubs that much now.

Savings clearly had to be made in the hedonism department because housing for students in recent years had entered a completely new realm. Sheffield was entering a new phase of private sector purpose built student accommodation. The rapid proliferation of student accommodation ringing the city centre had become one of the key features of this first decade of the 21st century. Standards were high compared to much of the private rents available in the 1980s, if more than a little functional. Prices were however challenging, hence the need for cheap booze, one to stop you plummeting further into debt and two so you could drink to forget that debt.

In the early 1980s things were different. Obviously some of those students who didn't avail themselves to the universities halls of residence and dived into the private sector lived in some decent places. It is just that I didn't. Cost being of imperative importance.

The Sheffield by-law terrace comes in a multitude of variations although it would be hard to gauge that from a cursory appraisal of any such terraced street in the city. Off-shot or not, two, three, four bed roomed, renovated in the 50s, 60s, 70s, or if you were lucky by the council direct works department during neighbourhood 'enveloping' schemes in the 1980s, Velux (aka skylight) or dormer. Anybody who has ever scoured the city to buy such a property will understand every nuance of the Sheffield by-law terrace, and how it affects its price.

The example I rented in 1984 in Sharrow was a three bedroomed single offshot model on Sharrow Street. At one time, for a short while, eight of us lived in it. I shared a double bed with my equally heterosexual friend Hog, who unfortunately had a predilection for avant-garde jazz and Hungarian folk music, late at night, most nights. This situation was up a notch or two from that of the six-foot plus lad who slept in the bath. OK this wasn't typical, but it wasn't that rare either. Anyway instead of drinking cheap lager in clone bars to try and help us address the existential questions of student life we brewed our own, grew our own and munched the Peak District's bountiful magic mushrooms in order to forget what the question was in the first place.

In some vague exhortation of that homemade hedonism, Sheffield musician and social provocateur Jarvis Cocker, has lent some verse to adorn, Unite's Student flat complex, 'The Forge', at the bottom of London Road. This sprawling student complex partially covers the site of the one of Sheffield's oldest nightclubs known in its numerous incarnations as the Locarno, Palais, Bed or the Music Factory depending upon which era you skipped the light fandango within its walls. Its defining architectural feature, a mock oriental pagoda, has been retained and is the centre piece entrance for a new branch of Sainsburys, which only goes to show that the area has really arrived. As is becoming traditional unlet retail units hem in the corporate consumer community bestowed upon the students of 'The Forge' by Sainsbury.

Jarvis's literary graffiti, warmly received by most local folk, can be seen behind the mock façade. It exclaims in two-foot high stainless steel letters;

> **"Within these walls the future may be being forged.**
> **Or maybe Jez is getting trashed on cider.**
> **But when you melt you become the shape of your surroundings.**
> **Your horizons become wider.**
> **Don't they teach you no brains at that school?"**
>
> **Jarvis Cocker**
> **Off The Shelf 2005**

Clearly a common thread of hedonistic absorption into your surroundings continues from generation to generation. Drugs change, buildings change, and perspectives change but endorphins and the rush of youth into a new world, a new unfolding year remains.

March

It is a cliché but the assertion that Sheffield is the biggest village in England continues to do the rounds. The currency for this assertion is the distinctly fragmentary collection of residential neighbourhoods that define the city. Some of these areas are based around swallowed up villages, others creations of the tramways that pushed out the boundaries of the city in the late 19th century. Other areas grew out of 20th century municipal decrees as partially self contained social housing estates.

Neighbourhoods are hugely influential in shaping our lives. Where we live in the city influences our children's education, access to services, physical well being, our mental health, even our self-image and identity. Most staggering of all is the fact that where you live in Sheffield can influence your life expectancy in quite a marked way. The Eton educated, linguistic polyglot and leader of the national Liberal Democrats Party, Nick Clegg, who represents the wealthiest area of Sheffield, the Hallam constituency, pointed this out in one of his first speeches as a political leader.

> **"In Sheffield, the city where I'm an MP, if you are a child born in the poorest ward in Sheffield, you will die, today in 2008, 14 years before a child born five miles down the road in the wealthiest ward".**

It is not new that there is concern about the health of people in different residential neighbourhoods of Sheffield. It was in the pages of the Sheffield 'Report on the Small-pox Epidemic 1887-88' that the moniker of 'England's largest village' first became attached to the soon to be anointed city. Assessing the character of the town and its role in the ability of a disease like smallpox to rip through its population the report observes;

> **"The population of Sheffield is, for so large a town, unique in its character, in fact it more resembles that of a village than a town, for over wide areas each person appears to be acquainted with every other, and to be interested with that other's concerns".**

It is interesting to ponder whether 120 years on from that convivial community that a rural, village-like, sense of attachment to place and people can still exist within the city, any city, let alone Sheffield, a city integrated into the hyper-mobile world of globalisation in the early 21st century. It seems unlikely. We are talking nearly 530,000 people, maybe 10,000 more if unregistered recent migrants are added to an increasing geographically fluid but gently rising population. That's a lot of people to be 'interested with that other's concerns."

When I first came to Sheffield as a student I moved into new areas of the city at least every year. Firvale, Sharrow, Malin Bridge, Crookes, Heeley and Grimesthorpe, (no really there is such a place and the name is apt). These were relatively fleeting sojourns, just long enough to upset the neighbours with a few decent sized student parties. We really weren't locals, just people who lived there. Briefly living in Hillsborough I joined the local Labour Party and was treated as the arriviste hippie student upstart who was full of shit, well if the cap fits wear it. I wore it. I stopped going to the meetings soon after it was suggested by the Militant inclined Ward officers that I could do with going on some political education courses. I did however once get to meet Roy Hattersley's mother Enid, she wasn't in Militant and was a very nice old lady and one of the few people who was outwardly friendly to the straggly haired youth with the rainbow striped jumpers who attempted to explain the thoughts of radical eco-socialist Andre Gorz in a southern accent.

Eventually at the very end of the late 80s house price boom I acquired a mortgage which immediately plunged into negative equity. It didn't really matter as I was buying a home not an investment. This time I was sticking around. Meersbrook that was going to be my manor, better cut down on the noise.

It was over the next few years that I started to grasp why Sheffield still thought of itself as a big collection of villages. I started to go native, become more of a local.

Meersbrook was a bit boho. Not exactly Haight Ashbury, but it was an eclectic mix of working class locals, many of whom could trace their families back to when the area was developed at the end of the 19th century, aspiring middle class teachers, social workers and other 'neer do wells'. Then there was the gay crowd, the eco-warriors, the dope heads and the schemers and scammers. Musicians and artists seemed to abound, Candida Doyle, the static keyboard player of Pulp lived over the back from our place, apparently. I never met her. Rave culture permeated the consciousness of just about everybody under 30 who hadn't already started a family. It was predominantly white but sort of yearned to be a bit more multi-cultural. It became so over time. It was a natural home of the growing black professional class.

I never thought of the area as particularly working class or middle class, it was urban class. Geographers would say it was being gentrified. Certainly there were a lot of skips in the streets. Velux made a lot of money, some from me.

Almost everybody met up in the park around which Meersbrook was gathered. When it snowed, and it did back then, the top end of the park became the coolest sledging site in the city. It could be packed well into the night, the 'piste' illuminated by streetlights. The notorious 'devils hump', in reality a small ridge halfway down the slope, launched careering sledge's into the air. Chiropractors gathered at the bottom touting for business, although being Meersbrook crystal healers could just as easily have been sought. These were the type of days when communities are forged. The moments when you interact with your neighbours, whether you like or know them, not just your friends.

Meersbrook Park also affords one of the best views across Sheffield city centre. This facility came into its own on Millennium Eve when hundreds of locals of all ages, my sleeping and snugly insulated 5 month old daughter being possibly one of the youngest, gathered atop the park to witness the greatest outpouring of explosive shenanigans since the Lufwaffe paid the city a visit in 1940. It was also an evening when the size of the starbursts didn't indicate the socio-economic status of the area from where it had been launched. We lit a firework so large that it created a small crater in the turf; they would have been impressed by its waterfall of colour even in Fulwood. People decanted from the Park into a myriad of house parties that lit up the surrounding streets and the music pounded away until a grey morning heralded the mother of all hangovers. I'm sure there were more dramatic, animated and sheer exuberant places to see in a new century but a bench in Meersbrook Park, surrounded by friends and neighbours hit the spot for me.

This was a neighbourhood without any pubs, a condition laid down by the Meersbrook Land Society who from 1873 started to lay out the road pattern. There was clearly a religious streak to the first members of this community, suspicious of the demon drink, fearful of the corrupting influence of the city. Then Meersbrook would have been a community of artisans, petit bourgeoisie, Methodists and

Asquithian Liberals.

The first tradition that grew to define the community was the Whit Monday community hymns that commenced two years after Meersbrook Park was officially opened in 1887. In the Edwardian period up to 10,000 gathered in the park to sing accompanied by local brass bands. The streets that surround the park have a multitude of chapels, all variations of the non-conformist tradition, many now in terminal decline or redeveloped into new uses. To my knowledge nobody had sung hymns in the park on Whit Monday for decades.

It was a genuine wrench to up sticks three months after the Millennium and move less than a mile across the Sheaf valley to Nether Edge. I had spent a decade in Meersbrook and had loved its convivial culture; I felt a part of a wider community. A community of activism and political participation where things had been achieved for all. A new community park to celebrate the Millennium, the re-opening of the Victorian walled garden in Meersbrook Park, the further development of Heeley City Farm as a beacon of sustainable development in the heart of a city; all were activities I had supported. It is through such endeavour that links to others and commitment to an area is grown.

It is striking that a move of a mere half a mile could so radically transform into a different, completely distinct community, separate entirely from Meersbrook on the sunset side of the River Sheaf valley. To get from Meersbrook to Nether Edge the narrow, flat valley bottom must be negotiated. That is a river, the mainline railway to London and two southward arterial roads from the city centre. This is a clear barrier. A linear line of industry had slotted into the spaces between the railways, river and roads.

A few years previous the opportunity to connect these two communities was spurned when the derelict land between the railway and the river was redeveloped with a soulless windswept prairie of car parks serving the small business barns that were built instead of the much needed housing that could have linked two vibrant and distinct communities. The land had been derelict since 1988 when the William Tyzacks tool factory that had stood there for just over 100 years was demolished along with a tradition that pre-dated this mere factory, that of Tyzacks, an immigrant family made good, who made their name making scythe blades for agriculture at Abbeydale Industrial Hamlet.

The acres of industrial wasteland had become a site of considerable urban ecological interest as nature claimed it back over 15 years. Foxes scurried past buddleias adorned with peacock butterflies. Sparrow hawks prowled the oxeye daisy strewn fractured concrete. The ginnel that crossed the factory site, connecting Meersbrook with Nether Edge, crossed over the River Sheaf on a footbridge onto Broadfield Road. It was notable for a fine range of feminist graffiti before the old factory walls were demolished. I preferred 'Women of the World Unite' to mindless tags put up like a dog pissing up lamp posts to mark out territory.

That ginnel was a well-trodden path when I lived in Meersbrook, with the Heeley Swimming Baths, Shahs culinary emporium, The Broadfield Pub and the 'local village hall, 'The Everyone Centre', nestled next to the river on the Nether Edge side. I rarely ventured up Sheldon Road beyond 'Cacti Martin's' house to the vegetarian and vegan delights of Zed on the Edge. Three types of organic rice cakes was more Nether Edge than Meersbrook. Nether Edge is an area of middle class ease.

Nether Edge is submerged under an urban forest, bequeathed to the city by its early Victorian developers. Chief protagonist in the creation of this decidedly un-working class, sylvan, inner-urban suburb was George Wostenholm, one of Sheffield's greatest cutlers. George was the complete Sheffield man, a middle class local hero. He was born in 1800 the son of generations of cutlers. His father moved his pocketknife business to Garden Street, in the burgeoning centre of Sheffield, soon after George's birth.

By the age of 27 George had been accepted into the Cutlers Company and been awarded the immodest trademark of 1*XL. It was this trademark that became synonymous with the knives that literally helped carve out America. It is alleged that it was a 1*XL knife that was found on the body of Colonel James Bowie at his ascension to American folk hero status at the Alamo in 1836. This was the ultimate in 19th century product placement. By the time of the American Civil War in the 1860s Wostenholm had secured 90% of the American knife market and the 'Bowie' Knife was the IPod of the day, a must have accessory. It was no surprise his factory in Wellington Street was named Washington Works in honour of another famous George.

What the enriched Wostenholm spent his US earned fortune on was first buying up a substantial tract of land south-west of the city centre from 1836 onwards, and then laying it out in tree lined roads centred around his own palatial pad Kenwood House. Many of Sheffield's newly wealthy businessmen invested in the area and local builders worked on perfecting a northern gothic Victoriana style from gritstone plundered from The Peak District. They did a fine job.

Where the wealthy went the middle classes followed, led by freehold land societies, organisations set up to buy big parcels of land that were sold on to individual middle class members. There was a political edge to this as property was a condition of the franchise and such land societies opened up an electorate to more liberal non-conformist traditions.

Conditions were imposed about the standards of building required. The grid of streets that stretch up towards wooded Brincliffe Edge from the centre of Nether Edge were all developed in this way. One might expect a uniformity of architecture remaining to the present day but the area was significantly damaged on December 12th 1940, when the first big bombing raid of World War Two targeted South Sheffield and the city centre. The gaps in the Victorian cityscape have been in filled with a wide selection of post-war housing styles, some fortunate that the more rigorous standards of today's conservation area status didn't nip their architect's aspirations in the bud.

Since the area's rise to prominence in the mid 1850s successive generations of gardeners have endowed the area with a range of greenery that has drawn in a startling array of urban wildlife. Robert Marnock, whose other local claim to fame was the laying out of the Botanical Gardens in the 1830s, was employed by Wostenholm to lay out the area's street plan. He planted the pavements of the wide streets with lime and plane trees. These trees are now fully mature, lifting pavements, dropping sticky sap on cars and providing a dappled canopy across the whole area during summer. Only in the winter is Nether Edge open to the sky.

As winter started to recede and light started to stretch into the early evening the more sedentary indoor existence of winter moved from early evening drawn curtains to a more outward perspective of home. People started to get out more.

March is the 'yellow' month. Daffodils were approaching their peak. The tete a tetes had been defiantly colourful all through a record sunny February but now the multitude of daffodils across the city were about to herald spring. They had been planted in swathes alongside roads and in sweeping banks throughout the parks. Forsythia, a common garden shrub across Sheffield, was starting to show with its streaks of yellow and the unknown bush that sits at the end of my garden that has bright canary yellow clusters of tightly budded flowers was about to make its annual mark on the year. March is undoubtedly a month of promise. A promise that the future will quite literally be brighter and sunnier. March was the month I moved into Nether Edge.

However what promise of the future the daffodils suggested was mitigated by a succession of vigorous storms running across the country. A conveyor belt of depressions was in business. Starting up just off the coast of Newfoundland these depressions spun an ever-tightening vortex as they arched their way eastwards over the Atlantic, pushed onwards by the jet stream.

Somewhat sheltered by the Pennines Sheffield has always been protected from the worst ravages of westerly Atlantic storms. However on the 10th a particularly nasty blast appeared to up its intensity as it ran into Yorkshire. On days like these you can clear three seasons in less than an hour. A grey blustery autumn, the torrential semi-vertical rainstorm of winter and sharp sunlight punctuated by scudding spring clouds. The only constant is the wind pushing through the weather system at breakneck speed.

The second Sunday saw much calmer weather, bright sunshine and blue skies. It also saw the first appearance of a new phenomenon in my neighbourhood. A 'Farmers Market' located in the small Victorian centre of Nether Edge, which was closed to traffic for most of the day.

This inaugural farmers market was a little short on farmers, clearly an oversight by local producers as the narrow street was packed with eager punters. Within a couple of hours some stalls had been cleared. In reality this wasn't a farmers market that could fulfil the criteria set down by the newly august National Farmers Retail and Markets Association that "all products sold should have been grown, reared, caught, brewed, pickled, baked, smoked or processed by the stallholder". A true Yorkshire market at this time of year would have had to of had some of Wakefield's finest, rhubarb. There wasn't a vegetable to be seen but at least there was wonderful and wonderfully expensive handmade Lincolnshire cheese, 'Poachers.'

Although lacking produce the market did not lack people. Sunshine helped but clearly there was a need, a desire for this community to get together. Chatter filled the streets, people reconnected, conviviality was the order of the day. This was Sheffield as a village. Ian a local priest stood behind me as I bought samosas from Atique, an ex-student of mine. Paul Bloomfield and his Euro MP wife Linda McAvan worked the crowd. In less than an hour I had met dozens of people I knew and bought some cheese and a loaf of rye bread.

Right across the city the summer saw an almost constant sequence of neighbourhood festivals. Pitsmoor multi-culturally gathered in Abbeyfield Park, Bhangra throbbed through Sharrow, where later in the year the community paraded through the streets with lanterns, Heeley was 'Green' and Broomhall these days was less dub and more Somali. Each of these festivals was a reflection of the urban village that supported them. A farmers market with few farmers, a lot of local evangelicals, a dash of samosas, a yoga stall and a packed Café #9 seemed aptly Nether Edge.

The highlight of the afternoon for me was my first visit to the 1867 Nether Edge Proprietary Bowling Clubhouse. Hidden behind a solid gritstone wall the Bowling Club is a delicious slice of Victoriana. I was transported back to gently decaying colonial clubs in Darjeeling or Shimla. The large bow window threw sharp light into the clubroom. Up a creaking staircase, following a display of historic snooker photographs - look Steve Davis as a child! - a large upper room reveals three full sized snooker tables. Solid, carved, aged tables draped with cloth. All four walls were lined with red leather pews on a slightly raised pedestal. A dusky gloom filled the unlit room. If I played snooker I would have handed over the £150 yearly membership fee there and then just to breathe in the atmosphere that had been accrued over literally centuries. I don't play at least not on a table you require a telescope to see the end pockets with. Maybe the crown green bowls would tempt me.

As an Englishman I have accepted that I have a deep-seated affinity for a good lawn. A quarter of an acre of 'poa' perfection sat in front of the clubhouse. It was a pure pleasure to gently stride across it. It was firm, uniform, moss free; we are talking serious lawn. Daffodils nodded approvingly in the surrounding flowerbeds.

I had walked past this undiscovered gem thousands of times. Never had I been inquisitive enough to explore its charms. I wasn't alone, one of my neighbours, who had lived even longer than my mere eight years in Nether Edge, also confessed that he had never been into the Bowling Club. I suspected that a life of bowls and allotments might await me if I am not tempted by a Mediterranean retirement. I know what Alan Bennett would choose, and I'm happy for my children to mock me if I spend the sunsets of my sunset years shambling across this clipped green carpet of this most quintessential of English spaces. I wondered if they had any local British-Asian members?

That thought was amplified the next night when after a blustery five-minute walk to the end of my street I arrived at St Peter's Church Hall.

Ninety odd locals had gathered to listen to Moazzam Begg, the released Guantanamo Bay prisoner, talk widely and eloquently about his experiences. This man, who claimed he was seized after going to build 'girls schools for the Taliban', clearly attracted few of the people who had thronged the farmers market the day previously. They were however as local. I deduced this by scanning the addresses on the petition that was passed around in support of a Cameroonian asylum seeker who spoke, in stuttering broken English, to the meeting urging support for his clearly open and shut case that had crashed into the unmoving Home Office.

This was part of a radical political community within Sheffield. Maxine Bowler, Respect Party head honcho for Sheffield chaired the meeting, Dr Jillian Creasy, Green Party councillor for Sharrow Ward spoke, righteous indignation coursed through the room. Palestine was the rampaging elephant in the room. The local Pakistani community was well represented; they were mainly the young men with beards in the room.

Mozzam Begg recounted his experiences as a detainee in Bagram, the US run detention centre in Afghanistan. He told how young men were seized in US raids and thrown into a system of abuse that made Guantanamo Bay seem a more enlightened regime. After months of abuse they were lobbed back into their communities, radicalised and bitter. He reflected, “It wasn't like here, family still matters in Afghanistan.” The accounts of torture and disdain within Bagram were quickly disseminated through the predominantly rural community in Afghanistan.

It may be that the religious conviviality of a socially and gender hierarchical society offered Mozzam a better model to live by; he at least considered it so for a while. Yet there is no doubt that this bore little resemblance to life in modern Britain as lived by most people. A society that Mozzam was clearly not a particularly big fan of. There was also an acknowledgement that such communities do exist within Britain, perhaps even within Nether Edge's Kashmiri community who lived predominantly on the terraced streets that edged the larger Victorian mansions of Wostenholm's grand design. Mind you it was not unreasonable to think most of that church hall room, regardless of ethnicity, were probably not that enamoured with life in Britain. Neo-liberal, racist, imperialist and oppressive would have been a fair consensus of the British state. A condition only to be escaped from with the dawn of a republican socialist state, although the lads at the back of the meeting might have preferred it with a dash of Sharia law thrown in for moral measure.

In the same week Lord Goldsmith reported his commissioned ideas back to the government about 'Britishness'. Ridiculed and derided as being essentially un-British in trying to actually think about and formalise a sense of national identity, Goldsmith suggested an oath of allegiance to the Queen, or simply to the country, and a national day. He suggested much more besides but it was these two points that were held up, rightly, to derision. However the issues he raises are important and are much more sharply brought into focus in a society that is increasing in mobility both internally and externally. Such mobility obviously reduces a geographic community's attachment to place. It becomes less of an inter-generational sense of identity linked to place and more a community of interests, or rather disparate communities of interest, sometimes conflicting, sometimes convivial.

Which event most reflected the identity of Nether Edge in the 21st century? Obviously both and neither. It could have been an evening of tambourine abuse with the evangelical King's Community, or whittling with the local Woodcraft Folk. Perhaps an ear-jarring evening of Dub Central vs Riddimation at The Everyone Centre. I'm personally probably closer to a relaxing evening of crown green bowls wrapped around with sedate Victorian splendour. All are communities that are both geographic and of interest. The city is like that, an overflowing Venn diagram of overlapping interest, sometimes defined by geography, at other times by class or ethnicity, religion and politics, interests and hobbies. It may be only half a million people but all life is within Sheffield, all possibilities, and the freedom to be what you are. From the voyeuristic sex of Attercliffe's 'La Chambre to the evangelical speaking in tongues of Pentecostal believers. How about the estate car driving suburbanites who devote themselves to model railways in Totley or those respectable elderly citizens who will still be drawn to a 'tea dance' at the City Hall.

Conviviality is the ability to just get on with it all. What could be more 'British'? To illustrate this point in lectures I have often referred to the day, many years ago, I saw a uni-cyclist wobble his way down Fargate, the pedestrianised centre of the city, dressed, on a less than tropical day, in just a glittery thong and carrying a Sainsbury plastic bag. Nobody blinked. Life went on as normal, except for a gaggle of wide-eyed Chinese exchange students who reached for their cameras. Nobody was going to believe them in Shanghai unless they had photographic evidence.

It was with the purpose of gleaning some photographic evidence of my own that on the third Sunday of the month I skipped a lie in and instead drove, early in the morning, to the Peak District village of Eyam, 14 miles southwest of Sheffield.

On the way I had picked up Martin and Richard, a couple of A level Geography students who had the added skills acquired by an AS level in Media Studies, a subject I unfashionably refuse to bemoan, of using a video camera, editing and sound recording. The eventual object of the exercise was to put together a short teaching documentary about change in a village. So best to choose a bitingly cold March morning with a sky of scudding grey clouds threatening rain to film the village looking at its best.

Eyam in many ways is not your archetypal English village. Its development owes much to minerals that lie within the limestone plateau on which it sits. It is not uncommon for Derbyshire villages to have an industrial basis for their development. It was way back in 1771 that Richard Arkwright built what could be said to be one of the first factories of the Industrial Revolution at Cromford. His water powered cotton-spinning mill. Its global importance underlined by a UNESCO heritage designation.

Eyam's industrial boom years were a little later and to some extent mirrored the unfolding industrial revolution in Sheffield. From 1800 onwards, lead mines, cotton spinning, silk weaving, boot manufacture and stone cutting all developed in the village. A turnpike road built in 1815 opened up the village to the world. However it was that world, in particular Broken Hill in Australia, that put pay to the lead mining industry in Eyam. In 1880 a huge new seam of lead in Broken Hill saturated world markets.

However lead is normally found in conjunction with other minerals like fluorspar, barytes, zinc and even silver. Eyam had deposits of the first two in abundance, alas no silver. The mine went on, this time extracting two minerals that are unknown to most people but are a benefit to nearly all. Fluorspar, or rather derivatives from it are used in everything from steel making, to coolants for fridges and even Teflon for frying pans. Barytes are normally used in lowly paint making. This industry continued until the 1990s at Glebe mine, right in the very heart of the village, a matter of 100 metres from the medieval church.

In 1982 this village along with neighbouring Stony Middleton could claim to be supplying a little over 1% of all the world's fluorspar. This time it was the Chinese who partly put pay to the mine. Unencumbered by niceties such as planning regulations in a national park, the Chinese share of the global market for fluorspar has increased by a whopping 400% from 1982 to 2003. This has squeezed the global price considerably.

The Glebe Mining Company, from its base at Cavendish Mill above the village of Stoney Middleton which nestles in a dry valley dropping down from the limestone plateaux on which Eyam is perched, is Britain's only commercial lead, barytes and fluorspar producer. Huge scars on the north-facing slope across the valley from Eyam testify to its continuing operations. As the company puts it; "As Glebe operate in a rural location we have a significant beneficial impact on the local economy providing quality, full time, non seasonal jobs." About 150 jobs contributing about £4.5 million to the local economy.

These jobs are precarious in that Glebe Mines operate within a national park, and not any old national park but the World's second most visited after Mount Fuji National Park in Japan. They are going to have to be good custodians if they are to survive the rigours of British planning laws; the expansion or just the survival of their business depends upon it. To that end the defunct Glebe Mine site in the centre of Eyam, one of the Peak District's less salubrious sites of industrial archaeology, was the centre of a rural rumble.

The mining company proposed turning the site over to a new housing development. Housing, a commodity much in demand in a village assailed by the twin pressures of being a mere 14 commutable miles from Sheffield and having the tourist potential to draw in both second home owners and the holiday let market. Then there are the retirees, an increasing phenomenon in an ageing society. Young, local, and yes working class village folk don't really have a prayer at getting onto a housing ladder. A ladder whose first rungs, social housing, were removed by the electorally inspired Thatcherite policy/bribe, the 'right to buy' legislation.

Back in the summer of 2003, I followed the story of Glebe Mines attempts to persuade the village of Eyam to change, expand, and move on by allowing them to build a new housing development on the site of their old mine. Although the Campaign to Protect Rural England argued that such a development would "destroy a significant piece of the Peak Park" this was not a view shared by most of the village. The Chair of the Parish Council, John Fox, described the site as an "overgrown concrete jungle". I showed my students the evidence, a series of photographs I took of the site in 2003. The C.P.R.E. clearly has rose-tinted spectacles. I was with Cllr Fox on this one.

Unsurprisingly the development was turned down but this was just the first stage in a long drawn out game of development strategy. Planning gain and the right mix of housing is what the village and Glebe Mines haggled over. Eventually, in 2006, the decision went the way of the developer and seventeen 4 bedroomed 'open market houses' and ten 'affordable' homes were passed by the Peak Park Planning Board, a scale of development within a village of 750 people unprecedented since the construction of two council estates which topped and tailed the linear village in the 1960's. With this development came a new extended car park for the village, a re-laid football pitch and the suggestion of further sports facilities at an unspecified point in the future.

What is intriguing about the change that Eyam has experienced since the 1960s is that, although the area covered by the village has expanded as a result of estate and single dwelling constructions, the population of the village has broadly stayed the same. Population density has declined. The notice outside one of Eyam's 16th century plague houses lists nine dead from a single two up two down cottage, three generations of one family. Late medieval affordable housing was achieved through high-density occupation.

At the same time that this areal expansion of the village has occurred there has been a gradual evolution in the population composition. It is getting older, wealthier, more middle class and more mobile. It is less likely to have roots within the village although that doesn't mean that an affinity for the place has been eroded. To some extent perhaps the advantages of living in a tight knit, community spirited village are appreciated more today than in the past.

John Davis, a resident of Eyam but also ex head of planning development for The Peak District National Park, when asked about the advantages of village life stated “most people know most people in the village, most people recognise people as being Eyam people and you wouldn't get that in an urban area”. This was, as Eyam resident Malcolm Beet put it a situation where “everybody knows your business...somewhere where you do know your neighbours... a feeling that this is a village, a community”. On numerous occasions locals cited with pride the fund raising in support of the village's elderly population. Surely this was a sign of a community that was at ease with itself.

I did not find a single resident that was against the Glebe Mines redevelopment. Comments ranging from “although it's an historic village that doesn't mean you can live in the past” to “most of the people born in the village cannot afford to live in the village” were commonplace. There was some concern about what 'affordable housing' actually meant, as John Davis observed, “they are not going to be cheap, but cheaper, things are not really low cost these days". The village awaits its new residents vetted by a housing association. New arguments about who gets what are suggested as demand will clearly outstrip supply.

It is ironic that one of the traits of a village like Eyam that makes it so attractive to in-comers is its conviviality. From the traditional events like well dressing to modern activities like its nationally renowned half-marathon this is a village that knows how to connect with itself. A week long carnival in August, a thriving sports association, a gardeners group, village society and the church, all contribute to its identity. As Sangat Bans, perhaps the only non-white citizen in the village observed, "you get out what you put in", although as a traditional beer loving Sikh Sangat also bemoaned the loss of three pubs in the village in the 14 years he had lived there, "the number of people going out socially has really gone down... it has changed from a working village to a commuter village". He is one of those commuters.

Village conviviality has been a central theme of the idea of a rural idyll. An idea extensively invoked throughout British history. What British child has not been exposed to this through their first picture book stories and more lately television programmes from Postman Pat (with its suitably modern spin of a single Indian family residing in Greendale) to Ballamory (disability, ethnicity and Scottishness). From literally birth through to school, it doesn't matter if all you see growing up are the stairwells of a vertical urban social housing estate or suburbia, that rural idyll idea will have been drip, dripping away into your evolving British consciousness. What was it he said when John Major as Prime Minister tried to invoke what Britishness meant as he, uncharacteristically for a Conservative, defended Britain's membership of the EU in 1993?

"Fifty years from now Britain will still be the country of long shadows on county grounds, warm beer, invincible green suburbs, dog lovers and pool fillers and - George Orwell said - "old maids bicycling to Holy Communion through the morning mist" and - if we get our way - Shakespeare still be read even in school. Britain will survive unamendable in all essentials"

This is an idyll that is by its very nature an unchanging response, as some have argued, to "ceaseless and accelerating change", set in train by the rise of the industrial city. The village is viewed as a place of "benign integration of history and landscape" where as Jeremy Burchardt in his book "Paradise Lost: Rural Idyll and Social Change in England Since 1800" argues life was "a landscape of enduring deferential hierarchy". You knew your place but that was OK because everything was right with the world, cricket was still played, the bells still rang out on Sunday.

Something of this idyll remains in thousands of villages across Britain as it does in Eyam. What has changed is that village life is not insulated from urbanism, mobility and globalisation by virtue of its isolation anymore. To some extent what happens in Eyam is about what happens in Sheffield. What Geographers refer to as a "sphere of influence". Eyam is part of Sheffield's hinterland far more today than ever before.

The tensions within a village, such as Eyam today, are the same tensions that underpin much of modern urban life as well, except in much less sharp focus and less outwardly dysfunctional. Malcolm Beet talked about youth disturbance, drunken disorder and even drugs, "What you can get in Sheffield you can get in a village like this".

The modern consumer economy has commoditised rural

communities as much as urban. Even small settlements are fractured into competing interests; farming vs tourism, commuters vs quarry workers, the old vs the young but mostly the rich, and thus more powerful, vs the increasingly marginalized poor. This is what the Glebe Mine Development in Eyam clearly illustrates; competing interests are being played out. Winners and losers.

If this all sounds suspiciously Marxist may I suggest a leaf through the 2004 Oxfam funded report 'Hard Times'. In this report the Peak District Rural Deprivation Forum presents the evidence that even that backbone of the Peak District, its hill sheep farmers are the new rural poor. These are the very people who three hundred years ago produced the raw material that set in train Arkwright's mills and the seeds of the Industrial Revolution, who's sheep shaped the very landscape that we now afford national park status and who's maintenance of that landscape is so essential to most peoples, whether rural or urban, perception of the continuing mythology of the rural idyll.

This report exposes the fact that such farmers generally live on some of the lowest wages in Britain, substantially below the minimum wage, are often tenants who cannot afford to retire near to where they have been custodians to the land and who can only survive through significant subsidy from either European or national government. It is a contemporary rural melodrama worthy of Thomas Hardy, that great myth breaker of the unchanging deferential rural society of the 19th century.

What remains above this constantly shifting social landscape, whether urban or rural, is an understanding that life is played out in communities. Communities made up of thousands of insignificant and sometimes significant social interactions. The people we share our lives with, the places that are common to us. Sheffield is not a collection of villages anymore than Birmingham or Bradford are. Yet it remains a convivial place where local identity remains closely linked to relatively small but overlapping neighbourhoods. This is what people still want whether a Kashmiri Muslim in Nether Edge, a middle class Sikh in Eyam or a retired ex steelworker playing crown green bowls in the verdant Victorian surroundings of a sepia tinged memory of times when this fact was perhaps even more so.

April

If Sheffield had been Cincinnati, or some such American city, a real song and dance would have been made. A museum, monuments, a tag line on a sea of merchandise, perhaps even a learned university research department with an endowment from a local millionaire allowing it to collect the rarest artefacts of the world's greatest passion.

It is difficult to grasp that even in a city as diffident as Sheffield that its status as 'the' home of football is so under played.

We could haggle over this fact. Cambridge University have sought this accolade and Barnes in West London has a credible claim dating way back to 1839. There are even dark mutterings from some club in Edinburgh. Yet F.I.F.A. and the Football Association both recognise Sheffield FC as the world's oldest football club and in 2007 they celebrated their 150th anniversary in the company of Pele no less. Do you need more confirmation?

Look it is a done deal, a fact. 'The Home of Football'. In December 2006 the FA adjudicated on the issue by declaring;

> **"Further to media reports this week, The FA can clarify its position on the world's oldest club. Earlier this week an illuminated script was presented to Cambridge University by the FA to recognise the university's key role in formulating the original code of rules for football. This year marks the 150th anniversary of the publication of the earliest set of Cambridge University rules still in existence. However, the FA, and FIFA, continue to recognise Sheffield FC, founded in 1857, as the oldest club in the world."**

There is no monument at the site of the potting shed near East Bank Road that initially was the club's headquarters at the time of its inception on the 24th of October 1857. An unprepossessing estate pub, 'The Ball' is as good a marker as any. However the exact spot is a bit of a mystery to me. In Cincinnati they would have built a Frank Gehry designed cultural centre as a minimum. Sheffield hasn't even rustled up a plaque.

The obvious question to ponder about Sheffield FC is if they were the first football club who did they play? The club's website anticipating this question outlines that the club's founding fathers, solicitor Nathaniel Creswick and his mate, a wine merchants son William Prest, organised its members into playing games against each other; married men vs unmarried men and professional occupations vs the rest. Not unlike park kickabout football today. A trip down to Endcliffe Park on a Sunday morning can still get you a game of students vs the rest or even Poles vs locals.

Sheffield FC were however, a bit more sophisticated than simply jumpers on the ground for goal posts. They invented the solid crossbar and even introduced to the game the radical approach of heading the ball. This was whilst playing London, at the Oval in 1875, apparently much to the mirth of the home team and fans. In fact the list of Sheffield football firsts is pretty impressive; the introduction of free kicks, corners and even the first ever game played under floodlights. Or how about the first ever football trophy, the Youdan Cup.

Bramall Lane, home of Sheffield United, is less than half a mile from The Ball and is one of the oldest stadiums in the world of football. The first fixture played there in 1862 involved Hallam FC, the world's second oldest club and now residents of the oldest football ground in the world. Their turf is in leafy Crosspool perched atop of Crookes

Hill gazing down upon the city.

Bramall Lane's position on the edge of Sheffield City centre is an increasingly unlikely setting for a major football stadium. The trend in recent years is to decamp to greenfield sites away from city centres whilst pocketing the real estate value of a large slice of city centre land. The ground has undergone a gradual evolution over the past 150 years to reach its current 32,600 capacity, a little shy of its record attendance of 68,000 in 1936. Host to an England Test match and home of Yorkshire County Cricket until 1893, cricket finally bowled out in 1973 when the current layout of a fully encircled pitch with stands tight to the wings came with the concrete construction of the monolithic South Stand.

The construction of a hotel adjoining the ground is the latest addition to what is becoming one of the best medium sized football grounds in the country. It has balanced modernity with tradition. Hemmed in by a grid of streets the stadium has reached its practical limit if Sheffield United desire to remain in a city centre location. Perhaps another tier on the 'Kop' end could raise the gate by a few more thousand but would it be worth the cost and disruption?

It is inconceivable that the club would be foolish enough to forsake a location so infested with the ghosts of football past, yet over the years such mutterings have occurred, driven not by sentiment but profit margins and ideas such as re-branding. What could possibly be a better brand than “The Home of Football”.

When LS Lowry painted his famous matchstick representation of fans arriving at Bolton Wanderers ground by foot in 1953 to watch them play, so one source suggests Sheffield United, it was an accurate representation of the reality of football in those early post-war years. Fans streamed towards the grounds in huge numbers using buses, trams and most of all their feet as they poured out of the tight knit terraced houses that inevitably surrounded so many of Britain's most famous old stadiums. Pubs heaved with working men whetting their appetite for the blood and thunder, which was to be played out in front of the massed standing terraces. Football has always been a predominantly working class activity. It grew out of a working class town.

I was reminded of Lowry's vision of massed ranks pouring towards the hotly anticipated game when I found myself, on a bright early April evening gradually picking up a crowd as I walked the mile and half from my house to Bramall Lane. I met up with my local curate and his sons in one of the numerous Asian owned local grocers on Abbeydale Road. We were stocking up on snacks to avoid the half-time crush. Ian asked me what I was most looking forward to as a neutral supporter. “Observing the visceral hatred” I replied. This was after all derby day.

Sheffield Wednesday - formed in 1867 and the first city club to enjoy national success - versus those Johnnie-come-lately laggards Sheffield United - formed in 1889. Bramall Lane had been home to both clubs during the 19th century and both clubs were formed from cricket teams, an even longer-lived sport significantly developed within the city. The world over, a match of this much pedigree, history and parochial antipathy was hard to find.

I was one of a few people within the seething cauldron of a ground who had vague pretensions of being neutral. I could not escape the fact that an accident of birth and upbringing had imparted a lifelong affliction to supporting Luton Town, currently plummeting down to the lowest reaches of the English league, mired in scandal and bereft of friends and finance. I had tried hard to shift my affections, once in the direction of Wednesday when living in Hillsborough and over the past decade towards the Blades. It was on occasions like this that I realised I'd never reach that spot of tribal loyalty that surpasses logic and sound mental health. When the 90% Blades in the stadium rose as one to scream “stand up if you hate Wednesday” I stood dutifully, moved my lips and turned to Russ my more fervent Blade companion and enquired; “what you do if you are ambiguous about Wednesday? Hover slightly above your seat.”

This was football not for the faint-hearted. A game with 36 attempts on goal, a see-sawing 2 all draw saved for United by a stunning free kick from a Lancastrian, James Beattie, with a mere five minutes to spare. For the neutral it went a long way towards justifying the eye-watering £28 a ticket, for the partisan supporter 90 minutes of agony and ecstasy. They would talk about it for months, probably years.

The crowd seethed with undisguised malice, fights broke out, riot police weighted in with batons to 'calm' the situation. The full range of Anglo-Saxon vernacular was spent. Missiles reigned down upon the beleaguered but happy Wednesday fans as they stretched their lead to two early in the second half. The Police helicopter chopped its way through the skies above the stadium. Then everybody went home to await a thousand work place and school room inquests across the city.

Even with its violent echoes more reminiscent of a time before the Hillsborough disaster this was a game that those giants of the early game of football in Sheffield would have been proud of. The lineage of the early pioneers, who could not have comprehended the remorseless global gravy train that the sport they plucked from its roots in medieval brutality which they moulded into something approximating to 'the beautiful game' we eulogise about today, was manifest in that derby game. It was a mere few weeks after the death of Derek Dooley, Sheffield Wednesday legend who lost a leg to gangrene after breaking it in a game against Preston North End in 1952 and then went on to become Chairman of Sheffield United. Another person who I feel might have been ambiguous rather than hateful about Wednesday.

Derek was born into Sheffield's industrial working class in Pitsmoor in1929. This was eight years before the demise of Sir Charles Clegg, who with his bother Sir William dominated Sheffield life in terms of both football and politics for over five decades. Charles Clegg would have probably claimed that his longletivity, for he was 87 when he died in 1937, came from his "militant teetotaller, anti gambling, anti smoking Methodist religious convictions". He played for Sheffield Wednesday and Sheffield FC, played in the first England Scotland international – although he complained that his predominantly 'Oxbridge' educated colleagues would not pass to him, "a man fra' Sheffield". This however did not stand in his way when he became the Chairman of the Football Association in 1890.

His younger brother William, who also played football for England, making the Cleggs the first brothers to play for the national team, went on to become leader of Sheffield City Council and Lord Mayor in 1898. Both brothers knew Nathaniel Creswick, Sheffield FC's co-founder, well. The Cleggs' father was like Creswick a solicitor and both boys played for Sheffield FC in the 1860s and 1870s.

Through two lives, Derek Dooley and Charles Clegg, the whole history of football, not just in Sheffield but worldwide, can be measured. It was no surprise to hear the heart felt condolences of the world's greatest and most famous player Pele on hearing of Derek Dooley's death. His life was the glue that pinned together football in its birthplace over generations. He was above the parochial aggressions that boiled over in the hothouse of Bramall Lane on a cool spring evening.

It was the intensity and passion that coursed through this game that has helped make English football a global brand, way beyond the expectations of those early pioneers in Sheffield. No event in the world surpasses the football World Cup for global interest, national patriotism and economic enormity. The football stars of today would have been an abhorrent horror to Charles Clegg who stood against professionalism all his life. Cristiano Ronaldo, the most stellar star of the football firmament in 2008 trousers close to £100,000 a week at Manchester United - a glaring, embarrassing miss at Bramall Lane two years previous is etched onto my memory as a rare error from this outrageously remunerated footballing genius.

Football in England had become an expression of the embracing nature of Britain to the forces of globalisation. It had already been a few years since Arsenal had fielded a team without a single British born player, let alone English. Foreign millionaires have invested over a billion pounds buying their way into the most prestigious sporting league in the world. This April three English teams were poised for potential European Champions League glory as they dominated the semi-finals of this most coveted of club football trophies. At club level English football was attaining a dominant power, sucking in capital and talent from around the world.

This Sheffield derby was in that context a time shift to another earlier age when football was more about 'localism'. A time when huge crowds ambled through terraced streets to pack heaving terraces, a sea of flat caps. Wednesday vs United had huge significance in defining bragging rights and local, and this really was local, pride. Very little of football's globalised product was on view.

Of the 26 players who huffed and puffed through this Sheffield Derby only one, Billy Sharp, was born in Sheffield. Yet nine players were born in Yorkshire, fourteen in England, two from Wales, a single Scot, although a South African born player had lived in Scotland since a baby, three Dubliners, a couple of Jamaicans, an Israeli, a live-wire French winger and a Pole - in keeping with the current migratory zeitgeist. Basically this was a British game of football played by some typically British footballers, full of furious pace, relentless see-sawing goalmouth action and some agricultural tackling.

Sheffield United may be more rooted to a sense of place than most football clubs, more imbued with a depth of history, a history unsurpassed by few, if any, other football clubs. They play in perhaps the oldest major football stadium in the world. Albeit a stadium that Wednesday used to play in before United had even been a twinkle in a cricket club's eye. Yet Sheffield United is no parochial club. In January 2006 they bought Chinese Super League club Chengdu as a strategic investment in what is potentially the world's richest football market. True to current global form Chengdu Blades squad contains a couple of Brazilians and a Jamaican. Few sports can readily assert the local whilst being open to the global like football, whether in China or Sheffield.

With what was remaining of the football season ebbing away, as April stalked its way across leaden skies, I took my eight-year-old daughter to her first football match. Like my first matches, at much the same age, this was played out in the lower reaches of the amateur game. For me, a long time ago now, Leighton Town's ground hidden behind Camden Motors garage and nestled next to The River Ousel. For Megan a far more uplifting experience, so I imagined, the legendary expanse of turf that is the oldest football pitch on the planet, Hallam FC, the world's second oldest club. I told her, if you are going to start watching football start at the beginning. She said “Do I get a bar of chocolate at break time”. She saw this as a lesson, a rite of passage to endure.

'Home' chapter 4: April

The Sandygate Lane ground of Hallam FC sits on top of the ridgeline that links Crookes Hill to the main body of The Pennines. This is close to where the Snake Pass route to Manchester slides pass the built up city boundary before plunging down into the Rivelin Valley. In the early 19th century this area boasted a pleasure gardens, where promenading perched precipitously above the Rivelin Valley was briefly popular. It was the major draw of this outlying area at that time. In the early 1800's this was countryside dotted with the desirable residences of the well to do. Breathing fresh air and gazing down on the spluttering poor in the valleys below.

A cricket club was initially set in motion in 1805, football only arriving on the scene a further fifty five years down the line in 1860. Even today the ground is shared between these two pursuits with the cricket square abutting the touchline. The antiquity of the setting is literally set in stone with an impressive old wall surrounding the ground in which a wooden green gate is set as entrance to the cricket club. For Hallam FC a more expansive entrance opposite the Plough Inn suffices. It was the landlord of this pub who in 1805 bequeathed the land to set in motion the cricket club as a good way of expanding business in this rather remote of locations.

Unsurprisingly given its lofty site and dramatic views over The Peak District this is a notoriously cold ground, although one wouldn't have expected it to be quite so cold given that it was the last home game of the season and May was not far from coming. This was Sheffield at its bleakest. Scudding clouds of varying hues of grey whipped over the ground driven by a persistant northeasterly wind. The only protection was the diminutive covered stand and the warming clubhouse next to it.

I had hoped that the Youdan Cup would be on display within the clubhouse. This Sheffield crafted silver claret jug was commissioned by Thomas Youdan, an Irish born, Sheffield based theatre impresario, to award at the culmination of a twelve-team tournament in 1867. It is the first football trophy ever awarded, the final being played out at Bramall Lane. It is the equivalent of a holy relict to the mass worshippers of this most global of games. If Sheffield FC's rule book of 1857 is the Dead Sea Scrolls then the Youdan Cup was footballs grail.

It was lost, forgotten for decades. Nobody can recall a credible story of the cups disappearance. Yet its rediscovery in the 1990's by a Scottish antiques dealer at a London antique fair and subsequent purchase for £2000 by Hallam FC reunited the club with the second most important artefact of football's early history. A recent BBC TV Antiques Road Show valued the cup at over £25,000 - a snip really for something that is essentially priceless - and it was partly as a consequence of this value that the Youdan Cup has now found a home in The Sheffield Assay Office, a hallmark of its importance not just to the city but the world.

A much better home would be the Millennium Galleries Metalwork Gallery which showcases some of the greatest craft to have been realised within the city. Here in the centre of the city the enormity of the local contribution to the creation of football as the world's pre-eminent sporting activity could be more openly and proudly expressed. Hallam FC's clubhouse has a framed, slightly yellowing, newspaper clipping about the trophy's rediscovery on its wall. This is perhaps a closer expression of Sheffield's relationship to the idea of the city being the home of football. It is joined on these walls by a framed signed shirt of Wednesday striking hero David Hirst and local boy Uriah Rennie's World Cup referees shirt. I drank a half of mild pondering all of this low-key memorabilia whilst my daughter queued for the toilet. That is the toilet, singular. It's a compact sort of clubhouse.

'Home' chapter 4: April

A crowd of 150 was scattered across the ground, leaning up against the gloss white metal railings that hemmed in the pitch and evenly distributed through the Lilliput stand. Megan observed that these were really old people, and broadly so they were. A young black guy sat behind us, an injured player of local rivals Dinnington so it transpired. A few children charged about oblivious to the huff and puff upon the pitch.

This was football without any razzamatazz. The pitch, holding up well after a wet spring, covered the players in cloying clay as they slid into tackles and wrestled with opponents. Hallam FC, playing in blue were soon in trouble when a confident Parkgate team, hailing from Rotherham, pressed forward and forced a despairing Hallam defender to handle a goal bound ball on his goal line. After a lengthy consultation with a linesman to identify the offender - who had merged with teammates and was wandering about as if butter wouldn't melt in his mouth - Hallam FC found themselves down to ten men and one nil down as the penalty was dispatched in a style which would of been the envy of Chris Waddle.

The departing Hallam FC player had no complaints but his club captain vented his spleen at the linesman who had snitched his man up. The language started to get a little industrial and it became handbags at dawn. I distractingly opened up a chocolate bar for my daughter, her look of boredom now being replaced by early onset hypothermia. Half time saw respite in a steaming hot chocolate and a quick stroll around the ground.

The football pitch and cricket ground were notable for their uneven topography. The second half would see Hallam FC play up-hill, metaphorically at 1-0 down and a man short, and physically by a measure of three or four metres or so. The cricket square was in pristine green seaming condition and was about the only absolutely level land to be seen. To the southwest the dark mass of Hallam Moor dominated, northwards the ridges that divide the northern tributaries of The River Don were set out along the horizon. The baronnial Scottish style home of Leng, the patrician editor of the Sheffield Telegraph and Conservative politician of the late 19th century, sat at the apex of the ridge with its turreted conceits attesting to the vanity of a self made man. More modest Barratt style new build executive homes infilled this solid suburbia.

It was interesting to consider the thousands of Sheffield folk who had toiled in sporting endeavour upon this turf. I suspected that many of the greying gentlemen who watched intently but with restrained emotion had once sped across this hallowed turf in what to them felt like a less than distant past on a Saturday afternoon like this. It was inconceivable that any other use could befall such a space, this was ground zero for football, and the fact was that its single redeeming feature was its relentless under-stated ordinariness.

Yet, like Hallam FC, I was defeated. They succumbed 3-0 as they ebbed confidence through the second half. I admitted defeat to my daughters increasing numbness, physically and emotionally, as the sky increasingly turned steely, threatening rain. We strided back to our warm air-conditioned car with ten minutes still to play.

Megan wasn't fooled by the exhortation that if you are going to start watching football you may as well start at the beginning, she knew it got more glamorous and impassioned, although she probably suspected it contained just as much swearing. We had swanked around Bramall Lane on one of Sheffield United's community days during the summer of 2006. With the pitch divided up into mini-football games, bhangra in the bars, a plate of samosas on your lap and thousands swarming unimpeded across the stadium it was possible to see how a club can be an integral part of a community.

Although it might be imagined that in its Sheffield home football might be rooted in the traditional this was a long way from the truth. This was still a place of development and one that increasingly grasped the global reach of the city's sporting imagination.

On the first Friday of April I had found myself in the Tunnel Bar tucked into the John Street Stand of Bramall Lane. 'Mooney' had tipped me off about this event. His band, Sparas, were joining forces with some lads from Zimbabwe, Khulu African Arts, who have been seeking asylum from 'Bob' Mugabe, to launch a 'Football Unites Racism Divides' event entitled from 'Sheffield to Soweto'.

Thirteen years on from its formation at Mount Pleasant Community Centre in Sharrow the charity Football Unites, Racism Divides continues to promote the idea that football can break down the barriers of prejudice not just in Britain but across the world. It has like many community projects in Sheffield been resourceful, persistent and successful. It started its endeavours by honouring Arthur Wharton, the first professional black football player who played for both Rotherham Town and Sheffield United in the 1890's by producing not only a biography of one of the first British black working class heroes but also erecting a headstone on his paupers grave at Edlington cemetery just outside Doncaster.

However FURD's real dynamism has been in its pro-active promotion of anti-racist messages, either through its mobile game Street Kick, which has travelled across Europe, or its promotion of teams and tournaments that bring together a smorgasbord of nationalities within and between countries. Even UEFA, the governing body of European football, acknowledges FURD as a model project. It's home is Sheffield United who since 1999 have hosted a fund raising community day with FURD in late May, when local Somali's, Pakistani's and any other local community in an increasingly globalised city charges across the Bramall Lane turf before it is re-seeded for the next seasons on-going saga of thwarted hopes.

This Friday FURD was raising money for the 'Football Between Communities Project' that works with orphaned children in the Democratic Republic of Congo. We got a great little film half way through the night made by FURD during a visit to this war ravenged country in 2007. Children, no older than my own, talked and dreamed about ripping down the wing in a World Cup for a victorious Congolese side. They were no different from thousands of children across Sheffield except their lives have irreversibly been shattered by death and destruction, blighted by gruesome poverty.

The band funked on, mixing up Brazilian, African and Yorkshire rhythms but I ended up leaving uncharitably early before they could unleash their reworkings of old Brazilian samba hits and their international anthem 'Love Football'.

Football has not always been so joyous in Sheffield. The ghosts of one of the worst disasters ever to befall the game in Britain still haunt the memories of many local people. It was on a warm sunny April 15th 1989 that I found myself seated, taking in the early warmth in Bole Hill Park on top of Crookes Hill. It looks down upon Hillsborough football stadium, at that time home of Sheffield Wednesday for ninety years. An impressively large stadium Hillsborough had hosted many FA Cup semi-finals as a neutral ground, on this day Nottingham Forest were challenging Liverpool for the right to reach the FA Cup final.

As has happened to me personally numerous times, shuffling so many fans through turnstiles to get into a ground was stiflingly slow. I was 5 minutes late into this years Bramall Lane derby after arriving 25 minutes before kick off, so even with the advent of electronic turnstiles and bar-coded tickets this problem remains.

Yet on this fateful day a frustrated lack of patience led to a series of events which culminated in the deaths of 96 people. 96, it remains a shockingly high figure.

These were people who literally had life squeezed out of them as they were crushed by the relentless surge of fellow supporters who were released into the terraces by the panicky act of opening the exit gates to relieve the crush outside the ground. This being the era of the football fan as sheep to be fleeced, as opposed to our more enlightened times when the football fan is simply a consumer to be fleeced, the relatively un-steep rake of the lower terraces were hemmed in by robust fan proof fencing. All means of escape were tantalisingly at hand but traumatically blocked.

This disaster unfolded not only in front of the increasingly disbelieving 40,000 crowd but a live television audience of millions. The familiarity of the situation resonating with anybody who watched football on the seething mass of standing terraces that were the hallmark of a big game in the 70s and 80s. A fissure of violence always close to the surface, sometimes bubbling up. It both frightened and fascinated me as a child even in the rather more bijou confines of Luton Town's Oak Road stand.

All these events have been picked over in the 'Taylor Report', numerous court cases and acres of newsprint, some of which possibly reached one of the lowest points, of many, in the journalistic history of The Sun, a publication that still harbours aspirations to be a credible newspaper. At the time I just recall thinking something must have kicked off for there to be that many sirens. I wandered off home and watched events unfold in front of me on TV.

Football took a long while to recover from this. Sheffield was dazed and it just seemed to be the last chapter of a decade that had seen the city freefall through de-industrialisation, throwing up a disintegrating urban fabric and air of general despondency.

Seventeen months later Meadowhall Shopping Centre opened and the 1990s really began. It took a further six years before Hillsborough was rehabilitated when 'football came home' with the European Football Championships in England. This was I believe the moment when Sheffield realised it had a future as a European city of some distinction and not simply a future built upon memories of a great industrial past managing a slow decline into the 21st century.

Three games were played at Hillsborough during a riotously exuberant and sparklingly clear, hot June 1996. All three games involved Denmark. The ground was now, post The Taylor Report, all seated. The fences had been torn down, capacity had been shrunk, fresh paint adorned surfaces and the newly opened Supertram line to Hillsborough unexpectedly gave the city an air of 'European city of sophistication'.

Much to my partners' consternation I had offered to put up three Danish football fans for the duration of their team's stay in Sheffield. Obviously she assumed, and I did wonder myself, that such football fans would come tattooed, belligerent and keen to replicate Nordic invasions of the distant past. We couldn't have been more wrong. Lesse, Thomas and Mikhal were model ambassadors for their country. Selflessly drinking beer at breakfast but never being raucously aggressive. Mikhal was the director of an African development charity.

The deal was that they would get me tickets for all the Danish matches in exchange for board and lodging. I became an honoury Dane for a fortnight. As the Danish national sport was 'drinking pubs dry', and this they took seriously and even improbably achieved on a couple of occasions, my liver took months to recover.

The Danes had nothing but praise for Sheffield, amazed not to find it a grimy industrial city, surprised by the beauty of The Peak District and in Thomas's view blessed to have a wonderful health service after he broke his ankle falling off a dancing podium at the Leadmill night club.

On our first visit to Hillsborough, a ground whose history was known to all of them, we crammed into a tram from the city centre. When the whole tram started to bounce off its tracks as in unison hundreds of Danish fans sang - in English for the benefit of the locals - that international anthem 'If you all hate the Germans jump up and down', the tram came to a shuddering halt. A pleaful voice came over the tannoy politely requesting that they stop their anti-German display because the tram was new and had never experienced such forces, to a Dane they all complied, some apologising to me. I declined to reveal that the trams were built in Germany just in case they were tempted to start up again. Denmark drew one all with Portugal and pubs were drank dry, the streets were peaceful if rather full of hefty men wearing Viking helmets.

Bizarrely Hillsborough never reached full capacity; most locals assumed all the games were the sell out that UEFA claimed. For the last game against Turkey, which although won by Denmark was not enough to put them through to the next round, only 28,600 turned up, 10,000 shy of capacity. Outside the ground numerous people were strolling around offering people unlimited tickets for free. UEFA still claimed the match was a sell-out.

'Home' chapter 4: April

In 1997 Sheffield Wednesday, in the last days of a Conservative government, reached the giddy heights of 7th in the Premiership. It has pretty much been a backward slide since then for the blues. If such a prestigious tournament was to be held in Britain again, say the 2018 World Cup, there is much debate as to whether Sheffield would be the venue for any of the matches. This is unthinkable. Who wouldn't want to play at the home of football?

At the considerable risk of provoking the blue half of the city, it is evident that Sheffield United's ground is a much better football venue today than Hillsborough. Its tight enclosed atmosphere is a cauldron in which a game can come to the boil. The city centre location an increasingly rare anomaly, bar Newcastle, for the modern game.

However parochial football in Sheffield remains, and this probably is a good thing, the game itself continues to bestride the world, its language one of brands, rates of return and product. The end of April saw the consolidation of the Premiership brand when Roman Abramovich Plc found themselves in the final of the European Champions League pitted against The Glazier family Plc in a re-run of the cold war; Russia vs USA. Thousands of Britons were going to bankrupt themselves to see the May final in Moscow. Nobody could ever accuse Britain of not embracing globalisation with anything other than reckless abandon.

Closer to home Wednesday were one must win game away from further relegation and Hallam FC achieved mid table respectability. My partner sighed with relief as a football free world intruded on our home for the duration of the summer.

May

If May 1st 1997 was a 'new dawn' for The Labour Party then May 1st 2008 might be considered dusk. Across England and Wales the incumbent party of government took a battering beyond a mid-term blip.

Much to the satisfaction of Liberal Democrat leader, Nick Clegg, control of Sheffield City Council was wrestled away from the Labour Party. Not since 1968 had the Labour Party taken such a beating in Sheffield. Then the Conservative Party had taken control away from Labour for a brief year as the rank unpopularity of Harold Wilson nationally and a split left vote locally did for Labour patriarch Sir Ron Ironmonger. Today not a single Conservative councillor exists in Sheffield. Their wealthy heartlands are now dominated by the Liberal Democrats who found themselves with 45 seats and overall control of Sheffield City Council. It was 1925 when the Labour Party last had an equally lowly level of representation with 36 councillors. A newly assertive Green Party made up the chamber with three councillors all representing the city centre, the most urban and least green area of the city.

It was quite clear nationally that the 'credit crunch' that had blown in during the winter was a key factor in confidence ebbing away from a beleaguered Gordon Brown. Circumstances, including rising global commodity prices, had scuppered any plans he may have held to make his mark after succeeding his political spar of the previous decade Tony Blair. A cohort of Tory Old Etonians increasingly looked capable of blowing his house down.

And what did I do to defend the party I have been a member of for the last two and a half decades? Bugger all beyond putting up a poster for my local candidate Mohammed Hafiz. I clearly didn't ride that wave of enthusiasm that Paul Bloomfield's selection meeting partially rekindled. I had seen Mohammed out campaigning; he really threw himself into it, got over 2,000 votes and still lost. I felt for him, he seemed to have a lot of zip and vim, he was keen, and keen is a precarious place to be in politics, local or otherwise.

Still because of Mohammed, and my fellow political travellers', glorious failure locally we were now living in Liberal Democrat times. Through my inactivity I had played a small part in their rise. They should thank me.

Strangely, and obviously with the exception of the British National Party, I find that I lack the instinctive hatred that true party hacks can drum up for their opponents. I have no particular dislike of liberalism or democracy. They both sound right up my street. As for 'Green', yes I can probably sign on the dotted line for that. I've just spent the best part of two and half decades teaching the fall gamut of environmental issues, from aviation to zooplankton. I probably have a Greenpeace badge somewhere at the bottom of a drawer. I've got an allotment with a proper composting system, if only I got time to turn it over more. It has been over a quarter of century since I ate meat. Even George Monbiot can't top that.

Apart from ushering in the Labour Party's biggest bloody nose since William Clegg bestrode the corridors of the City Chambers an intriguing political 'B' movie was also played out in the run up to the election in Sheffield; a rather unseemly spat between our local Liberal Democrats and the local Green Party.

Now I expect my bi-yearly Liberal Democrat 'Focus' to have photographs of earnest councillors craning their heads to inspect faulty streetlights or looking indignant at some mindless tagging. A good whinge about Labour favouring this area or that and a graph showing how many seats/votes they need to grasp victory. I don't expect them to slag off the Green Party as well. This time they did. "Greens vote against recycling!" was the rather unsettling claim. Surely some sort of post-modern joke.

I wanted to get to the bottom of this but first I had to get married. This was a reality that was accepted when 'Jack' died. A partner dying within an unmarried but long-term relationship, unless you have legally tied up all the loose ends, is not advisable for those that remain. The simplest solution was to indulge in a dash of conformity to the powers that be.

The intrusive state and its laws had tempered the liberal, free-spirited ethos that remained a significant hangover from my student days. This was also, to some extent, at the heart of some of the struggles between liberalism and environmentalism that I was increasingly perplexed by. Free choice or mediated choice, if any choice at all. This was a debate that would develop as the century unfolded. We would, more and more, need to wrestle with the increasingly universal and complex problems of our material existence. It would be a debate that would be played out at all levels. The neighbourhood, the city, the country and globally. This I would return to once spliced.

Mind you we had held out for 22 years. I couldn't help but struggle through a justification when my youngest daughter, Ingrid, demanded why?
"Err...we love each other",
"Yes but why?"

This was a bit awkward as it was the morning of the wedding and she had decided she was against the idea. I guess telling the kids on the morning of the wedding wasn't such a great idea after all. Still she came round after I'd placated her with a bar of chocolate and some I love you hugs on a father and daughter bonding trip to get the car washed at Tesco's. We all had our 30 minutes of public acclaim and made our declaration of undying love in front of a small but distinguished, or is that delinquent, group of friends.

We gathered outside the late Victorian splendour of the Town Hall where we mingled with the Saturday shoppers. Inside the Town Hall the suitably grand Hallam Room, located on the ground floor looking across Pinstone Street, served us. Richard Hawley, on tape, serenaded us into the room. In my eye line, as I solemnly declared, was the bus stop I normally used to get home from the city centre. Above was Vulcan the god of fire who sits perched on the Town Hall's loftiest heights. I was proud to be married in Sheffield, the Maldives would have been nice, whilst they are still above sea level, but home was just fine.

The sun blazed unseasonably hot as we strolled out of the side entrance of the Town Hall onto the packed Peace Gardens. Kids scooted about through the jetting fountains; M and S sandwiches were being devoured on the pristine lawns. We retreated to the slightly more sedate Winter Gardens, gathered photographic evidence and went home and drank more champagne than was necessary.

The early May sun had woken the city up. The heat tempering canopy of green was unfolding as the mercury zapped up to 26C. The vividness of the early green of the limes that line many of the roads in Nether Edge was a sharp burst of colour set against the clear blue sky. Stately horse chestnuts in full flower adorned the city, their flower spikes reminiscent of a decorated Christmas tree. Hawthorne covered the hedgerows like spring snow and pink cherries shed a confetti of blossom across paths. As the daffodils faded the city was springing into life. Grey to green. I think May is my favourite month, it is so life affirming.

At this time of the year when high pressure builds, diverting northwards any inclement depressions scudding across the Atlantic, I suspect there can be few finer places in the world to be than home. With the first warm breezes from the continent house martins and swifts begin to sore above our houses, the trees stretch out their canopy above woodlands carpeted by bluebells. The city centre is flush with eagerly hedonistic students fresh from the year's final exams and the evenings stretch into velvet twilight. That moment before summer sets in has always been for me, as somebody who has nearly always worked in the world of education, a time of promise and adventure. It is drawing towards the end of an academic year. Exams starting just as the pollen count goes stratospheric.

I figure it is uncommon for most urban dwellers in the modern world to have the opportunity to be so in touch with the vagaries of seasonality as that presented by living in Sheffield. They claim that Sheffield is the 'greenest city' in Britain. On a sparkling late spring day with the swifts returned and the sun high it is easy to buy into this claim.

Yet who are 'they' that claim it? What is it that they are claiming exactly? And is it true?

The first of these questions is hard to pin down in terms of who made such a claim first, however a recent assertion of it came at the full meeting of Sheffield Council in February 2008 when Councillor Bryan Lodge - Labour Party - started off a wide ranging motion basically patting the soon to be departed Labour administration on its back about its commitment to the city's parks by stating;

> **"That Sheffield provides more public parks and open spaces per head of population and has more tree cover than any other City in the Country, making it the greenest city in the United Kingdom and a great place to live."**

This seemed highly authoritative. More public parks and open spaces per head of population. More tree cover than any other city. Could this be so?

I spent a couple of evenings on the Internet working every angle I could think of to see if I could turn up any such data. No joy. So I e-mailed Warwick Toone, Communications Manager at Sheffield Council, to see if he could throw any light upon these claims. Either Warwick is stunningly efficient or he is sitting around all day waiting for any scrap of work to fill his waking hours; he got back to me in less than a day. He suggested that the source of this claim probably originated from a strategy document produced in 1993 for the council by Dr Alan Barber, who is currently a commissioner for the Commission for Architecture and the Built Environment (C.A.B.E.). In this document he states "Sheffield's wealth of parks and green spaces is second to none".

Warwick conceded, "today, many towns and cities make claims about being the greenest". He then set out Sheffield's credentials. They are pretty strong. One third of the city within a national park. OK so barely a soul lives on those heather clad moors that come within the cities administrative jurisdiction, but they are there, constantly on the horizon of many a city street, sparsely populated with sheep, but Sheffield sheep.

Then there is the level of public open space provision, with up to 6 hectares of public green space for every 1000 citizens (national guidelines are 2 ½ hectares). The City council managed 45 parks, 16 recreation grounds, a couple of playing fields, four golf courses and nine woods. Then there were the three gardens, one each of a moor, spa, brook, ravine, pond and common. There were even green spaces that went by the name of 'Tongue Gutter' and some 'Deep Pits'. Of Britain's large urban areas Sheffield has more ancient woodlands and Sites of Special Scientific Interest than any other, either in absolute or percentage terms.

This was pretty persuasive evidence but then Warwick pointed me in the direction of Adrian Middleton who, in 2004 whilst working as a volunteer at Sheffield Galleries and Museums Trust was asked to look into the claims that Sheffield is "the greenest city" in Britain.

This was a task he took seriously and with even more rigour than his website investigation into the 'teashops' of the Peak District. The result is two in- depth papers worthy of a degree dissertation. Not peer reviewed assuming you don't count my careful reading of all 27 pages of data analysis (this is sound science - Karl Popper would have aproved of it). Really all you want to know is what he concluded. Well, with a string of caveats preceding the tentative conclusions Adrian eventually states, "Sheffield can justify its claim to be the greenest 'major population centre' in Britain". He does however acknowledge that Kirklees, West Yorkshire, although not a city as such, does give Sheffield a run for its money.

All things considered although Councillor Lodge's claims cannot be definitely verified through a single piece of 'killer' research, if what is meant by 'greenest' is some measure of vegetation within an urban setting, trees, parks and biodiversity, then Sheffield is probably the greenest city in the country.

Adrian Middleton is first to damp down such a claim, first by questioning whether quality might be more important than quantity and then by stating it is not what you have got but what you do with it over time that really matters. The amount of trees per head of population is not 'greenest' within a political context. Sheffield is not an English Curitiba, the Brazilian 'eco-city' that is like a Mecca to urban planners intrigued at how to make their cities more sustainable.

In October 2007 a report by the 'Forum for the Future', an environmental charity whose explicit aim is the promotion of sustainability, Sheffield trundles in 7th out of the 20 largest cities in England and Wales in a league table of sustainability. So not number one there if that is what 'greenest' means!

Like the concept of sustainability itself the overall sustainability score of the 'Forum for the Future' research is subdivided into component parts. Gro Harlem Bruntland, an ex-Norwegian prime minister, was commissioned by the United Nations in 1983 to head up an investigation into “the accelerating deterioration of the human environment and natural resources and the consequences of that deterioration for economic and social development". That is 25 years ago. Let's just remind ourselves that 'green' is not some new idea, Chesterfield born Frank Fraser Darling, spelt out the fundamentals of climate change way back in 1969 in his Reith Lecture for the BBC.

Four years after the United Nations set in train its investigation the landmark report of Bruntland entitled 'Our Common Crisis' set out the first clear definition of sustainability. It was human development that “meets the needs of the present without compromising the ability of future generations to meet their own needs”. A more wide ranging explanation of this simple idea involves not simply environmental considerations but considerations of social equity as well. What really 'frightens the horses' about sustainability is that it does suggest that a significant and dramatic re-distribution of resource consumption is required. Not just at local and national scales but internationally as well if the world is going to be a truly sustainable place. This is where the real global inequality lies. Every citizen of Sheffield is almost certainly within the richest 15% of the world's population, richest 10% for most. Why are there poor people? Because there are rich people. It's a simple enduring truth.

What is wealth if not the store and use of global resources; minerals, energy, food, information? Some people think that sustainability sounds like a new form of 21st century Marxism, after all how else are you going to persuade a population of resolute consumer capitalists to get a little, actually make that a lot, poorer, at least in terms of their resource consumption. As George Monbiot, environmental activist and provocateur who also ignites argument within the pages of The Guardian observes; "what does a sustainable economy look like, well a bit like a 'third world' economy". This was something that I guess would have to be high on the enquiry list if I could ever persuade any of the city's leading Greens and Liberal Democrats to talk to me about their efforts to claim the 'green' high ground in the battle for Sheffield's hearts, minds and votes.

What they all could be proud of, as politicians, is that in the 'Forum for the Future's' calculations of sustainability Sheffield was awarded 3rd place, behind Brighton and Hove and Edinburgh, for what is known as 'futurity', another component of sustainability. This was calculated by looking at each cities commitment to tackling climate change, their action on recycling, the level of biodiversity within the city and the number of 'green' business's operating within the city. Considering the wealth of Brighton and Hove and Edinburgh it was not that surprising that they took the top berths for 'quality of life' whereas Sheffield was a meek thirteenth. A clear marker of the economic inequalities that are so evident, still, within Sheffield.

Wherever Sheffield fits into the increasingly assertive view that sustainability is the key notion in whether an area or a population is 'green' there can be no doubting the raw material that the city has endowed itself with. For a city that almost choked itself on malodorous fumes as it raced to define the very idea of an 'industrial revolution' it is heartening to know that through the efforts of both private citizens like J. G. Graves and an enlightened council throughout most of the 20th century, that the seeds were sown to allow the city to aspire to re-invent itself in the 21st century as Britain's 'greenest city'.

It may not be necessary to quantitatively confirm such a proud assertion, at least in terms of trees per head of population. Your own eyes should suffice. A good starting point might be one of Sheffield's 45 public parks. How about the oldest?

When the 13th Duke of Norfolk decided, in the 1840's to plant up an avenue of turkey oaks leading into what was originally his deer park on the edge of Sheffield he could only have imagined just how imposing and regal they would become over time. Nationally Britain is a treasure trove of wondrous trees, which connect the present with the past in a tangible, living and breathing way, and so this collection of turkey oaks might be deemed nothing particularly noteworthy by national standards. Yet within Sheffield they remain one of the arboriculture highlights of a city that is perhaps as famous for its multitude of trees, some two million of them, as its buildings. This avenue of turkey oaks lines the entrance into Norfolk Park from Granville Road.

Norfolk Park, less than a mile from the city centre, is one of the oldest public parks in Britain. Its inception in 1841 came just one year after what is considered Britain's oldest public park outside of London, Derby's Arboretum, was opened. The official opening of Norfolk Park in 1848 was some seven years after its layout was engaged upon. The 1849 Ordinance Survey map of Sheffield shows its planned layout clearly and also indicates how the park was linked to the city via the avenue of turkey oaks and Norfolk Road, which in the early years of Queen Victoria's reign, must have been a surprising dash of grandeur rising out of the slums and tanneries of the Sheaf Valley.

The early Victorians had become increasingly concerned about the rapidity of urbanisation and its impact upon the morals of the working poor. It was thought that parks would have a socially beneficial function, encouraging a more contemplative temperament among working people, and decreasing public drunkenness.

Sheffield had already started to develop a botanical gardens some two miles west of its centre in 1836 but this was not open to all and sundry, requiring a membership subscription to enjoy its pleasures. That so many of the migrants to the city at that time had rural roots is explicit in the extensive 'garden plots' that ringed the city in the mid 19th century. These were the forerunners of allotments. The formal grandeur of Norfolk Park was at that time for Sheffield's working poor the only insight they had into the landscapes of the grand houses that the aristocracy and the new captains of industry created for their pleasure.

Possibly the finest example in Britain of these arcadian visions of a tamed and compliant nature is to be found at Chatsworth House, the historic seat of the Dukes of Devonshire, some 14 miles south-west of Sheffield. For Sheffield's poor at that time this would have been almost a mythical place.

Norfolk Park today has never been more splendid. The trees planted as acts of faith in the future have reached maturity. Substantial investment in the park has seen it transformed from a down at heel amenity to one of the city's best kept secrets, even from most of its residents. I had lived in Sheffield years before I paid it a visit and barely any of my students are aware of it, let alone have visited it. My kids vouch for the quality of its playground.

The hub of Norfolk Park is its 'Centre in the Park' opened in 2000 courtesy of Single Regeneration Budget funding from central government. From its curvaceous frontage sweeping grassland flanked by woodland opens out onto a vista of Sheffield city centre and the Pennine moorlands on the horizon. The view is breathtaking and every bit as interesting, although a tad less historical than that of Florence from the Piazzale Michelangelo perched above The River Arno. One can only imagine what Queen Victoria made of it when, in 1897, she was serenaded in the park by 50,000 children in honour of her jubilee.

An even more dramatic view of the city is afforded from the promontory above the Sheaf Valley on which the city's Cholera monument is located. Lit up at night, this needle like memorial to the dead resulting from a devastating outbreak of cholera in 1832 hovers above the city, offset by the surrounding darkness of Clay Wood.

Cholera was a recurring hazard of the urban poor in pre 20th century Britain. With sewage systems still to be developed and on street water taps shared by hundreds of people it is not hard to understand why. Sustainability was in nobody's lexicon then, not even on the horizon. Such a grand monument to even a sizeable contagion such as that which raged in 1832 would have been unlikely to have been proposed if not the Master Cutler of Sheffield at that time, John Blake, not succumbed. Previously cholera had been associated with the 'drunk and idle', that was clearly challenged by so eminent a man's death, not that the rich were not also prone to bouts of drunkenness and idleness.

It wasn't until the York born physician, John Snow, demonstrated the spread of cholera in Soho, London, being linked to use of a water pump that a real appreciation of the unsanitary conditions in which the disease bred was arrived at. Such moments were instrumental in persuading the munifence class that the 'undeserving' poor deserved more, if only to avert a riot, a revolution even.

On top of the graves of 339 victims of cholera a neat formal garden has been created. From here in the summer the extent of wooded Sheffield is plain to see beyond the city centre. Looking due west towards the Pennines, the suburbs are obscured by a canopy of foliage broken by rising spires and the monolithic bulk of the Hallamshire Hospital. This canopy was largely the creation of Victorian gardeners who not only planted native species but increasingly turned to a multitude of exotic plants brought back as botanical plunder from the far reaches of empire. Some of these, such as himalayan balsam, have established themselves so aggressively in Sheffield – helped by its tactile seedpods that explode when touched - that they are considered a threat to endemic flora.

However it is native species that pre-dominate; birch oak, ash, sycamore, lime and alder. Within this urban eco-system niches have been exploited by what might be considered rural species. Foxes of course, scream their way through mating in February, deer are numerous in the woodland fringes, even badgers excavate their way through suburban gardens across the city. And then there are the birds. My best 'twitch' in the city was an over-flying osprey that I spotted from my back steps. Yet jays, sparrowhawks, goldfinch, long-tailed and blue tits, wrens, robins and tawny owls are all regular visitors to my handkerchief-sized garden.

Although I was drawing closer and closer to accepting Sheffield Council's 'greenest city' boast disquiet over the claims made by the council about its green credentials seemed to be constantly breaking out.

A long running saga over whether St Luke's Hospice, a place I've always had a deep suspicion I might see more of than I might like, could relocate its peerless efforts at striving to give death some dignity to Graves Park, in contravention, so many argued, of the original 1920s trust from alderman J G Graves, which gifted the park to the people of Sheffield. The problem was the area concerned, although within the bequest, it was not really in the park but a walled adjunct that had served as a municipal nursery for many a decade and presently is home to 'Green Fingers', a horticultural charity, and a fair degree of under use verging on dereliction. The move of St Luke's was not an unreasonable proposition but vehemently opposed by many in Sheffield, some of whom were buying into the idea that the council was selling off the family silver or rather our prized begonias. This idea was probably put to bed by the arrival of the Liberal Democrats at the Town Hall; they had been consistently opposed to St Luke's proposition.

One particular protest showed the conflicts between perception and reality when the concept of 'greenness' was being haggled over. In February the Friends of Loxley and Wadsley Common had declaimed in The Sheffield Star that those who believe the “Propaganda from Sheffield City Council about our green city and the number of trees they plan should take a walk on Wadsley and Loxley Commons”.

Well this seemed a reasonable suggestion, as I had not visited this area of the city for probably over twenty years. Then, walking up from Malin Bridge, where I lived at the time, you traversed a large imposing house, which I recall being derelict, into some youngish woodland before topping out over some tumbled down rocks up to a triangulation point cast amongst a small open patch of heathland. I was always on the look out for adders, thinking this a likely spot after spotting lizards basking on the rocks during hot days. There were rumours, records perhaps, of nightjars, churring into the dusk. I never heard them. It was a great place on a summer day to laze back and listen to the hum of the city in the valley below.

There had been change, as only is to be expected after nearly a quarter of a century. On what 'had' been the heathland plateau the detritus of management was all too plain to see. Large stashes of cut birch were left scattered about the heath. From the proliferation of birch stumps a rapidly establishing wood had engulfed the heathland over the past decades. This was clearly an attempt to reclaim the heathland from the expanding woodland. Creating a diversity of habitats to allow wider biodiversity would have been the pitch of the conservationists who probably proposed such action.

Some species had already searched out their new niches and a sign next to one large heap of brushwood stated it had not been moved because of breeding blackbirds. Clearly not much more could be done until the breeding season came to pass in mid July. The sign had been adorned with graffiti shouting out 'more lies'!

The basic beef of an uncontactable group called 'The Friends of Loxley and Wadsley Common' is that Sheffield Council are imposing a top down management regime upon this area and that such an approach is characterised by removing/destroying - choose your own description - the recent silver birch growth.

To confuse things further another local group 'Wadsley and Loxley Commoners' is broadly supportive of the council's management, in fact has been active in shaping policy. Their near neighbours at Wharncliffe, a few miles further north up the River Don had a similar birch invasion problem around its crags and a local conservation group had taken to organising voluntary days 'birch bashing' to try to get it under control.

What the 'Friends' drew upon, beside a deep antipathy towards Sheffield City Council, were the views of Dr Mark Fisher, a self styled advocate for nature. The position of this greener than green environmentalist and evangelist for permaculture is set out on his website entitled 'Self-willed land'. In his 'manifesto' the aim of 'rewilding open spaces' is centre stage. This is not a nuanced appraisal of the conflicts between human activity and the development and maintenance of the biodiversity in which we as humans live and dominate. Rather it is a call for humans to butt out of nature, to leave it to its own devices, for it to become self-willed. Technically speaking it is an argument for what is known as climatic climax communities to increasingly reassert dominance over plagioclimax communities of an agri-environment. Well that is what I would tell my students.

I'm sure Mark Fisher is a nice bloke who cares passionately about nature but his grasp of the interacting pressures on green spaces that are in close proximity to major urban areas is brief, or to put it another way, is not his brief. Yet his fingerprints crop up again in the arguments being marshalled by Friends of Blacka Moor, another one of the myriad 'Friends' groups in the city that draw those within the wider community interested in specific places and spaces together. Such groups are increasingly common across the city. They broadly are not spokespeople for the wider community but rather the loudest specific voices within a community. They are a vital cog in any democratic process; they certainly stop any council officer having an easy ride. As such, they are probably a good thing, regardless of whether the campaigns they engage in are campaigns that the broader community might support. In the case of Loxley Common two such groups are in opposition to each other. They are the non-political part of a participatory democracy and are normally concerned with single issues.

I drove down to Blacka Moor on the last Sunday of the month, calling in first to see some friends whose house has extensive views looking southwards over the moors. I then continued on, up Penny Lane, past the text book pretty Cricket Inn which unsurprisingly overlooks an achingly picturesque cricket pitch, up the romantically named Strawberry Lee Lane until arriving at the rough hewn car park at the foot of the moors.

I strode out up the main track passing an imposing collection of introduced beech trees way-marking the track beside a tumbling brook. Woodland dominated much of the lower slopes of the moorland, deceptively wild looking, but partially tamed woodland. The track opened out into a bracken and bilberry landscape with plenty of heather to add vivid purple hues come August. I continued on up to Blacka Hill at just over 1000 feet without seeing a single person; northwards up to half a million people's homes were in my horizon. Here skylarks serenaded my climb and red deer probably watched my progress. This was not wilderness as such but it was easy to see how rising out of the city the sense of such apartness could wash over a lone individual. The 'Blacka Blogger', who writes almost daily of his walks upon the moor sets out both the beauty he senses in the place and what he believes to be its threats. He sets out his position in his blog preface;

"Blacka Moor is on the South West edge of the City of

> **Sheffield. It is 445 acres of mixed landscape. A fine place to escape from the madness of modern life, its noise, its hyper-activity and the over-managed work places. Here, for a lifetime, nature has done its own thing. It has not been driven by other people's plans and targets. This has been where to come to re-charge the battered spirit. But it seems nowhere can long remain free from the influence of managers, specifically self-serving land managers and conservationists. And they have arrived here bringing their barbed wire, their farming practices and their self-justifying management plans intent on controlling that which cries out to be left alone."**

I met up with Blacka Blogger, Neil Fitzmaurice, a couple of weeks later. It was a cool, overcast Friday mid afternoon. It was a 'blind date', I had no idea who he was although I had a good idea where he was coming from after following his incredibly place specific but engaging blog for the past couple of months. His posted photographs of red deer grazing on the moor had impressed me. As Neil himself observed a recent national newspaper guide to British Wildlife had suggested that the wild highlands of Scotland were the best place to spot this largest of British mammals, not so. Sheffield would do nicely.

I was also a bit sceptical of his position because he had a tendency to intemperately rubbish those who worked in 'the self serving conservation industry'. He had a view about how Blacka Moor should be managed and the Sheffield Wildlife Trust, who managed the land on behalf of the city council, had thwarted it. It was clear he wasn't happy about this.

We strode out from the Strawberry Lee Lane car park, climbing up to the moorland on Blacka Hill, Neil in sturdy walking boats, myself embarrassingly in a slight pair of work shoes. Neil set out the recent history of Blacka Moor and the substance of his conflicts with Sheffield Wildlife Trust. The core of this was the conservation manager's proposals to enclose the moor and stock it with highland cattle. The intended purpose of this was for the cattle to trample the bracken that dominated parts of the moor, weakening it and thus, in theory, arresting its spread. Obviously for the dog owners, one of the most regular users of the moor, such a proposal was one that might restrict their or rather their dog's freedom. Not only that but highland cattle are quite intimidating beasts who have a tendency to shit all over the paths.

The paths were dry and shit free thankfully for my prissy Italian footwear. We climbed up through a beck and came to a crossing at its apex where the tell tale signs of red deer were clear, a dusty area of flattened vegetation with considerable damage to the surrounding trees. Clearly the red deer could do the same job as the cattle if only there were enough of them. We stood around speculating where the deer would have come from and settled on Chatsworth a few miles south across the moors. On top of the hill sweeps of cotton grass gave sudden bold light to the moor. We looked back across Sheffield watching the darkening skies of a storm trundling across the city centre. Neil suggested that you could see Lincoln Cathedral from here, thirty miles or so eastwards, not today.

On the walk down to the car park we chatted about Ethel Gallimore, who more than anybody is responsible for this expanse of rugged countryside belonging to the citizens of Sheffield. Back in 1927 when the Duke of Rutland offered Blacka Moor up for sale it was a surplus grouse moor. It was Gallimore who persuaded the wealthy alderman J. G. Graves to buy the land and gift it to the city. It is said that when Graves finally complied with Gallimore's entreaties, he said, "Will you leave me alone now?" She declined and Graves, who made his fortune developing one of the first mail order shopping companies in Britain, employing over 3,000 people in the city at its height, became perhaps the greatest philanthropist that Sheffield has ever known. He found that Blacka Moor was just the beginning of his generosity towards his adopted home. Along with Sheffield City Council Graves bought land right around Sheffield's boundaries in order to stop unchecked urban expansion. In the 1930's they practically invented the concept of a 'green belt', which then got exported down to London and across the country. Graves went onto gift an art gallery, further parkland and the central library to the city. Gallimore set her sights further afield and set about the task of bringing Britain's first national park into existence, The Peak District National Park.

In his own way Neil Fitzmaurice was carrying on that local tradition of cussedly digging in his heels in order to protect and enhance the 'golden frame' that surrounds and sets off the city of Sheffield. I'm sure that Ethel Gallimore would have warmed to his commitment.

The Sheffield Wildlife Trust (SWT) were less sure about Neil, on occasion they had effectively barred him from meetings about the future management of Blacka Moor. Some bad blood had flowed over the years. If I thought that some sort of rapprochement was perhaps in the offing this was quickly dispelled by recent blogs that showed a consistent relentlessness in its attacks upon the SWT. It was under this backdrop a week after my stroll with Neil Fitzmaurice that I met John-Paul Ward, the acting SWT site worker for Blacka Moor. Now here was a very pleasant young man whose only 'self-serving' perspective appeared that he liked his job and he wouldn't mind hanging onto it. It was a really worthwhile thing to do, it made a difference. When I pulled up in the car park he was collecting up litter to past the time of day waiting for me.

It didn't take us long to broach the subject of Neil. John-Paul sighed. “Well” he replied “Neil is certainly passionate about the place, active, committed.” I sensed he wanted to say 'bitter, relentless, really causes me grief'. He politely declined to follow that line. Instead he set out what SWT were hoping to achieve. The bracken-trampling cattle would be on site next week, about a dozen. What their impact would be was hard to say however this, along with hand removal and some selective spraying, should have an impact on the amount of bracken, over time. John–Paul didn't think there would be much of a problem with dogs and they certainly were not going to be restricted. This was good news for nearly all those we passed that day as dog walking seemed the predominant activity this Friday afternoon. Whatever happened at Blacka Moor it was happening after four or five years of consultation debate and reports. I suggested you might get planning permission for a nuclear power station more quickly. Twenty years ago this would have passed as a quip now it was more likely to be a statement of fact.

I think it is fair to assume not everything in this process was handled with aplomb by the SWT. I also think it is not unreasonable to consider that the friends of Blacka Moor are not representative of the views of most of the moor's users. The most vocal, yes. The most assertive, without a doubt. However I suspect most of the remarkably few users of Blacka Moor that I 'good afternooned' over 4 visits in a month cared little for the arcane machinations of moorland management and the politics of conservation. They would have cared that such expansive land of remarkable beauty was in essence the property of the people of Sheffield, in perpetuity. The legacy of J G Graves aroused serious passions within the city as St Luke's Hospice would testify as they cast their eyes across the city to find an alternative site to Graves Park.

The heart of the St Luke's Hospice debate is what JG Graves intended with his legacy. For Blacka Moor he set out his ambiguous position in a letter to the Sheffield Telegraph on 28th February 1933.

> **"The object of the purchase is to preserve the moor in its natural state and to prevent any alteration to its present character by building operations or any other form of interference. I have the pleasure of offering Blacka Moor as a gift from the Graves Trust to the City of Sheffield, with the condition that the moor will be allowed to remain in its present natural state."**

Why ambiguous? Well what is natural about moorland? It has been created through generations of active management, grazing by sheep. Natural would be self-willed, woodland in time. However clearly Graves wanted it to remain moorland so management it must be.

What this fascinating, and I use this word indulgently as I suspect that only Geographers and their like might use the word fascinating in this context, about this snapshot of conservation and conflict is that it illustrates, in a small way, the essential contradictions of liberty, as represented by Neil, and environmentalism, as pursued by the SWT. It also helps illuminate why Sheffield became and remains the 'greenest city' in Britain.

Should our beautiful green places in this densely populated island be managed, intervened in, controlled and for what purpose? Or should they become self-willed, truly natural in their dynamic progression. Our responses to virtually all our environmental challenges in the future will be determined by a similar dichotomy. How much should human choice and individualism be restricted in order to achieve some balance and dare I say it 'order' that will lead towards a more sustainable future. Liberal greens, like Sheffield based Joe Otten argue that individual freedom and the markets should not be suppressed in a doom laden sub-Marxist centralism that he suggests is the ultimate perspective of The Green Party. Perhaps he has more insight than most as he once served on the executive national committee of The Green Party. He now is a cyber cheerleader and local activist for Nick Clegg. He is one of the thinkers behind the claim locally that the Liberal Democrats were more 'green' than The Green Party.

As to the specific claim that Sheffield Green Party were voting against recycling. Well it will be no great surprise that this was all a bit of political smoke and mirrors. A part from the fact that this Liberal Democrat proposal to extend doorstop recycling services to glass collections was only presented to the Green Party a matter of hours before the budget vote, technically there are issues that suggest this proposal might not be as successful as it might be imagined. Glass is heavy and expensive to recycle, most of it is recycled into aggregate for building not for making new glass and this was yet another recycling bin, the fourth for many in the city. Great in the large gardened west of Sheffield, a bit more problematic in the inner city terraces. A more 'green' response would be a polluter pays approach but the incoming Mr Scriven flatly rejected charging for the amount of waste a household produces. Let me guess this might cost the higher consuming residents of west Sheffield a bit more. The arguments no doubt would continue.

One thing the Liberal Democrats could be a little confident about was the ability to claim that their administration was presiding over the 'greenest' city in Britain. It is true, fairly asserted by a multitude of organisations and individuals promoting Sheffield's charms. The issue was how these places and spaces that are so contributory to the quality of life in the city were to be managed. Whatever path was to be taken community gatekeepers were waiting to keep those choices honest and transparent. It seemed to me that democracy was alive and kicking whether I liked its outcome or not.

June

We arrived back from four days camping in Dorset - a county so quaint there are even thatched bus stops - to a garden and an allotment bursting into almost uncontainable growth. A prolonged dry spell for the first three weeks of May had been replaced by a sultry grey rain. If a plant couldn't grow now it would never grow. The slugs went into overdrive.

It seemed improbable but not impossible that a repeat of last year's June floods in the city could be repeated. In an attempt by the council to offset this possibility, culverts and storm drains had been cleared in preparation for a 12-hour deluge on the 3rd. The previous year on June 25th some 75mm of rain fell into the tight river valleys dropping out of the Pennines that feed into the River Don. It resulted in surging rivers, unprecedented in my memory, breaking their man made constrictions throughout the city. It was described as a 1 in 400 year flood, I'm sure the odds are narrowing quickly with the continuing onset of global climate change.

My local park, Millhouses, stretched out in a narrow linear strip in the River Sheaf valley, was particularly hard hit. A 14 year old boy was swept away to his death whilst on his way home from school. The ad hoc memorial to Ryan Parry remains even though the ripped up asphalt the treacherous water destroyed has been repaired. A more permanent memorial to this unfortunate school boy is arriving soon.

The flooding was at its most dramatic in the Lower Don Valley where The River Don has carved out a wide flood plain as it travels northeast towards Rotherham and eventually The North Sea. The city was almost cut in two as the river rose up. A friend who worked in the north of the city took his life in his own hands as he tried to make his way home to the south of the city. The city centre was divided in half for many hours. With many central roads awash and the river continuing to rise he negotiated the new footbridge just upstream of Lady's Bridge. A few minutes later the police stopped anybody that foolhardy attempting it again. Meadowhall was awash, stock floating in aisles; helicopters swooped to rescue workers from factories bordering the river and a man was swept to his death in The Wicker as he tried to escape his inundated car.

I found out all this after I got home from work and turned on the TV. The rain did feel especially intense as I got off the bus. I think the fact that I sloshed my way down the pavement and nearly lost my footing in the cascading water coming down the steep cobblestone ginnel up to my house should have suggested to me that this was something a little outside of the ordinary. Friends and family rang to see if we were OK but frankly if our house flooded you would have built an ark by then. Like most people in Sheffield we live on a hillside.

Of course it shouldn't be entirely surprising that a flood plain floods, even one with a now highly engineered river. This is the natural response of a river under extreme conditions and a month's rainfall in less than a day constitutes extreme, especially as the antecedent conditions were wet, wet, wet. It was upon this flood plain that the industrial fortunes of Sheffield were built; The River Don was the lifeblood of the steel industry that exploded into life in the mid 19th century and led to Sheffield being forever labelled 'Steel City'.

It was the wide Lower Don Valley that had the flat land that was required to scale up Sheffield steel making when in the 1850s Henry Bessemer developed his technique for bulk steel production opening the doors for the industrial age to go truly global. The first to take advantage was John Brown and he developed Sheffield's first mega mill in 1862. Following fast on his heels was the family firm Vickers who opened the River Don Works in 1865. It remains to this day. The floods of June 2007 one of the few events to quash its fiery furnaces, a feat even the Lufawaffe could not achieve.

The River Don Works is Sheffield. The reason it is a city and not a town. If a city could have a heart this for Sheffield is that place. It is as complex and pulsating as that organ. It has sustained the lives of tens of thousands of Sheffield folk, perhaps hundreds of thousands. It's main aorta, The River Don, feeding it the cooling water to damp down its blazing core. To get to grips with the significance of this reticent symbol of Sheffield's past and perhaps to understand something about the city's future this was one of the key places that I wanted to visit in my year mulling over my home.

The sixty acres of blackened hanger like buildings that are stretched out across two sites adjacent to both sides of the River Don was a place of mystery and intrigue to me from my very first months in the city in 1982.

The amount of times I had driven down the Brightside Lane 'canyon', the public road that goes through the centre of The River Don Works, is far too numerous to recollect. The works towered over the street, shattered iron sides, blackened beyond comparison, allowed fleeting glimpses of fire and light accompanied by the insistent thump of drop forges. The view down Brightside Lane was a linear cityscape hemmed in by these vertiginous hulks that looked directly towards Vulcan on top of the Town Hall some three miles distant.

It had been the route the mini-bus took that whisked me out to the Polytechnic's Wentworth Woodhouse site. At that time I wasn't aware of the significance of the site that I was travelling through. It didn't attract the cache of a Cadburys in Bourneville, Port Sunlight or

Saltaire in Bradford. No enlightened religious entrepreneur was driven to make a working atmosphere that he hoped would touch the soul of man. This was the inferno, the dark heart of industrialisation. It had helped to make Sheffield's name and became a place of legends, ghosts and myths.

It is also a working steelworks, still. Even people in Sheffield need reminding of that. I suspect that a significant number of locals really have very little idea that the River Don Works is still up and running and punching well above its weight. I had been following its convoluted history in the local paper for two decades and I sensed that now after nationalisation, privatisation, renationalisation, merger, predatory venture capitalists and a dilettante foreign owner something was growing that was beginning to remind the world that Sheffield steel had not evaporated in the 1980s under the triple onslaught of globalisation, Thatcherism and de-industrialisation. Furthermore this was not a story of 'new' Sheffield, the city centre flats, call centres and the culture and leisure that had come to the fore in the last decade. This was 'old' Sheffield, but old with a very modern twist.

I thought it would be tricky to get a visit; I'd only managed it once before when I visited a GCSE student on work placement in the main furnace shop. I was awed, he was awed. It sure beat double science. Although brief it remained seared into my memory. This time I e-mailed their media team and in a matter of days the non-executive director Peter Birtles replied and said fine, when? I was starting to get disconcerted by the sheer efficiency and helpfulness of those I was asking for help in getting to grips with my city.

The first thing Peter said when I sat down in his spartan, utilitarian office beside the reception of Sheffield Forgemasters gate No 1 was that I clearly wasn't a threat as I had to be cleared by the Defence

Ministry to gain entry. They had sent my name off and hadn't got a reply, so that was OK. Forgemasters was a defence secure area, I would find out why later. I immediately confessed that my father was a 'self styled Marxist' and trade union firebrand, Saltley, Grunwicks and all that. We reminisced about George Caborn, father of Richard Caborn, the soon to be departed Sheffield Central Labour MP. George, a lifelong communist had sat across the negotiating table from Peter haggling over the minutiae of pay and conditions when Peter was starting out his career in management. This was a career that had begun as an apprentice at Samuel Osborne's steelworks right in the heart of the city on The Wicker. It was a good start; I liked this guy, an unabashed capitalist, a self-made man and a pragmatist. There was reams we could probably disagree about but today he was going to show off his patch, I sensed he was quite proud about doing it. Frankly the pride was understandable.

This was the oldest working steelworks in the world. The rest of the competition in Sheffield had all gone under the bulldozer yet here was a business that could trace its roots back to the mid 1750s and on this site since 1865. The River Don Works came into being at a time when Sheffield was at the height of the industrial revolution. As I have already outlined the city centre sites of the early metal trade pioneers were constrained by a lack of space and in a period of five years in the 1860s the city expanded with huge rapidity along the Lower Don Valley towards and into Rotherham. Jessop and Cammell joined Vickers and Brown in constructing huge steelworks to take advantage of the seemingly exponential world demand for Sheffield steel. Carlisle Street departs the inner urban suburb of Pitsmoor straight as an arrow for two miles along the north side of the Lower Don Valley, it became the 'de rigueur' address for global steel makers for a few decades in Britain's imperial heyday.

Why then? Why Sheffield? Well there is no escaping the fact that

Britain's colonial aspirations and projection of power were built upon military muscle and transport for trade. Sheffield supplied the wherewithal. Armaments, iron for ships and railway track. And although the city had grown up on its rivers, with huge reserves of coal literally under its feet, its location even then owed as much to tradition, skills and innovation rather than hard headed geographical logic. Every drop of iron ore had to be brought into the city along first canals and then railways from North Sea ports, shipped in mainly from Scandinavia. It was to be expected that from 1880, when Wilson Cammell relocated its steel making activities to coastal Workington in Cumbria (Cumbria, what were they thinking?), that the pull of the coast would be irresistible for bulk steel production in the long term. Workingham steelworks are now derelict. Sheffield forges on.

The history of Sheffield Forgemasters is to a significant extent the history of industrial Sheffield over the past 150 years. From the humble beginnings of Edward Vickers, who ran a corn mill on the River Don close to the centre of Sheffield in the late 18th century, it took less than half a century for them to become a global giant, part of a conglomeration of steel makers that by 1870 produced half of the world output of steel.

For a brief while the railway tracks that were opening up North America were sourced from Vickers. However the United States, although in many ways a perennial 'Johnny come lately', once they get going on something have tended to blow the competition out of the water and steel is one such example. The steelworks at Carnegie in Pittsburgh rapidly eclipsed not only Sheffield but also the rest of Europe.

This is when Vickers started to specialise in what at that time of empire was one of the nation's core businesses, 'war'. David Hey,

Professor of local history at The University of Sheffield has described the Lower Don Valley as being "the single largest concentration of armaments manufacture ever witnessed in history". Companies within walking distance of each other competed to manufacture even more destructive shells and even more resilient armour plate.

Vickers diversified into shipbuilding at Barrow in Furness (again in Cumbria, why?) and The River Don Works fed it the plate steel and shells to help construct the fearsome British Navy. They cast the steel for the world's first submarine, the first machine gun and generally exported the means for death and destruction, colonial subjugation and imperial might to the four corners of the globe. If it was pink in the atlas the River Don Works was partially responsible.

The scale of this might is one of the great sights of the city. The River Don Engine commissioned in 1905 to power a plate steel rolling mill has been moved to Kelham Island Industrial Museum, one of the best provincial museums you are ever likely to stumble upon. Like Forgemasters they too were shut down by the floods, unlike Forgemasters they remain closed. When they reopen later in 2008 The River Don engine will remain their chief attraction, it is awesome. The first time my youngest daughter saw it fired into action she ran screaming from the museum, nothing would coax her back in. The power is tangible, the building rumbles, the vibrations rising through your feet. What really staggers is the speed at which its motion power can be reversed, forwards, backwards, forwards, backwards, rolling out 90 ton ingots into plate steel for battleships. Every child in Sheffield should be taken to gaze upon its power.

The build up to World War Two pulled the Sheffield steel industry out of a slump. Rationalisation had occurred bringing together Cammel Laird and Vickers. Once war commenced The River Don Works were a key target as they were vital to the war effort producing amongst a multitude of armaments, crankshafts for both Spitfires and Lancaster bombers, the bouncing bomb that took out the Ruhr reservoir dams and the 10 ton grand slam bomb, at that time the single most explosive conventional bomb ever produced. They all came to pay homage including Churchill and King George VI. The Luffwaffe came but missed, twice. If only the Germans would of carried on this tradition into penalty shootouts.

The post-war period saw the company move through a series of changes that created an incredibly unsettled company. Renationalised in 1967, becoming part of the British Steel Corporation, The River Don Works started to concentrate on producing huge castings for the expanding North Sea oil industry. Ironically they also produced the rolls for rolling mills in the foreign steelworks that would help drive much of the rest of Sheffield's steel industry to the wall in the 1980s. Another new and growing line of business was casting components for the expanding nuclear industry.

The 1970's were a time of strikes with a “management culture that was not focused on profitability” according to Peter. In fact Peter confirmed to me that the steelworks only made a profit in a single year in the second half of the 20th century. It was a strategic asset and as such propped up by successive governments, blue and red.

In 1983 Forgemasters came into being with the privatisation of parts of the steel industry under Margaret Thatcher. Its workforce then numbered 6,500, a fraction of the 32,000 employed by the amalgamated steel works of what had been Vickers and Firth Brown prior to nationalisation out of which the new company was grown. Losses continued, strikes continued. Even though this amalgamation project was dubbed Phoenix the company did not rise gloriously out of the ashes of de-industrialisation. It did however stagger on until

1998 when the cavalry were thought to arrive in the shape of Aitchson a US steel company who added Forgemasters to their business portfolio. They really didn't know what to do with the company, in fact they hadn't much of a clue about anything as by 2005 they filed for bankruptcy.

Such a state of affairs certainly raised a few political eyebrows and a management buyout of Forgemasters was encouraged. Up to £60 million of government money helped ease the transition, primarily in the underwriting of significant pension liabilities built up over generations. Dr Graham Honeyman led the buyout and now he presides over a company which in 3 years is turning over a multi-million profit on the back of a packed order book stretching many years into the future.

After an hour in Peter's office we donned overalls, a hard hat, earplugs and goggles and set forth into the land of blackened hulks. Huge open plan hangers that clearly had rhyme and reason but one that would be impossible to comprehend without an expert guide. They were filled with activity. We started in the pattern shop, light, airy spacious and full of complex abstract structures made out of wood. Now I've put up shelves, built raised beds and can wield a saw with bodgers aplomb but these guys - and apart from the secretarial staff and an enigmatic woman sneaking a fag outside the door of the finishing shed everybody I saw was a man - these guys are the people you want to build your new kitchen. What they must earn moonlighting can only be imagined. These were abstracts in plywood that would have had Barbara Hepworth drooling.

Across the yard everything changed when we entered the forge, which fitted just about every stereotype of a grimy, noisy, hazardous environment. Crunching across the slag we peered down into the cavernous pits into which metal was cast. The molten metal did however have a considerable journey from the farthest reaches of the works to get to the forge. Across the river, down a public road - obviously shut for such an occasion - transported in huge crucibles, not quite Heath Robinson style but certainly not what you want if you were designing an ultra efficient steel plant from scratch.

These vast spaces appeared to the uninitiated to have a chaotic and perplexing sense of purpose. Those men who inhabitated the forge went about their work unperplexed and purposefully. They briefly acknowledged the presence of 'tha' boss and turned back to the task in hand. A lot of welding seemed to be going on. This was potentially an extremely hazardous place to work; only recently a member of the workforce had lost their life in an accident. This was a place where procedure and practice were essential in order to get things done safely, to be able to walk through the front door of your home after a hard days work. I wondered what the health and safety would have been like back in the day. I have some film footage of a melt at The River Don Works taken in the 1920s. White-hot molten steel splashes dangerously close to a flat-capped 'melter' while tens look on in rapt attention. For some reason I am reminded of a matador in the ring as the thermometer is thrust into the open furnace door.

It was easy to see from even a cursory visit to the foundry how such work would set up a thirst. This was hot, dry work. Physical, tough. The Lower Don Valley had spawned tens and tens of pubs to service such thirsts. Few remained in business today. I had heard that at one time one of the steelworks had actually had its own pub on site.

It wasn't until we crossed over Brightside Lane on the works internal footbridge that it was possible to see the elemental beauty of the castings that were created in the foundry. The machine shop was an engineer's heaven. My father, who was an engineer in the car industry and my wife's father (this is one of the first times I have used that descriptor-wife - how odd it seems after 22years), who was a marine engineer for the MOD would have been transported to engineer's heaven. A micrometer precise, polished and oil slick atheist heaven.

In the machine shop the raw metal was treated and machined into the components that Forgemasters supplied worldwide. 80% of what was produced went on its way via Immingham Docks. The metal gleamed, pristine and precise.

Here was a giant propeller, there a propshaft for a French navy destroyer at least 20 metres long. Parts for nuclear submarines, warships and hydroelectric turbines were on our itinerary. I was particularly taken by the three men intently examining a huge abstract metal shape chained up from the roof that in the end would somehow lie at the heart of a nuclear reactor. It was as big as my house and weighed, I don't know, a lot. The engineers seemed pretty confident of the chains as they stared up at the casting from below. A few years previously a similar casting had fallen from a crane in Antwerp docks whilst being delivered from Forgemasters. It sunk the barge beneath it in seconds, resulting in the death of two crew. Eventually it was hauled back ashore by massive cranes and sent back to Sheffield to be re-machined.

As I admired the engineering I was increasingly grasping why there was a significant level of security required for this site. I didn't even suggest I took a few photographs. What exactly did that huge gleaming chunk of metal do inside a nuclear submarine? Or that massive metre thick container that was part of a nuclear power station? I also started to realise that a fair amount of the future for this scale of forging and engineering was dependent on certain strategic choices that were coming to a head in government. Was the country going to embark on a new nuclear power programme in response to both climate change and an energy crisis that was growing more tangible by the day? Petrol had reached the uncharted territory of £1.20 a litre. Gas and electricity bills were driving new inflationary pressures that were proving almost impossible for the government to get a grip on. Although wind turbines were beginning to march right into the heart of cities and solar technologies were touted as a possible panacea, some hard decisions were going to have to be made, and soon. The Labour Government had sat on these choices for a decade seemingly hoping not to have to choose. Later this month a report would be published outlining these choices. I sensed Peter had a fair idea what it would contain. Which way the wind or even the atom would blow.

Then there were defence contracts. A pair of aircraft carriers was awaiting government confirmation. They were to be the single most expensive bit of military kit the British government had ever commissioned. The River Don Works fully expected a slice of the action, after all if not them then whom? Even the French government placed significant defence orders with Forgemasters and you just know this was probably done through the gritted teeth of a French defence minister.

This was the point of Forgemasters in the 21st century. It was a bespoke, one stop shop for extremely large, extremely tough and extremely well made bits of metal. It had few competitors globally, Japan Iron and Steel definitely and China Steel increasingly. How long before Tata, the Indian steel making multinational giant that had recently secured a massive foothold in Sheffield with its purchase of Corus Steel would muscle onto Forgemasters turf? The Russians also couldn't be discounted in the future. But the cachet of Made in Sheffield, one of the world's first global brands, still mattered especially when it was backed up by innovation and engineering verve.

At present the company has seen its turnover rise from £45 million three years ago to £140 million in the last substantially flood affected year. It's order books were filling, a £60 million deal over ten years to supply steel casks to transport and store nuclear waste in Germany (The Germans send their radioactive waste to France to get reprocessed and then get it back to bury in their own territory - Britain does the same for some of Japan's nuclear waste). Turbine blades for huge hydroelectric dam projects in China and India. Steel rolls for mills in South Korea and Russia. If they could surely these countries would make their own stuff I suggested to Peter. He replied that it is a question of quality, sure they can make this stuff, it's just they want the best and when it comes to extremely large bits of shaped metal Sheffield still led the field. Actually he acknowledged that the Japanese were up there as well.

In 2007 the company hosted the World Forgemasters Conference and showed off their technology to the world's leading steel makers, just as the city had in the 1850s with the Bessemer converter and in 1913 with the invention of stainless steel (a fortuitous experimental accident). More pertinently for the city over 250 jobs have been created in the last three years and this year alone some 60 apprenticeships are being offered in everything from laboratory technicians to steel makers in the melting shop to marking up. Whatever 'marking up' is, it takes three years to learn it. Blue-collar jobs. Well paid, highly skilled.

It has been years since such skills were being passed on within the city. If it didn't happen now some of these skills would be lost. I wasn't surprised that they got 50 applications for each position. It's the graduate jobs they find hard to fill; recent recruits in this area have come from Mexico and Germany. Peter lamented that they didn't have strong enough links with the Metallurgical Department of the University of Sheffield. This I was a little surprised by as I knew the University of Sheffield were collaborating with Boeing Aerospace at a high-tech machining factory built on top the site of the 1984 Orgreave riots during the Miners Strike.

Forgemasters made a profit last year, about £20 million. This is modest by the standards of BP and the real global multinationals. Yet all of it is going back into the company, no dividends were paid. The idea is to plough everything they make back into the company for several years. Peter suggested that their London based financial advisors found this a little strange. A new forging press costing up to £70million will be installed. The whole strategy is based on export lead growth, the weak pound certainly wasn't doing the workers any favours when they flew off to Tenerife or Greece for their summer holidays but it was certainly making exporting a lot easier.

I could have quite easily lingered much longer but a lecture beckoned and Peter probably needed to get back to proper work. I missed the melt shop in action, I angled for an invite back but Peter with a lifetime working in a steelworks didn't hear me. I wanted to see the crucibles of molten steel rumbling in the dead of night through the cordoned off streets of Attercliffe. I imagined it to be akin to the trundling of the massive 'juggernauts' that are paraded through the streets of Puri, India in celebration of Hindu deities. Except this was discreet, uncelebrated and largely unknown. It seemed an apt metaphor for Sheffield steel today.

The day previous to my visit to Forgemasters, a warm sunshine filled Sunday, I declined the attractions of another 'farmers market' in Nether Edge and the Meersbrook Park walled garden open day and instead set forth with the intention of walking all or at least some of the Five Weirs Walk.

This is an eight-kilometre footpath that hugs, as best it can, the route of The River Don from the city centre along the Lower Don Valley to Meadowhall and on to the border with Rotherham. This project was instigated in 1987, promoted then by the Thatcherite quango the Sheffield Development Corporation. It has taken over two decades to piece together the geographical elements that make up the walk and as Donald, my walking partner and fellow Geographer and I immediately discovered, it remains a work in progress.

We had intended to set forth from Lady's Bridge, the geographic centre of Sheffield from its medieval days, but were halted by a forest of temporary railings. This bridge, which was William de Lovetots big infrastructure idea in the twelfth century, has effectively joined the north and south of the city together for generations. Rebuilt on numerous occasions, the bridge still contains elements over 500 years old. It was hard to judge as the consequence of the battering it took in the 2007 floods was a shroud of plastic and scaffolding, its base buttressed by huge bags of sand. It was showing its age. Whatever its fate it would forever be immortalised by local balladeer and occasional rocker the bequiffed Richard Hawley, in his highly acclaimed, 2007 CD *Lady's Bridge*. More of Richard later I hope.

For all its local significance the Golden Gate it is not! After all Lady's Bridge is barely 20 metres wide

Mind you in the sparkling early summer sunlight we should have been thankful for the leaps and bounds of progress that had come to the River Don over recent decades. As the town of Sheffield grew into a city in the 19th century the Don was not its palatial waterfront as The Seine is to Paris or The Danube to Vienna. No it was its toilet, the Pennine rains flushing it seaward. Professor David Hey uncovered this contemporary description of The River Don around Lady's Bridge from 1861.

> **"Rivers sluggishly flowing through the town are made of conduits of all imaginable filth...polluted with dirt, dust and carrion, the embankments are ragged and ruined."**

This national report in '*The Builder*' observed that where the The Sheaf entered The Don, a matter of metres from Lady's Bridge:

> **"A plank bridge over the Sheaf here shows dead dogs and cats floating on the slimy waters, and a terrible condition of the partially-walled banks, through outlets in which fluents of excremental slush ooze into the river"**

Things didn't improve over the rest of the 19th century. Samuel Osborn built an ever-expanding steelworks a little downstream of Lady's Bridge inexplicably in the style of a castle and then expanded it on cast iron stilts over the river. The extremely tall chimneystack of Osborn's was immortalised in 1916 by Stanhope Alexander Forbes in his oil painting "Sheffield: River and Smoking Chimneys" which sometimes hangs in The Graves Art Gallery. The artist's palate is restricted to brown, oh and a touch of grey. It never made it onto tourist posters, until today. A postcard reproduction of the painting is pinned to my notice board courtesy of the Gallery's shop. I'm looking at it now, oh go on a dash of white as well but that's only smoke rising from the crucible chimneys.

However through all this grime the area also was home to a brewery (from 1852 onwards Tennant Brothers and later Whitbread's from 1962 to its closure in 1994) and more improbably a Batchelor's canning factory that is reputed to be the birthplace of the mushy pea. Beer, mushy peas, and steel truly this place lies at the very heart of Sheffield culture.

Currently most of the area is a work in progress. A jumble of bollards, paths blocked by metal grills, towering cranes and scaffolding. At the centre of this activity is the I Quarter building; a 15-storey glass tower perched across the River Don from the vaulted outflow of The River Sheaf. This is the next stage in a continuing reclamation of The Don waterfront. In much the same way Newcastle has rediscovered The Tyne and Manchester its canals. Developers have been drawn to water in the urban renaissance of England's northern cities.

Thankfully the River Don does not still flow with dead dogs and shit. It is still recovering from the floods with plastic still clinging to the branches of the crack willow's that have colonised the loose islands of sediment that fragment the river; at least ten feet into the canopy. A surprisingly large amount of traffic bollards had also found their way into the waters. But it was clear water and a family of ducks were scooting across the weir. Once I had seen a kingfisher flash under the bridge.

This area around Lady's Bridge was fast evolving into a major office quarter for the city. A host of law firms and The Home Office had moved in upstream, downstream a clutch of speculative offices waited to be finished and let. The whole area was in flux. The Wicker chocked of it's through traffic due to a new traffic management scheme and then cut through by the new inner ring road was fast changing. The street had been at the heart of the squalid Irish slums during the Industrial Revolution. Families huddled into damp cellars cheek by jowl to the relentless industry. It had retained its pre-eminent place at the heart of Sheffield's incoming global diaspora. Pakistani, Afro-Caribbean and African hues enriched life here. Fresh barracuda, no problem ditto lamb kebab. Yet even the kebab houses that lined the road were changing. Black marble frontages were replacing the hand painted signs.

Our second obstacle was a battered railing that had been placed across the entrance to the Spider Bridge. This post-modern architectural flourish took the route of The Five Weirs Walk through the arch that the River Don slips through to pass the grand Victorian engineering of the Wicker Arches. This bridge is suspended inside the arch that once supported Sheffield's Victoria Railway Station. The railing was a minor obstacle as it lay crushed to the floor. It wasn't until we were 10 metres across the bridge that the reason for this thwarted closure dawned on us. Where were the aluminium sides to the bridge that reduced the probability of plunging into river below? At rogue smelters we guessed. It seemed that all across the city, metal, if wasn't nailed down and even some that was nailed down, was being recycled illegally back into a rapacious global economy. The lead roofing of my local swimming pool had disappeared last year, closing it for five months. Damn those Chinese and their booming economy.

The other side of the Wicker Arches the city centre became a distant memory in a matter of metres. The landscape turns instantly to one of industry. Few pedestrians venture this way. After a quarter of a mile of Effingham Road we cross back over the river on an original Sheffield manufactured Bailey bridge. This is a transportable bridge that was strung across European rivers to aid the progress of the Allied armies on their way to Berlin. The bridge's metal strut work was still jammed with a beaver like agglomeration of woody debris washed up a clear twenty foot above the normal water line in the floods and still not cleared. A year on I'm a little surprised. A new riverside path planted up with clematis takes us up to Norfolk Bridge. This survived the deluge well.

The overhung river path was proving to be a cool place to be as the clear blue skies kept the temperature rising. A niche of urban heath land, a plant community developing on the impoverished soil of a levelled slagheap, slots in beside the river. Although this area is called Salmon Pastures three young men were bashing their way through the dense riverside vegetation hoping to catch brown trout. Not a fanciful idea I have seen them in nearly all of Sheffield's rivers in recent years.

We are then sent on a diversion through the uninhabitated back streets of Attercliffe. This is because the next section of the walk has been washed away. As we walk down sun bleached Washford Street a garage band provides a soundtrack from their rehearsal space tucked away in a seemingly derelict building sitting in a scrap metal yard. It is a cinematic moment; the light is sharp, the chords angular and the outlook ambiguous. We turn a corner peering up Bessemer Road, cobbles, and factories of uncertain provenance, red brick and corrugated iron, dusty and decaying. And a single extremely clean and shiny top of the range Mercedes parked intriguingly alone. There is nobody but us and a distant middle eight. We scurry on thinking we have just walked through the opening shot of a new Guy Ritchie movie, the one where Brad Pitt plays a murderous Yorkshire scrap metal dealer.

Attercliffe has, since its hey day of back to back slums, sulphurous skies and bustling shopping street replete with its own 'department store for the poor', Banners, developed a notable reputation for sleaze and legal ambiguity. Massage parlours, sex shops, gay clubs and 'La Chambre', a private members club of intriguing national repute hold fort. There had been some attempts to draw more mainstream nightclubs into the area. Vogue, Hotshots and Pulse all came and went in the 1990s. To far from town. Even the Art Deco gem of a cinema, The Aldephi, in the centre of Attercliffe had once played mine host to all night drum and bass sessions. This club was a dark, thunderous place, with an edgy vibe not unlike the surrounding steelworks. I went only once; getting a taxi home, spannered and numbed by sub-bass, at four in the morning, in

Attercliffe, was a genuine challenge.

Tucked away in this low rent landscape was a varied menu of sexual peccadilloes, apparently. In many respects it was an ideal solution to a perennial problem. Hardly anybody lived around here; neighbours to annoy were thin on the ground. Prostitutes were sunning themselves outside a massage parlour as we passed. It was Sunday lunchtime, trade was slow.

When we rejoined the riverside path we witnessed the scale of the damage that had created such a disjointed Sunday stroll for us. On the opposite side of the river the retaining wall had been demolished as the river had attempted to extend its meander, as rivers do when they flood. This substantial wall was now adding to the debris washed by the river but it had done its job, beyond was the mainline railway on a raised embankment, unscathed.

Soon the immovable presence of The River Don Works would interrupt our progress and the temptation of a pint at a pub pulled us over into Attercliffe proper, ' *The Cocked Hat'* our destination, one of the remaining boozers in the valley. It was very quiet, a complete change to my last visit when The Rolling Stones were playing next door at The Don Valley Stadium.

Just beyond the pub the Sheffield canal is transported above Darnall Road within an aged but solid metal bridge. We joined the towpath here and returned into town. The canal towpath was a much busier thoroughfare than the Five Weirs Walk, fishermen - one with his partner stripped down to her underwear silently beside him, joggers, Sunday strollers and a wistful junky propped up on a seat with a thousand yard stare were all greeted in a rapid return to the city centre.

The dominant landmark on this part of the walk, apart from the canal obviously, is the towering presence of the Sheffield heat and power incinerator. Its chimney perhaps higher than even Osborn's fabled totem. I have a clear view of it from my home some four miles southwards, it's plume a clear indicator of the wind speed and direction. Mainly the smoke is going towards Rotherham, steadily.

The controversies surrounding this plant have driven Greenpeace activists to scale it and drape it with banners berating its existence, it remains the bete noir of the local Green Party who would rather reduce, reuse and recycle. Admirable but the incinerator does extract energy from waste, distributes that energy locally and reduces the volume of landfill needed. It meets some pretty stringent EU pollution guidelines, the like of which would have filled the early steel makers with horror. I wouldn't choose to live next door to it but I like the idea that the city deals with its waste within the city rather than dumping it out of sight and out of mind. It's an impressively sizeable building. I see it as a symbol of the cleaning and greening of a valley once so polluted barely a blade of grass could survive its atmospheric tortures.

It is common to think of Sheffield as a post-industrial city, the result of shaking out some 100,000 manufacturing jobs between 1971-2001, some 73,000 of which were based in the metals industry. However this is only a partial truth. Clearly the fog of pollution that hung over the huge steelworks of the Lower Don Valley is largely dissipated like the thousands of jobs whose endeavours created the fumes. Yet industry is far from dead and buried in Sheffield. Forgemasters is one example, a major example, of the tenacious ability of Sheffield industry not simply to hang on but to continue to thrive.

Diana Buckley, a researcher for Sheffield City Council produced a report at the beginning of this month entitled "Modern

Manufacturing" which set out to "challenge the continued perception of decline in the manufacturing industry" within the city. She sets out the facts; 29,000 people employed in 1,600 manufacturing businesses, three-quarters in companies of less than ten employees. Over half of these companies are concerned with metals and engineering. As Buckley observes "the success of the manufacturing industry is often measured by its ability to generate employment, thus employment decline has led to a prolonged perception of an industry in decline". Yet it is the output of this declining band of manufacturers that we should consider and here Sheffield has excelled. Between 1998 and 2004 a 38% increase in productivity was achieved creating some £3 billion of production across the Sheffield City region.

Where is this productive dynamism happening? Not just in blackened hangers clinging to the sides of the River Don but also in newly constructed industrial parks on the edge of the city.

On top of the cleared Handsworth site of the Orgreave Coking Works, scene of King Arthur's biggest battle, is the Advanced Manufacturing Park. Opened in 2004 by Prince Andrew, under the backdrop of an Apache attack helicopter, this is a cutting edge manufacturing environment. Boeing, Rolls Royce and Alcoa all do business here in anonymous sheds in the style of Milton Keynes. Still making things out of metal that threatens and destroys, just they do it in cleaner buildings today.

Steel city is not an epitaph but a continuing reality. On the last week of June I found myself driving down the Carbrook canyon as an orangey-brown haze of fumes hovered above Forgemasters foundry. I should have been repelled but instead found it strangely comforting.

July

The entrance to Frog Walk sits anonymously on the five-way round-a-bout that brings to an end Psalter Lane's progress towards the city centre. An Edwardian gaslight illuminates the narrow entrance. The mature trees that overhang the walk as it drops down steeply into the Porter Valley darken its constricted confines. This is a classic short cut, a ginnel, connecting Nether Edge with Ecclesall Road. To venture down this defile requires some local knowledge, you would have to be shown, you wouldn't stumble upon it.

Frog Walk is potentially intimidating on a dark night, with the ghosts of the adjacent general cemetery and the fears of the Daily Mail entering into your imagination. I have no doubt that its gritstone walls could tell many tales, macabre to merry. On a bright summer evening it is slither of rural tranquillity, the city locked out until you see the debris within the River Porter (a full sized basketball hoop on this occasion!) and the wall of graffiti that abuts the riverside path. You emerge next to the 1836 Victorian gated bridge whose Greek Doric columns act as the main entrance to the General Cemetery.

On the last day of June the short run up Cemetery Avenue to Ecclesall Road contained one of the fleeting sights of summer in the city. A street full of rubbish. Black wheelie bins acting as the core for the mounds of discarded detritus of departed students. In some streets, particularly in the tight terraces off Ecclesall Road and areas like Crookes and Broomhall, levels of student occupation almost reach the level where the adjective 'swamped' might be considered. Barely a property on Cemetery Avenue was now occupied. Undrawn curtains revealing bare rooms punctuated by stripped beds and cleared desks. Old posters, discarded lecture notes, impressively large collections of beer cans and a microwave oven that had never seen a cleaning spilled out of sacks. Considering that a number of prosecutions had been pursued nationally for incorrect bin filling - lid partially open, put in wrong place that sort of thing - this was an exhibition of anarchic student non-conformism, of sorts. In the 1960s they occupied universities and built alliances with striking factory workers to pursue radical utopias now the 'right to party' and litter with impunity was as libertarian as many students aspired to.

It was a group of students that I was off to meet. The end of course drinks for the 2nd year Humanities and Social Science Access to Higher Education Certificate. This was a tried and trusted route for mature students into university. Social Work, Law, Education, Psychology and Criminology degrees were all destinations for the year of 2008. These were no run-of-the-mill middle class students; Ecclesall Road was a broadly untrodden path for them. They had mainly travelled over from the eastern estates, Waterthorpe, Richmond, Darnall, Hakenthorpe and The Manor. Talking to a few of the students as we sat outside in the warm sunshine it was clear that my easy familiarity with Ecclesall Road, on occasion referred to as the city's 'golden mile', was not something that they shared. This was the main artery into the heart of Sheffield's wealthiest districts, the couple of miles it stretched from the inner ring road to Banner Cross the home to the full range of opportunities to dilettantely dispose of cash: champagne bars, designer chocolate shops and a casino. What is there not to like about Ecclesall Road apart from the traffic, oh and parking and the way it makes me feel skint!

The bar that they had chosen was at the city end of the road, close to the Collegiate Crescent site of Sheffield Hallam University, a place that for many of them would become a second home over the next three years. It felt a bit like a reconnaissance mission.

We would not have had to travel far up the road from our lager and black and soft young red wine to Laurent Perrier vintage champagne and Chateau Haut Brion. We were at the cusp of west Sheffield, wealthy Sheffield and east Sheffield, working class Sheffield. Gown or town. 4X4 or weekly saver bus pass. There are not that many cities in Europe let alone Britain that can display such a sharp geographical disparity of wealth as Sheffield. It was as if the city suffers from some kind of economic bi-polar disorder.

At the very core of modern Geography are three key ideas, globalisation, sustainability and inequality. They are interwoven ideas. None can really be comprehended without comprehension of the others. They are also ideas that traverse the commonly perceived distinction in Geography between the human and the physical. All of this was very much in the forefront of my mind as the summer holidays slipped into view. In previous recent years I would have been dusting down the passports, filling up on Euros and looking forward to a thousand miles of French motorways. Last year 999 miles took us to a villa on the hills perched above the Gulf of Saint Tropez. Work forgotten for weeks. This year work was going to nag away at me all summer. September would see the launch of a brand new Geography A level syllabus, a complete modernisation since the last change a mere eight years previously. No bad thing in principle but a pain in reality, a lot of work. No foreign holiday beckoned.

This new syllabus offered differing routes to students heading towards their GCE A level. In the first term a choice had to be made between “Unequal Spaces” and “Rebranding Places”. For me this was a no brainer, the very phrase 'rebranding' brought me out in a post-modern sweat. Sure it was interesting to see how change, or regeneration, was altering both our cities and countryside. However the idea that 're-imaging' was at the forefront of understanding our changing world was an idea that required context. Part of that context was inequality and a topic that "explores the social, political and economic causes of disparities and identifies the 'haves and have- nots' " was a core idea. It remains to be seen but I suspect that rebranding will be the most popular option nationally as Geography teachers attempt to 'rebrand' their numerically declining subject with a 'sexier' take on the subject. I guess I'm a bit old-fashioned thinking that inequality still really matters.

What all of this did mean was a summer mainly at home and to start with the need to get to grips with inequality in Sheffield and to come up with some 'all singing and all dancing' fieldwork which would allow students to both understand the research process and the issue of identifying inequality whilst examining the ways in which it is addressed.

Ironically inequality came into this decision. Many, perhaps most schools and colleges tackling this syllabus would 'franchise out' – to keep in step with modern ideas - most of their fieldwork. This normally means a week at field study centre where the in-house staff take over those onerous tasks of thinking through meaningful fieldwork and resourcing it. The cost of such trips could be a considerable financial burden; £200 would be cheap, £400 not uncommon. A reputable private school (radicals might suggest that this is an oxymoron) in Sheffield was willing to take its students to Nepal at significant, four figure cost, to, amongst other activities, help build schools in one of the poorest countries in Asia. Thousands of pounds to help comprehend global inequality, humm, is it just me or does this all seem rather bizarre?

My A level students were not in that financial league, in fact a good proportion were in receipt of an Educational Maintenance Allowance paid by the government to help economically disadvantaged students to continue on with their education post 16.

Financial accessibility was at the forefront of any ideas that I could come up with. So with a couple of days planned in Skegness looking at coastal issues such as managed retreat, resort development and physical challenges to the coastline (don't panic traditionalists there would be a healthy dose of coastal morphology in all of this), the idea was to come up with some fieldwork in Sheffield concerning inequality. Where to start?

Last year much was made of a report by Barclays Bank that ranked UK locations according to the living standards of their resident populations. This piece of research was more nuanced than most because it was based upon buying power, taking into account price differentials in housing and other consumer markets. When using this technique to compare the economic status of different countries it is commonly referred to as purchasing power parity. In other words it's not simply what you earn but what you can purchase with what you earn.

Nick Clegg's Hallam constituency, that lies at the heart of the west Sheffield 'wealth belt', rolled in 4th (£39,697 net spending power per individual) in this research. This was much to the surprise of London based journalists. It is hard to credit but 4th was one place above Hampstead and Highgate. Wealthy northeast Leeds came in 8th (£37,931). Top, no surprise, was Kensington and Chelsea (£50,438).

That such wealth exists within Sheffield should also be of no great surprise. I would consider it credible that if such a calculation included all wealth, fixed and liquid, west Sheffield would not be too far shy of over three thousand millionaires calling it home. I know a few, but this is really a hunch rather than a verifiable fact. Not that it is quite the fiscal accolade it once was as a result of the staggering increases in property values over the past decade. Even I, in 2003 and 2004, earned more from the increase in the value of my property than I did in wages. 'Earned'? Rather sat on my backside, paid a relatively benign mortgage and felt smug about my ability to ride the crest of a capitalist wave. 2008 was proving to be the year people were being reminded that capitalism was about the downs as well as the ups. For a nation without a recession for 16 years, nearly a couple of generations, this was becoming a challenge for people to get their heads around. It was bizarre but it felt like modern capitalism was about privatising profit during the good times and nationalising debt in the bad times.

Yet that real wealth was still here, and in a city like Sheffield, where flashy shows of wealth were limited and still rather frowned upon, was sometimes surprising to people. Sheffield wealth was rather stolid and under-stated. Even millionaires asked for discount and eyed up a bargain. Or is that just the ones I know?

Some local millionaires didn't quite grasp the Yorkshire diffidence to being flash. Prince Naseem Hamed, pugilist extraordinaire, local Yemeni boy done good, had spent a decade cruising town in a succession of ostentatiously bling sports cars. After wrapping one around an innocent fellow traveller and residing at Her Majesty's pleasure for some months he was selling up his pile of Victorian splendour, Castle Dyke House, out on the Ringinglow Road, for the not inconsiderable sum of £2 million plus and moving down to Surrey where such displays of wealth are probably still considered cool.

However it pays not to get too carried away. Wealth in Sheffield is very concentrated in local, specific areas. When we take into account small areas, 'Lower Super Output Areas', the smallest level at which census data is collected, and fit Sheffield's wealthiest areas into a national index of multiple deprivation - bare with me on this, it is the sort of wonky number crunching beloved of geographers -

Sheffield's top area, Fulwood, yes I know you thought it was going to be Whirlow or Dore; Fulwood only comes in 470th in England. That's more like it. OK in the top 5% in the country but with a significant slice of London and its southern environs between it and number 1. E01016709 is the identifier of an area in Wokingham, Berkshire, which is officially the least deprived area of England.

It is worth dwelling on the fact that 'least deprived' is not quite the same thing as 'wealthiest'. Deprivation is a multi-factorial concept. Sheffield Council considers seven variables in drawing up its in-house definition; economic activity, education, housing, environment, access to services, health and social care and community safety. It has engaged in such exercises for decades, I can recall looking at 'Areas of Poverty' data back in the 1980s. In fact back in the 1980s I lived in a couple of such designated areas. Recently it has been 'The Closing the Gap' agenda that Sheffield Council has engaged in which has created such an intriguing database.

Nationally central government nuances deprivation by calculating different scores for child deprivation and elderly deprivation as well as overall calculations using just about all the same criteria used by Sheffield Council. Using these huge data sets you can deduce that for children Forest Heath in Suffolk is the best place to grow up and some part of Westminster - one of the social housing estates tucked on the edge of Pimlico? - the worst. As for the elderly you would prefer to live in The Mole Valley in Surrey rather than bottom ranked Tower Hamlets. It is intriguing how significant geographical variations occur for both groups at the beginning and end of life.

In Sheffield the poles of these two age defined types of deprivation surprise a little as only one comes in the top ten highest or lowest deprived areas overall in the city. For the elderly Bents Green comes out top, which will please Julie, my fellow lecturer in Geography at

Norton College, who lives there. Where she will not be moving too are the flats that run parallel to the inner ring road in Broomhall, this really isn't the place to be old. Are you surprised?

As for bringing up your kids, and I hesitate a little here as such knowledge probably will add a few thousand to the price of a house in this area, is Quarry Hill. Where? Well Quarry Hill is a collection of new suburbs out on the Mosborough Road where I imagine most of the kids will cross the county border to go to school in Eckington, Derbyshire. Burngreave is the 46th worst place to raise your kids nationally and the worst in the city. Recently a couple of 'gang' murders of youths barely out of school only confirm the popular perception that this is an area out of control with drugs, guns and gangs. With the huge data base files of the 'Communities and Local Government deprivation indices' uploaded onto my computer I could bore for Britain on this. Did you know that St Albans? No best to leave it.

However I imagine that the Gucci heeled citizens of E01016709 in Wokingham would recognise much of what they would find in Sheffield's E01007958, or Fulwood as we call it round here. This is overall the 'best'; or rather least deprived area in Sheffield. It is not an area that shouts wealth at you, rather it mumbles it discreetly in your ear. I suspect that it isn't the domain of the wealthiest folk in the city but what it clearly doesn't have is poverty. Pretty much none at all.

When I spent a few hours on a midweek afternoon walking around the area, of the dozen people I spoke to all were surprised that the neighbourhood could be considered one of the most well to do in the city. This is solid suburbia, gardens front and back, detached and semi, a legacy of the 1930s and the rapid expansion of the city courtesy of increasing levels of car ownership. It was such developments that Ethel Galligan and J G Graves fought against as they bought up land on the Pennine fringe concerned that housing would spread out into the moorland.

From the small strip of shops on Brooklands Avenue, that pass as the centre for Fulwood, Hallam Moor hovers on the horizon. At 700 feet above sea level it is but a spit to the Peak District. It is a resolutely ordinary range of shops that serves the area. A Co-op store that has stood here since Fulwood, in the early 1930s, was primarily developed, dominates. The original manager's house still attached. What Tesco would give for such a pitch? The lead aisle display was for Australian Brut sparkling wine. A discount champagne. It felt appropriate, sort of posh but great value. Gathered around the Co-op was a butcher, greengrocer, GT News, Threshers wine store, an optician, hairdresser, a locally owned hardware shop, a small shoe shop and that staple of any British neighbourhood in the 21st century the Indian take away. Ordinary, non-descript. No gastro-pub lurked touting balsamic drizzled fennel and white truffle salads, no designer togs winked at 'ladies who lunch' passing by in their soft top Saabs. Even the local church, Christ Church, whose first stone was laid in 1837 is a unprepossessing and rather squat church which has had its architectural lines disturbed by several later additions, not unlike the proliferation of extensions and conservatories that the surrounding homes appear to have in abundance.

Christ Church's packed graveyard is the last resting place of generations of pious but essentially bourgeois believers, their names sometimes hidden by an abundance of 'ladies mantle' and a riot of grass. Such tranquillity of course hides schisms. Christ Church had been at the forefront of opposition to the ordination of gay priests promoting an orthodox Anglicanism, arguments had ensued and a city centre offshoot, Christ Church Central now led the more literalist members of this conservative flock. A few weeks after this visit I was talking to a friend whose daughter attended one of the primary schools local to Fulwood and they expressed surprise that most of their fellow parents were regular and vocal church goers. This underpinning religiosity is a core value of such west Sheffield neighbourhoods, even today. Notre Dame, the city's leading Catholic School is but a short hike, or rather dash in the Audi, (the 4x4 parents are more drawn to the private options). Its popularity assured through year on year results the envy of my humble FE college. Supply teachers wax lyrical about its calm studious ethos. It's enough to make you Catholic, or is for some families so I hear.

Walking through the streets of Fulwood in high summer is an object lesson in why the country can support so many garden centres and helps answer the question why the Tatton Garden Festival is one of the great middle class rituals of the north. Unlike the church graveyard there is barely an unkempt garden to be seen. Shrubbery, bedding plants, annuals and perennials from across the face of the planet, act as makeup for a surprisingly dull selection of suburban housing. This is the constituency of Alan Tichmarsh and Sunday visits to the garden centre. Lawns are neat, hedges cleanly sculpted, borders blooming. To fail to wield a pair of secateurs at least once a month is a social faux pas of such great merit barely a soul would cross that well clipped line.

Such gardens do serve the role of drawing the eye away from the architecture It is neither Arts and Crafts nor Art Deco, nor modernist, nor anything really. How about mid 20th century suburban vernacular. Some is 30s bay window mediocre, further up the hill at over 900 feet 60 and 70s mediocre dominates with its clean boxy lines and efficient central heating systems

Safe, solid, utilitarian with a dash of chintz, this is a community that author Philip Hensher makes the backdrop for his late 20th century set Sheffield novel 'The Northern Clemency'. An area he knew well as he grew up in it. The cover of the book shows some blousy blooms hiding the roof of a church. Clearly his graphic artist also knew the area well. The novel, it was announced at the very end of July, was long-listed for the 2008 Booker Prize. Fittingly for a novel set in Sheffield it is the rank outsider. At 700 plus pages of intimate family goings on it is so submerged in suburban nuance that the few times the book ventures into east Sheffield it appears as if it is entering another distant and rather foreign land. It took me the first three weeks of the month to read, with a great deal of pleasure and the odd exasperated grumble - come on Philip 'Forge Dam' in the Rivelin Valley! - I'd blame the editor or roof reader, as I will for all the scurrilous slurs, duff grammar and limpid statements of fact that I hope don't litter this book.

What is clear is that Philip Hensher knows the Sheffield middle class well; he has an eye for its details and its mini morality plays. His contemporaries as young white middle class lads being excessively well educated amongst the begonias include Sebastian Coe, Michael Palin and Michael Vaughan. Alan Bennett's 2004 play The History Boys is set in the fictional Cutlers Grammar School in Sheffield, think Tapton, Silverdale, High Storrs or Notre Dame RC as equivalent schools today. It is infused with the bourgeois insecurities of the area many of which are probably amplified today a quarter of a century on from its historical setting and sharpened by school league tables. The Headteacher of Cutlers is mortified by the fact that his degree is in Geography, from Hull University, although he did 'try' for Oxford. Pederast Hector - it still goes on as a contrite ex-head of a 'good' private school in the area admitted in court earlier this year - admits he will have to get through life with a degree from Sheffield University. Oh shit my 2:2 from the local Polytechnic isn't going to pass muster around this neck of the woods.

For me, Sheffield's real suburban architectural pleasures come a little further into the city. Walking back towards town I edged eastwards along the south facing valley side into Stumperlowe, the western edge of the Victorian and Edwardian suburbs of the city. Now this appeared a much more affluent area than Fulwood, and to be fair it is the 4th least deprived neighbourhood in the city. Stumperlowe for me is really a place of social mystery, of privacy. Houses are significantly detached, gardens are extensively sylvan in structure and that shady maturity hides prying eyes. Expensive alarms wink at the head of curvaceous gated driveways. What would Stumperlowe House, a minor early 19th century mansion cost in Highgate? Who lives there? What on earth do they do to afford to live there? I mean what must it cost to paint the outside of the house? Let alone keep that lawn, sweeping and moss free, snipped to literally an inch of its life?

For a solid mile eastwards towards Broomhill this slope, whose visible cityscape is obliterated by trees in the summer is full of quirks, quiet corners and surprising opulence. I'm particularly fond of the iron bridge that discreetly carries Stumperlowe Crescent Road across Storth Lane. Who, why did they do this? Damp, hardly trodden steps drop you down into the gorge like confines of Storth Lane, you wouldn't notice it at all if you were in a car.

At the top of Storth Lane the meeting of five roads in unmanaged confusion is perhaps the heart of this monument to Victorian architectural values. Blocked off from your car is the one way street of Ranmoor Road, described in the Pevsner Architectural guide to the city as “a most harmonious assembly, from vernacular cottages of the 17th and 18th century to neoclassical”. This has got to be a contender for one of the most liveable city streets in the firmament. It drops down to St John Ranmoor, Sheffield's finest ecclesiastical edifice, its elegant spire way marking Ranmoor to the city through its forest camouflage. It is backed by the 'Ranmoor Cliffe' a minor gritstone outcrop submerged by towering Beech trees. It is but a stagger from West Ten's wine list and of course an Indian restaurant goes without saying. I think I'll move in if only I could earn enough money to employ an accountant to help me avoid as much of my tax liabilities as possible.

If I did install myself in my discreet Victorian pile in Ranmoor I would find a copy of Westside magazine shoved through my brass letter box once a month. Distributed free to "20,000 AB homes in the west of Sheffield" this magazine sells a lifestyle that befits such solid money. Fed by advertising and aspirational journalism Westside would at least provide me with a few rules and opening conversational gambits over a Cape Sauvignon Blanc in West Ten. Mind you when I strolled in mid afternoon for a cool glass of South Africa's finest I was greeted by West Ten's genial host Johnnie Higginbottam with the announcement "look out here comes a communist". I'm not sure I'd blend in.

If I was going to ask the students to compare and contrast the poorest areas of Sheffield with its most well to do I felt it was only fair that I reminded myself what this involved. Strolling around Fulwood and Ranmoor was a breeze now I wanted to search out the most deprived, least salubrious areas of the city. Of course I knew what they were, everybody did. Ask a class of students to write down the three 'worst' areas of Sheffield and everybody will get areas in the bottom ten, The Manor the most commonly cited. Ask them why these areas are 'worst' and crime predominates. Not poverty, or poor opportunities, or low quality housing, nor even lack of education but fear. Fear of crime. Those students who live in these areas are perhaps a bit more measured about the risk but even so they tend to be under few illusions about where the area they live sits in the social-economic pecking order.

Again there are a few differences between Sheffield Council's data and that of central government when identifying the poorest areas. The council cites Darnall as the district with the highest level of deprivation, the greatest need to 'close the gap'. Darnall borders the lower Don Valley, the area developed to house the workers who sweated their livelihoods in the steel mills. In recent decades it has been a hub for incoming migrant populations with nearly 50% of the population belonging to an ethnic minority, predominantly Bangladeshi and Pakistani. It is a mixed housing area with half of the residents being tenants of social housing but the centre of the district is dominated by late Victorian by-law terraces, some in extremely poor condition and overcrowded.

Perhaps more typical of the sprawling municipal suburbia that is a particular feature of east and north Sheffield is the Manor Estate. Built from the early 1920s onwards first at the behest of 'The Citizen's Party' and then continued and expanded when the Labour Party first seized control of the city council in 1926, this estate at its peak housed over 30,000 people. The significance of The Manor is that it was one of the first large scale housing estates for working class communities provided by any local authority. The ambition and scale of the project showed great vision and from 1926 onwards the quality of construction was high. The residents of this estate were moved on mass from the cheek by jowl slums of Attercliffe and were a community already, except when they moved they became a community with gardens, wide roads, inside toilets, space and a secure future.

Unlike the 'garden cities' of Letchworth and Welwyn ringing London, or even the earlier Bourneville in Birmingham, The Manor was not conceived with any idea of integrating services and work into the new estate. An education committee report in September 1926 revealed that of 3,000 school age children on The Manor only 1014 were able to attend school because of a shortage of places. Addressing this was a major priority of the new Labour Council, it took time and erred towards piecemeal rather than planned.

For 50 years The Manor was the heart of working class Sheffield conviviality and community, underpinned by the trade union movement and a culture of work. It was a man's world. Then the 1970s happened, and then Thatcher and things were never quite the same. Cradle to grave certainties passed on from generation to generation began to unravel and an ageing Manor began to unravel with them.

The Manor Estate has a reputation. It goes beyond the city. Like most reputations it is a mixture of perception and reality, occasionally simply prejudice. What frames most of this reputation has been the estate's appearance in the wider media. The 2006 BBC TV series 'Traffic Cop' gave the estate a national reputation for car crime. After tearing up the streets of Sheffield in pursuit of teenage 'twockers' the voiceover invariably came back with a "meanwhile back on The Manor" refrain.

The estate has also provided easy pickings for London based journalists looking to demonise and sensationalise urban poverty. Amelia Hill of The Observer has trundled through the estate, I'm not sure she got out of her car as nobody connected to the estate was interviewed, in order to piece together her 'expose' "Council Estate Decline spawns New Underclass" (30 November 2003). More recently and clearly urged on by the Traffic Cops series, The Daily Mirror (27 April 2007) put together an 'exclusive' "What life is really like on one of Britain's worst no-go estates". If this wasn't such a scurrilous piece of journalism it would be funny. Turning up at 9 o'clock on a midweek evening, this amazingly persuasive journalist is abused by local kids, interviews old dears chatting over a garden fence, sees babies in buggies hurtling unattended towards main roads and checks out the local off licence. All pretty much in the dark. They're 'hard' these Mirror journalists or maybe they are just good at creative writing. The article concludes, “Everyone has turned their backs on us”, that's not a quote from a resident but from the journalist. Clearly they are one of 'us'.

Now to be fair The Manor is obviously not 'my manor'. I have no friends who live there, although I have taught a fair number of people who did live there. I haven't been invited to summer barbecues, house parties and the like. Over the years my experience of the area has been restricted broadly to 'fieldwork' visits, tramping around with nervy students, pointing out dereliction and renewal. My 'window' into the area was to have been Jack, whose sudden death dominated the start of my year. He had worked up on The Manor for many years with an organisation whose government-funded role was to persuade and place the long term unemployed back into work. This was quite challenging work but I figure Jack was pretty good at it, over a number of years he rarely despaired about what he did. On the rare occasion that his frustrations and a drink or three got the better of him he advocated a level of draconian imposition, normally involving a 30-foot high fence and searchlights that would have been considered outlandish even by fascists. In the morning he was sober and measured. I really missed his waspish humour but at the moment I really missed a sure-footed guide to the estate.

One of the key problems in getting to grips with The Manor is its scale. This estate sprawls and merges into neighbouring estates, Woodthorpe and Wybourn, which although similar in appearance, in that they follow the 'garden suburb' template, both were built a few years after The Manor. Where one begins and another one ends was not always obvious to my untutored eye.

'Home' Chapter 7: July

I went on a few walks around the estate, mid afternoons. On the surface all was calm and suburban. Visual cameos of the stereotypes of council house culture were there as well. Young children bombing down the roads on bikes, swearing like dockers, tattooed teenage mums hiking prams down the pavement. Dogs, big dogs, frightening dogs, I don't much like dogs, they clearly do in The Manor. Yet apart from the dogs, I didn't feel that this was some sort of threatening environment, a ghetto, a 'no go area' at least on a sunny mid week afternoon. Obviously I might change my tune if I'd lurched up late on during a winter evening.

The data wasn't great. In 2007 The Manor threw up 1611 recorded crimes. That is one every six hours. Obviously these were only the reported crimes; let's call it a reasonable assumption that the real rate was significantly higher. However is that 'significant' in the sense of double the recorded rate or treble; it is impossible to say. By its nature there is no data on unrecorded crime. Furthermore much of what perhaps made residents lives in The Manor difficult wasn't criminality as such but broader issues of 'anti-social' behaviour.

Mind you the good thing about data is that it allows you to construct other perspectives. Even though The Manor has the 3rd highest level of recorded crime in a residential area within Sheffield (Parson Cross the gold medal for deviance goes to you in 2007, Darnall silver) it only constitutes 2.4% of all crime citywide and levels of violent crime are 750% higher in the city centre than on the estate (that is the CCTV watched city centre). The Manor doesn't sound so bad when you put it like that. That is the thing with statistics, they don't lie but you do have the option of selectivity so you can put on what spin you require.

I went to see one of the local councillors for The Manor to see what their perspective was. Jan Wilson had until recently been leader of the council and since May was now leader of the opposition. She had represented the Manor Ward since 2000 and had deep roots in Sheffield's working class culture. She had worked at Osborne's Steelworks just off the Wicker alongside George Caborn the legendary socialist trade unionist; his was a name that seemed to crop up time and time again when researching the political landscape of the city.

Jan gave me an hour of her time in her ungrand and rather sparse office in the guts of the old Town Hall. We talked about The Manor and the decision by the new council to stop the 'Closing the Gap' approach to addressing deprivation and inequality in the city.

The Manor and its problems were, unsurprisingly something Jan had given a lot of thought to and her considered perspective was that it was community safety and an extremely low level of educational achievement that lay at the heart of the estates problems. This despite falling reported crime, although fear of crime was paradoxically rising. Furthermore there had been investment of millions in 'Sure Start', primary and secondary education including the arrival of an 'Academy' the governments much vaunted response to failing schools. Mind you looking at the results of the new 'Christian Academy' I can't help wonder what happens if its results do not reach the 'floor target' below which a school is deemed to be failing, 30% of Y11 students achieving 5 A to C's at GCSE. Get a new religion in, let's say Confucius, to see if it can do a better job?

Jan pointed to the breakdown of a working class culture that had pinned estates like The Manor together in the past. The structure and continuity that it had created in the community. Male, hard drinking, parochial but ordered. Within The Manor in 2007, of 4,084 household some 47% were in receipt of housing benefit and 37%

dependent on welfare benefits of one form or another. Jan pointed out that this statistic didn't acknowledge those who wholly lived outside the system, neither formally working nor claiming any form of welfare, living by their wits illegally. She pointed to a recent study by Sheffield Hallam University sociologist, Alan Mc Gauley, in which he observed within geographically tight hot spots within the Manor Estate virtually all households contained people who had a criminal record, some significantly so. Educational achievement in such areas was on the floor below any 'floor targets'. I suggested what was happening here was what some called 'a culture of poverty'. Jan wasn't prepared to go that far, although she didn't dismiss the idea out of hand.

What was actionable? Was there a catalyst that would set in train a progressive change in The Manor? Jan pointed out that even though her electorate often harangued her saying “this is a forgotten estate” the reality was that tens of millions had poured into the area in the previous decade. Rebuilding huge parts of the estate, refurbishing what was left standing, new schools, a raft of social projects and an audacious attempt to 'green' the estate - most evident in painterly blocks of riotously colourful wild flowers in areas where once housing had stood. All had made a significant impact yet the area still remained poor. How could this be so?

You need to go back to statistics to get a grip of this. In the first eight years of Margaret Thatcher's tenure as Prime Minister, 1979 to 1987 the richest 10% of Britain's population saw their weekly disposable income rise by 25%, the poorest 10% by a mere 3.8%. Contrary to popular perception the first nine years of Tony Blair's government saw the poorest 10% of the population's average household disposable income rise by 21.4%, higher than the richest 10%'s rise over the same period of 19%. No matter the gap between these two groups in respect to weekly income widened from £468 in 1997 to

£553 by 2006. To close the gap would involve a significant transfer of wealth down the income spectrum and given that all of that poorest 10% are receiving welfare benefits in one way or another it is as simple as taxing the wealthy to pay higher benefits for the poor. Anybody think that's a vote winner? The alternative approach is to provide those on benefits a route out of state support, employment. With the best of times for unemployment figures past and an impending recession threatening to strip a million plus jobs from the economy this approach was looking increasingly problematic. Especially for low skilled, poorly educated, work history limited citizens on the Manor or anywhere else for that matter.

I suspect plenty of people probably think all of these income figures aren't accurate anyway. Well their original source is the Office of National Statistics but I first spotted them in The Daily Mail on the 29th of July. They were using them to paradoxically berate the government for allowing the inequality gap in the country to grow. I look forward to this bastion of radicalism advocating a policy of radical progressive taxation and improvements to welfare benefits.

This took Jan and me onto the broadly cosmetic but ideologically important policy that her council had introduced in 2004, 'Closing the Gap - A framework for Neighbourhood Renewal". As its introductory document unambiguously stated;

> **"Another important feature of Sheffield is that any map of social indicators for Sheffield shows the same broad pattern: a deprived Northeast and affluent South West. This means that to successfully close the gap between these areas and ensure that every neighbourhood is successful, we need to improve the most deprived areas faster than the city as a whole."**

In reality this was a policy whereby the limited money available to Sheffield Council for neighbourhood renewal, about £20 million a year, was targeted into the city's poorest areas. Furthermore when allocating certain other resources within the council's remit a form of positive discrimination for those poorest areas existed. It was in Jan's words "a bit socialist".

It was one of the first things stopped by the incoming Liberal Democrat administration. Jan thought this was because "they believe that poverty was individual and not neighbourhood based". The Liberal Democrats in their winning manifesto state it as being based upon the observation that "There are pockets of deprivation in all parts of the city." This is essentially true but essentially disingenuous as well. There will be a handful of households in Fulwood who are struggling, yet they will not be in the poorest 10% of the population, at least a third of households on The Manor are.

The Liberal Democrats labelled the policy "Labour's favoured areas policy", implying it was a bribe to their 'favoured electorate'. Jan suggested that if that was the objective then the Labour Party would of been better off directing monies into the marginal wards that had just given the Liberal Democrats control of the city, areas such as Walkley, Hillsborough and Wisewood.

The Liberal Democrats core focus was on what they saw as unfair allocation of the street scene budget; street lights, filling potholes and cleaning out water gullies. As Sylvia Dunkley, Liberal Democrat cabinet member for street scene put it "faulty street lights in an area with high night-time crime statistics could have been neglected due to streetlights in a 'favoured' area getting a higher score". No example of such a practice has been given. I have asked for it. In fact I spent a fair amount of time trying to illicit a response, an interview, in fact any sort of comment from the new council on the reasoning for this policy change of heart. I had not had any sort of reply by mid August, maybe I'll have to come back to this later in the year if a reply arrives but I'm not holding my breath.

I was particularly interested in how much real difference such a policy would make, Jan thought not huge amounts as the sums were relatively small. However I was also interested in what was the underlying message about inequality within Sheffield that the new council wanted to convey. The Liberal Democrats national leader clearly thought it important if he mentioned its outcome in the city in his maiden Parliamentary speech as party leader, perhaps this concern was not so eagerly shared by his local party.

Maybe the reason the Liberal Democrats would not communicate with me on this issue was because they thought I'd stitch them up, they knew I was in the Labour Party. Whatever, I'll keep trying. Yet by the end of this month I was starting to give up caring who was right and who was wrong. I was meant to be on holiday and all I had to show for it was folders of data, reams of notes, a pile of discarded books and five PowerPoint lectures for my new geography course.

I admired Jan's resilience as I left her office with my scribbled notes clasped in my hand. I broached the grand foyer of the Town Hall and stepped into the sharp light of a bustling Fargate. I needed a holiday; my ability to grind on in the face of adversity was far below that of Jan's. It was time to take a break. Now would that be Skegness in the style of The Manor, or Tuscany in the style of Fulwood? Wherever I went I would still come back to a divided city and I probably had no better idea of how to address it than I did a month ago when I started contemplating the scale of inequality in Sheffield.

August

'"But there's lots more to see" Katherine said. "There's much more happening in London". She didn't want anyone to think they were stupid lumps, going on about the wonders of Sheffield.'
Philip Hensher: 'A Northern Clemency'

It is indisputable that there is much more to London than Sheffield. The odd seven million people is a good starting point. A few thousand years of history and the fact that it stuffed with monuments to glory, despair, avarice and plunder give it a few laps head start against Sheffield. London is in the premiership of truly global cities. Globally Sheffield is probably not even second division.

I recall reading a few years ago the results of an international survey, whose provenance now escapes me, it concluded that London was the most popular global location for a tourist visit. I hadn't been as a tourist to London in decades, my children never. This despite it being a mere two and a half hours down the train line that sometimes lulls me to sleep through the open windows of a warm summer night.

At the end of the line is St Pancras station, a destination in itself. A contender for the greatest railway station in the world, its old Victorian glories and its cathedral like steel roof, the 'Barlow Shed', a masterpiece of its age. On its completion in 1868 it became the largest enclosed space of any building in the world. It was now spruced up and its status enhanced further by it becoming the international Eurostar terminus. Paris Nord, Bruxelles, Leeds, Sheffield and all points north and south can be reached via the platforms beyond its stretch limo of a champagne bar.

In the past decade conferences and meetings have made up the few times I have visited London. I always try to wrangle an evening or better still an overnight stay and often, if possible, try to walk to where I have to go. I love walking in London; you could do it for a lifetime and still have somewhere new to go. In the 1980s I particularly enjoyed demonstrations that wound themselves through the city. It was a great way to see London, although Trafalgar Square didn't look quite at its best at the fag end of the Poll Tax demonstration in 1990.

At the start of August I went down to London with the family to be a tourist. The Natural History Museum, Science Museum, The London Eye, St Paul's Cathedral, The Tower and Greenwich. As well as a Grayson Perry look-a-like flash mob in Camden, a Brick Lane curry, peregrine falcon watching on the roof of the Tate Modern, Saturday night watching the buskers in Convent Garden and a stroll through the diminutive graveyard of St Olave's in the eerie quiet of a becalmed weekend evening within the vertiginous 'City'. As Samuel Pepys, who is buried in St Olave's graveyard, is often quoted as saying; "When a man is tired of London he is tired of life".

I wished I had lived in London for a few years when I was younger, a month dossing on the floor of a friend's flat in Lewisham when I was 17 hardly counts. I'm glad I don't live there now. That it is the world's greatest city is indisputable, that all life flows through its streets a given, its wealth a marvel of our times, its poverty more shocking than anything Sheffield can muster. This is the city as a living organism, assailed by decay yet vibrantly alive. Ever mutating but cloaked in the ghosts of history. Why wouldn't you want to go there?

We had a great time but I was glad to get home.

'Home' Chapter 8: August

Sheffield railway station, although no towering beauty like St Pancras, is a fittingly proportionate entrance to the city. Bustling and bright, its revamped Victoriana hemmed in by the brooding presence of Park Hill Flats and Sheffield Hallam University. Outside the new station Sheaf Square attempts to invoke elemental Sheffield. Tumbling water and shinning steel. At six o'clock in the evening the square performs a minor light and sound show. The only time I was witness to it I was loitering outside smoking a cigarette and then all of a sudden red lights pulsed through the water and dry ice rolled across the concourse. I had to check what I was smoking, I half expected Def Leppard to emerge in a crescendo of power chords. I've not stumbled upon 'the show' since. Did I imagine it?

What definitely is imagined is the Andrew Motion poem that gazes down on Howard Street, the main link between the railway station and the city centre. After its imagining from the Poet Laureate it has been made real in foot high letters on the blank end wall of Sheffield Hallam University's nine storey 'Owen Building'. I have met folk, people who write poetry, go to readings and all that stuff, and they have bent my ear long and hard about what a poor effort it is by such an esteemed poet. I pass on this as I know as much about poetry as Serbo-Croat grammar, or even English grammar some might say. Yet I am quite struck by the last passage of the poem and the idea that you can adorn walls with more than 'tags' is always appealing.

> **"To greet and understand what lies ahead -**
> **The city where your dreaming is re-paid,**
> **The lives which wait unseen as yet, unread."**

Perhaps the graffiti loitering on a wall in Sharrow might be more apt this year "Noah says build your own ark!" It was raining as we returned home.

'Home' Chapter 8: August

We went into the city centre the day after arriving back from London, the first Monday of the month, it seemed so compact and Lilliputian after the capital; and quiet. Where were the multitudes, the throng that filled the streets of central London? The streets of Sheffield were far from packed and we idled an hour away snaffling tapas outside Platillos in the new, and barely animated Leopold Square. Where was everybody? How were these businesses that had spent a minor fortune revamping the old school board offices ever going to make their money back?

The days when whole northern towns decamped to a traditional seaside resort on mass, a 'wakes' week, were a nostalgic notion in our 24/7 21st century. There had been talk of a mass stay at home as a result of the 'credit crunch', of heaving beaches at Blackpool and Brighton, Cameron Tories scoffing their way through 'Padstein', or Brownite policy wonks trudging the sand and gazing at the endless skies of East Anglia. All dreaming of power and Tuscany, and all of them having to be seen to plug into the economic zeitgeist by prudently holidaying at home. Wherever people had gone on holiday it wasn't in Sheffield. Rather, it appeared, the locals had left on mass to somewhere, anywhere else.

Apart from a few jaunts out of town, five weeks of the school summer holiday, pretty much the whole of August was going to be spent 'in town'. Not even a fortnight sheltering from the rain in amusement arcades in Cornwall or a week in the statics of Sheffield by the sea, Skegness. The question that was perhaps more prominent in the minds of my children than myself was "what do you do when you go on holiday in Sheffield?"

Children under ten require a certain level of organising and entertaining to thwart their onset of boredom, although a bit of boredom, I feel, is a perquisite for a real school summer holiday. How else might it seem so endless? There were a range of activities that could be brought in for the offspring of the less fiscally challenged; art, craft, acting, sport and adventure. Some parents spent hundreds especially if both were working full time and the school holiday stretched out like a second mortgage. However a fair amount was free, recreation play workers toured the city dropping anchor on patches of grass to biff balls and fly kites. Museums, parks and allotments were mainly gratis, except for the ice cream and inevitable 'stuff'.

Then again it was raining, most of the time. It became, yet again, the most talked about aspect of the summer, rain. The crap weather generally. I wondered whether it was wetter than last year in the same way that I might have tried to work out whether 1998s Glastonbury festival was muddier than 1997s. It didn't really matter both were knee deep. Holiday Sheffield, damp and quiet, same as last year.

It was in moments like this it becomes easier to comprehend the desire to up sticks and decamp to southern Spain. The bright light, barmy star soaked evenings and crisp morning shadows of Andalucía vying with the endless swoop of one Atlantic depression after another across the British Isles. A pattern of meteorological uncertainty that makes togging up before going out a bit of a lottery.

Not to fret, given an hour or two in a car or train a stunning choice of holiday entertainment was set out before us. Sheffield is as central as you could get in England, about as far from the sea as it is possible to be on this island. Cleethorpes is the nearest possibility to paddle your feet. Actually Immingham Dock is the nearest piece of coast to Sheffield, the city's port, with its views across to Spurn Head, which hovers in The North Sea like the lost island it almost is.

Connectivity is a core 'buzzword' in business and in Geography. Basically the concept is concerned with how accessible a place is. In the past this would have been determined by distance and topography. Technology has shrunk distance beyond the imagination of our grandparents. Today the idea of 'time geography' is just as important. How long does it take to get from here to there? For instance, not withstanding hawk eye traffic police I can drive from Sheffield to Leicester Forest East services in an hour, 60 miles at a mile a minute. Getting to Manchester, two thirds of the distance takes 30% longer. The Snake Pass is part of the challenge but the array of speed cameras stretched out from Glossop to Marsden delivers not only safer roads but longer journeys.

We took a day out in Liverpool, just over two hours away if you drive through the centre of Manchester. It would be truly fanciful for Sheffield to be awarded European City of Culture but Liverpool, even though it might be about to bankrupt itself for the honour, has the shapazz to carry it off. It's a waterfront thing, those docks connecting the city up to the whole world. The 'Three Graces' of Pierhead, a mini me of the Shanghai waterfront. The Albert Dock, a genuine multi-faceted visitor attraction that can keep your attention all day. We came for the gilt-edged opportunity to see Gustav Klimt at the Tate Gallery. Later we went onto Crosby Sands to see the battered bronze of a hundred Anthony Gormley 6 foot plus male, very male as my daughters pointed out, figures. This is public art on a grand and imaginative scale. Open, not just to the elements but to public ridicule and playfulness. Nearly as surprising were the wonderful sea front houses of Crosby, a long row of mid Victorian terraces with wrought iron verandas and intricate balconies one of whom was the home of Captain Edward Smith of Titanic infamy.

Even with a short diversion up to the wooded dunes at Formby to go red squirrel watching we were home in just over two hours with dusk spreading across the Snake Pass as we climbed above the twinkling lights of Glossop. A few days later it took about the same amount of time to get to the car park in the upper River Dane Valley in Staffordshire to pay a visit to Lud's Church, one of the natural wonders of the Peak District. This immense natural cleft in the steep gritstone slopes of Back Forest has the power to bewitch. From the top it is invisible, hidden below a sea of bracken and woodland. A dark opening drops you down through living green walls of moss. Then out of the dank gloom appears an open topped chamber which could easily accommodate a hundred people. A freshly cut vase of flowers nestled on a natural rock shelf. It is a romantic and mysterious place with much folklore and rumour swimming around it. A hiding place for Robin Hood, perhaps? That's Robin of Loxley, Loxley the suburb of Sheffield. Mind you, a bit of a way to come and hide.

Of course the reason that Gradbach, where the car park for Lud's Church is found, takes so long to reach is that it is a journey right across the heart of the Peak District. Retracing out meanderings we go back up the Dane Valley to Flash, England's highest village at 1518 feet. Past the jagged peak of Chrome Hill, the sleeping dragon of the Peaks, and on down into Longnor sitting at the head of the lushly grazed Manifold Valley. Then climbing back onto the limestone plateau, past the 4500 year henge of Arbor Low and sliding down into Bakewell. The rest is plain sailing over the eastern moors into Sheffield. We met a herd of cows, horse riders, cyclists galore and a few toddling tractors. There are many English rural idylls, and all of them have their underbelly of deprivation and inequality so hardly stand up to the test of a true idyll but the Peak District really does stand up if only for the fact that, surrounded by the great cities of the industrial revolution, assaulted by some of the worst pollution thrown at the natural world for over a century and trampled over by millions of near neighbours from those Victorian terraces, it is still rural. Majestically so. Amazing.

At the far reaches of the Derwent Valley, beyond the visitor centre, slowly traversing the spurs of Howden reservoir until you reach the end of the public road is the most accessibly rural spot in the Peak District. A short 20 minute walk past the blocking five bar gate and through some nicely maturing woodland takes you up to an old packhorse bridge. This was moved up the valley from the village of Derwent when its original home was flooded to provide England's rapidly expanding population of the early 20th century with water. The place where the bridge crosses The River Derwent is called 'Slippery Stones'. The flat stones that make up the river bed here have a viscous quality that make crossing it rather than wading through it a welcome option.

On a rare blue skied morning we set off to Hathersage village outdoor swimming pool. As somebody had left the plug out of the pool draining all the water away and shutting the pool at the start of its busiest weeks of the year we found ourselves at a loose end. We went and paddled our toes at Slippery Stones. This was our own little bit of wild, remote Britain. Well for ten minutes or so and then phalanxes of cyclists lycraed past us. Then there were the planes coming into Manchester Airport overhead and... Sod it, this is as wild as it's going to get in the heart of the modern industrial world. You wouldn't fancy making your way eastwards from Slippery Stones over Featherbed Moss and down into suburban Bradfield village on a rapidly darkening winter's afternoon. It would be a journey of some foreboding. Early August it is breathtaking and benign. You can begin to imagine yourself deep within the wild and rugged landscapes out of which much of the 'north' has been carved.

I still have to remind myself what a beautiful place England's first national park is. You can get complacent about it when it has been such a large part of your life for so long. Like so many Sheffielders I have a store of Peak District places for seasons and moods. Its variety was revealed to me in the glorious summer of 1986 when I was hauled out of post-graduation unemployment to count wildflowers for the National Park Authority. I visited just about every wood in the Peak District and decided whether bluebells were dominant, abundant, frequent, occasional or rare. Occasionally we found something incredibly rare. Herb paris in Monks Dale. Deathcap fungi in the Derwent Valley. Really such a job existed; the interview involved successfully identifying a dandelion and a daisy. This was all courtesy of 'The Community Programme', a graduate employment scheme for those harsh economic days. It was possibly the greatest positive contribution Margaret Thatcher made to my life, her negative contributions being far too extensive to bore you with. My love of flowers I owe to the 'Iron Lady'.

The Peak District is in reality a managed ecological construction. It is however cited as Sheffield's greatest 'natural' asset. It is the simple reason that there is no possibility of a fast road or rail connection to Manchester from Sheffield. Why, even though Britain's, in my opinion, second city is a mere forty miles away, it sometimes feels like four hundred and anything but a near neighbour. A public enquiry in 1967 considered the possibility of a motorway. A report in the early 1970s discussed stretching the M67 past Mottram and over the northly Woodhead Pass finally connecting to junction 35A of the M1. You wouldn't even consider such a scheme nowadays unless you were Jeremy Clarkson. Beyond the cost - would you get any change out of £2 billion? - it would galvanise every tunnelling, climbing, superglue wielding eco-warrior in Britain. And quite right to. We are going to have to live with our twisty-turny, mad BMW driver overtaking Snake Pass for a great deal longer. Fortunately Manchester isn't a place most Sheffielders are over-excited about visiting. "You know it's a bit like London". But poorer. Oh and smaller.

The rise of Sheffield as a city occurred in spite of its limited connectivity. Industry developed in close proximity to raw materials and like so much of northern Britain coal, water and limestone defined where was developed and where was not. There were massive coal deposits under Sheffield, limestone in the Peak District but only modest amounts of iron ore so this has been bought into the city from Scandinavia through North Sea ports for centuries. The nearest of these was the river port of Bawtry which had started exporting wool from the 14th century. It was a short lived era as the river silted up. Today it is twenty five miles from the sea.

The Sheffield Canal was the first serious transport infrastructure project in the city. Taking three years to construct it was opened on 22nd February 1819. Its construction was funded by private investors led by the Duke of Norfolk and the Earl Fitzwilliam both of whom were extending the wealth of their hereditary lands by sinking coal mines to fuel the industrial revolution. The canal connected Sheffield to the Don Navigation which gave Sheffield access to the Humber estuary and the world. Exports, especially to North America, rose dramatically.

The time of the canals lasted a little over three decades before the railways arrived and then the complex criss-crossing of development in the giddy boom years of railway building put Sheffield and Sheffielders in touch with just about everywhere in the country. You'd probably have to change a few times, and get a Hanson cab at the other end, but you could get there, wherever there was. Resorts such as Skegness and Scarborough grew up planned at the end of newly built railway lines. Never had more people gone somewhere else with the express purpose of whatever the Victorians considered 'having a good time'. Geographically millions were liberated from the idea that 'home' was all they would ever know in their lives. Blackpool was invented.

Today, our horizons are even greater. Even as little as 35 years ago I was the only person in my primary school class to have been abroad, it would be an unthinkable state of affairs today. The Airline UK Market Report for 2007 states that 131.2 million passengers were carried by all UK airports. A little over 2 flights for every person in the country. This cost us £17.32 billion and resulted in us clocking up a cumulative 315.87 billion km, on average 2407km a trip! And everything is up, regardless of environmental exhortations to cut back on flying. More passengers, more frequently, we're flying further. Of course it is unfair to cite an average figure. In reality flying remains an activity of affluence, 90% of all 'budget' airline flights are consumed by the wealthiest 10% of the population.

For a city to be connected into the hyper-mobility of globalisation it appears that an airport is an essential accoutrement. Sheffield is currently the largest city in Europe without an airport.

There I have said it. It wasn't so bad.

From 1997 to April this year this had not been the case, an airport existed, developed and paid for by the Sheffield Development Corporation, the last act of this central government quango. It had been felt for decades that the city required an airport, there was much political discussion about this right through the 1960s and 70s.

The S.D.C. enabled that aspiration to be fulfilled albeit in a rather compromised way. The essential problem was always where? Sheffield is a city noted for its topography, the flat slice of land that abutted the Tinsley railway marshalling yards was just big enough to fit in a 1200 metre runway. Any further north-east was halted by the M1, south-west by Darnall. And there lay the seeds of the airports demise.

The business model that the airport was developed around was a pattern of transport geography called a hub and spur. KLM, the airports anchor carrier was going to ferry people on small STOL planes to Amsterdam where flights to every corner of the globe were available. Friends flew to Delhi in this way. It was a business model out of step with the time. The zeitgeist of air travel has been low cost European city connections with big players such as EasyJet, Ryanair and BMI Baby influential in redirecting our holiday aspirations. None of these companies was interested in Sheffield, the economics didn't stack up. The workhorse of low cost airlines was the Boeing 737 and Sheffield's runway was too short to accommodate it.

With so many airport options for carriers to explore and with such a competitive market it was a matter of years before KLM, British Airways and the Belgium carrier Sabena gave up on Sheffield. Scheduled flights ended in 2002. A little previous to this Sheffield City Council, who had taken control of S.D.C. assets, sold the airport site to two companies one of whom was Peel Holdings who not only owned Liverpool airport but had acquired the old nuclear bomber RAF base at Finningley, six miles south-east of Doncaster.

This is the source of some suspicion. When this deal, cost £1, was made it was 5 years prior to what was initially set out by the S.D.C. as the time frame for whether a going concern could be made of

Sheffield airport. The Sheffield Star at the time reported the initial contract between the S.D.C. and the airport operators stated that "all reasonable efforts should be taken to attract airlines and the airport should be maintained for at least 10 years." There is some ambiguity about this, especially if, as some argue, the land asset could not be transferred for the nominal sum of £1 unless this condition was met.

Well of course Peel Holdings could be accused of predatory practice because they also were running Sheffield's nearest competitor, Doncaster Airport. I personally would not make that assertion - do you think that is good enough for the solicitors? - because whatever way you spin it Sheffield Airport was at best always going to stumble along as a rather minor 'airfield', the preserve of private planes, rather than a globally connected city airport.

Doncaster, Doncaster/Sheffield, Robin Hood, whatever name will eventually fall into common usage holds all the cards. A runway 2,893 metres long and particularly wide at 60 metres compares favourably with most major airports. It can cope with the largest of wide bodied jets, even the new Airbus Superjumbo and Antonov 124's. The airport is an area of low population density with extensive lowland moors to the north and marshy agricultural land eastwards. You could double its size, lengthen its runway and apart from the Pringle sweaters at Bawtry Golf and Country Club it would hardly cause a stir. One day a link road will be built from the M18 or better still the rail connection restored into Finningley village and the time geography of getting there from Sheffield will be shrunk. It will be the local airport.

Does it matter whether Sheffield has its own airport? Well think on this. If you want to get from central London to Heathrow, or Gatwick or Stansted for that matter, whether you went by car or public transport you are talking about a journey of 40 minutes minimum, given congestion and unplanned chaos, I'd give myself an hour and a half. You could get to Leeds/Bradford, Manchester, Humberside and East Midlands airport in that time from Sheffield. Given a link road Finningley is 40 minutes maximum, about 18 miles from Sheffield city centre to the airport.

If you get a Ryanair flight to Barcelona you'll actually end up in Girona or Reus airports north of the city by respectively 64 miles and 66 miles. From there the Ramblas is at least two hours drive time. Ryanair's boss Mr O'Leary calls that Barcelona, and you know what? Most of the people who get these flights think it is too, until they get there.

The key is not whether the airport is in Sheffield but whether Sheffield has good connectivity to an airport. It remains a significant issue in the city, letters digging over the entrails of the deal have been in the paper all summer, threatened but hastily aborted legal action against the closure and some wounded civic pride all testify to this. It is a done deal, time to move on. To questions like why aviation fuel is not taxed, or whether local authorities committed to sustainability should support such ventures with tax payer's money? Maybe we should ponder whether we can actually afford to keep growing air travel - could we not ration it and let those who don't use their quota trade it on an online market? Dangerously redistributive but if we do want to 'close the gap' it may be through allowing people to trade 'rights or rations of resources' when they do not want to or cannot afford to use them. I must stop reading those George Monbiot columns in The Guardian or I'll end up chaining myself to coal fired power stations.

Actually towards the end of August people almost did end up chaining themselves to the detritus of a coal fired power station in Sheffield. The parabolic cooling towers of the old Tinsley power station, the oldest remaining example of such industrial architecture in the country, a key component of the industrial east-end were given notice of their demise. Destruction day was the 24th early Sunday morning, 3am. 12 hours before the event contributors to the internet site Sheffield Forum were suggesting a mass drive down the M1 motorway to halt the destruction, this after a campaign several years long to save this rather dubious but affectionately thought of artefact of the city's industrial past.

I had wondered about going to see their demise but my feeling was that their destruction was an opportunity missed. As Go.Sheffield, the op-art agitators whose two Toms, James and Keeley, have put together ten 'fanzines' which are “about Sheffield, about its buildings, about its regeneration and its soul” argue “Sheffield never misses an opportunity to miss an opportunity”. What they promoted was the idea that the cooling towers could be used as a canvas for an innovative piece of public art. For a 'leftfield' idea it garnered a significant amount of support, local politicians, local bands, Britain's leading public artist Anthony Gormley and so it appeared many, perhaps most, locals.

The real reason I didn't take an early morning spin eastwards on the 24th was that I was soundly sleeping off a delicious dinner and copious amounts of wine. A couple days later when I found myself driving southwards along the lower deck of the Tinsley M1 viaduct I regretted my lack of self discipline. There were still folk lined up along the pavement photographing the jagged stumps, traffic slowed to a crawl. The papers were full of invective against E.O.N., the German managed power company who owned the site, the council, the lack of imagination, anything, everyone.

Of course the idea is one thing, the realisation another. E.O.N. state categorically that the cost of making the cooling towers structurally sound for the future, bearing in mind their proximity to Britain's major motorway was prohibitive and that is without the cost of the artistic makeover. You might argue that a company making profits on a scale that even the government is eyeing up a windfall tax on to trim its sails, can afford to make such a public spirited offer. Probably but it isn't the sort of thing a foreign owned private company tends to do.

Then there is the issue of the art itself. Personally I wouldn't have minded a huge Banksy, preferably a replication of the piece he recently donated to the Labour Party to help them raise funds; schoolchildren, hand on chest saluting a Tesco carrier bag being run up a flagpole. I'm not sure Meadowhall would agree. My eldest daughter suggested painting them to look like vases and then building huge white roses sticking out of them to signify to the world 'you've arrived' in Yorkshire.

Of course one of the problems of such huge statement art on structures almost kissing the motorway is that it might be a distraction. From a personal point of view I found this the case when I once drove past Gormley's Angel of the North outside Gateshead. It was so bloody spectacular that my eye was constantly being drawn to it. There is no doubt that if the towers had been re-cooled by art that it would have been a huge statement. The M1 is devoid of visual interest as it crawls northwards. The domed rock-salt store at Newport Pagnall services, err... the Ratcliffe on Soar power station on the River Trent, that's about it until Emley Moor telecommunications tower offers itself up as you motor on up past

Sheffield to Leeds. It's hard to miss, Britain's tallest structure at 1,084 feet, concrete, utilitarian and grade 2 listed. Remind you of anything?

Sheffield has been a bit fickle about public art, once, in 1999, turning down a free offer of a sculpture by Shirazeh Houshiary courtesy of the Arts Council to sit at the top of Fargate at the site once adorned by the Goodwin Fountain. Actually adorned is too nice a word for a woeful piece of public water sculpture which eventually turned into a huge municipal rubbish bin. However, once the new sculpture was unveiled - a substantial metal pillar that was not wholly unlike a huge multi-coloured twist drill - public opinion was whipped up against the idea and a timid Labour Council fearful of losing the local elections later in the year, a fear not misplaced, scuppered the idea. A similar piece by Shirazeh Houshiray now sits outside the British embassy in Paris.

I think one of the strongest reasons to have kept the Tinsley Cooling Towers has to be folly. Britain has a long history of buildings which are constructed for no good purpose. A repudiation of Benthamite good sense. Once the towers had rhyme and reason, today they were pointless beyond their visibility and bulk. They were a signifier of home. Landmarks come and go and quite often it is time and familiarity that sets them into the public consciousness not aesthetic considerations. The Eiffel Tower was derided by the public when it was constructed in 1889. A letter written at the time observed that “stretching out like a black blot the odious shadow of the odious column”. A view few would share today.

But the cooling towers were now gone, just like the school summer holidays. No tans were acquired and the kids weren't too bored.

'Home' Chapter 8: August

Bikes were ridden, parks frequented and the Peak District rediscovered.

September

It was raining, again. It had been raining an awful lot. Everywhere you went people were grumbling about the weather. Normally the main reason that weather is such a talking point in Britain is because there is simply so much of it. Hot, cold, wet, dry, hail, snow, windy, calm, possibly all in one day. How dull it must be to live in LA, to get up, throw open the curtains, and lo' yet another clear blue sky, day after day. British weather is a constant battleground of the elements, a constant topic of conversation.

Yet this summer a rather unfortunate regularity had settled in. A repositioning of the jet stream, the high altitude tunnel of wind that drags maritime depressions across the Atlantic Ocean, had occurred. It had set up camp in the central Atlantic, further south than we would expect at this time of year. Some talked about the 'El Nino'- the fickle South Pacific oceanic current oscillation that creates offbeat weather patterns - others chuntered about climate change and the extreme weather events that climatologists associate with rising atmospheric temperatures. Everybody agreed it had been a crap summer.

So much rain had fallen and with such monotonous regularity that the apple tree in my allotment, weighed down with abundant ripening fruit, keeled over. The soft, saturated soil unable to support it. Slugs had invaded the greenhouse stripping the green peppers and clearing out the salad crops. Blight had hit the potatoes. The autumn raspberries were going mouldy on the canes. The tomatoes were hardly ripening and the pitiful progress of my grape vines should be an object lesson for anybody who thinks that onrushing climate change will herald the dawn of English winemaking. 2008 was not going to be a vintage year for wine or weather.

The first week of September continued this pattern, rivers rose and flood warnings were issued. Nervous eyes were cast over the rising River Don. Was a once in four hundred year flood going to become an annual event? Across the world reports of extreme weather, far more impactful than anything that might assail Sheffield, were coming thick and fast. Hurricanes swept through the Caribbean and the southern coast of the U.S.A. New Orleans was evacuated, Galveston submerged and Haiti relentlessly battered. Of course it is not possible to attribute a single extreme weather event as being specifically set in train by climate change. Weather is a time specific event; climate is the pattern over time. However, it is notable that although England in August saw a rainfall total that was 152% above the long term average it also experienced an average temperature 0.8C above the same long term average. It was simply the dullest least sunny summer month in living memory. 60 hours short of the August average for sunshine hours, that is 5 whole 12 hour days of sunshine lost in a month. It was carrying on into September. Hopes of an 'Indian Summer' were dissipating fast.

It was also the start of the 'New Year'. The academic new year. The significance of this is substantial. Every person who has been through the British school system is aware of the temporal guillotine that sets apart year group from year group. The 1st of September. For anybody working in education September is the 'New Year', my diary runs from September 2008 to August 2009, as does my holiday entitlement and my life for the past two decades had revolved around this cycle.

I started the academic year in the company of David Attenborough, who helped me explain the impact of human activity on biodiversity. Unfortunately it is but a film, 'State of the planet: Why there is a crisis'. Attenborough sets out the five ways in which human activity is reducing biodiversity at such a rate that it is considered to be akin to the great extinctions such as the one that wiped out the dinosaurs 65.5 million years ago after 165 million years of them strutting their stuff across Earth. This is serious. A jolt into reality for the students after a summer of sloth.

Islandisation, alienisation, over harvesting and pollution - particularly climate change - are wreaking havoc on an unknown and potentially unknowable amount of biodiversity. However it is habitat destruction that Attenborough cites as the most impactful human activity of all. 6.3 billion humans and growing; all demanding an ever increasing amount of resources to sustain them. Our planet is pretty much a fixed entity as far as most resources go. We can't just invent land, create soil, mine forever, keep pissing in our water and drinking it. As the 'Club of Rome' environmental group so alarmistly put it way back in 1970, there are "limits to growth".

It pays to be a little cautious about dramatic claims of impending environmental doom. Paul Ehrlich, the Stanford University Professor of Population Studies claimed in 1969 that he "would take even money that England will not exist in the year 2000". He predicted, surprisingly precisely, that the population of the USA would fall to 22.6 million by 1999. However Sir, Lord, Saint, David is a little more measured, just. He doesn't predict impending doom but a greyer, drearier world of lost opportunities.

Attenborough goes to Chaco Canyon in New Mexico, U.S.A. to make his point. Here the Anasazi culture reached its pinnacle about 1000 years ago. It wasn't a desert then, as it is now, but wooded, fertile and able to support a sophisticated urban culture capable of building multi-storey structures using the resources around them. They stripped the land of its trees, cultivated the soil into submission and saw their population grow beyond sustainability. This of course is a story that will sound familiar to anybody who has looked into the collapse of the Easter Island society that erected the Moai statues. It is the story of Harappa the very first urban civilization founded in the Indus Valley 4600 years ago. There are many lessons from history for humans to ignore.

In Britain the pressure on biodiversity is continuing apace. An E.U. report released in the first week of September suggested that the population of Britain would rise to 77 million by 2060, making it the most populous country in Europe. In Britain this would mean an increase in population density from 240 people per sq km in 2001 to 311 people per sq km in 2060. Of course in reality this isn't an even distribution, the south-east and the major urban areas like Sheffield are where the majority of the population is to be found and that is also where the growth will be focused. Put it another way it is equivalent to 30 Sheffields being created somewhere in our green and pleasant land in the next half a century. If Sheffield takes its fair share of that growth it will mean a population of around 650,000 in 52 years time. Are you really worried about house prices falling in the long term? Just think supply and demand.

How are we to respond to this challenge? Well part of it is to be seen with a cursory scan of the evolving skyline of Sheffield. The view from the front bedroom of my house is due north across Sheffield city centre. All year I have watched the daily progress of St Paul's Apartments as they have edged towards becoming the tallest building in the city centre. When in 2009 this residential tower block, that is a component part of the city council's 'Heart of the City' master plan, is topped out it will reach 32 floors and 101 metres. It will dominate the city. It will be the landmark building that will define the city's visual image. Its functional architecture probably precludes the use of 'iconic' in any future description of this, Sheffield's first true skyscraper. The only way is up!

Or maybe not!

At the end of June City Lofts, the company that were developing St Paul's Apartments ran out of finance and went into administration. £130 million of debts were left for the administrators to wrestle with. Most of this debt was owed to Lehmann Brothers, who with the German based Hypo Real Estate Bank International, effectively owned City Lofts. In the third week of September Lehmann Brothers became the most spectacular casualty of the credit crunch recession, so far. With the US treasury refusing to bail them out Lehmann's have fallen with bankruptcy awaiting them. The size of their debts are unknown and the fallout is global. Somewhere down the line somebody is going to have to divi up Lehmann's assets in an attempt to partially pay off its creditors.

Even the lines of insurance that were put in place to protect the construction of St Paul's Apartments from such financial hiccups were allegedly with AIG, the US insurance company that was facing the possibility of becoming a defunct shell. By the first week of October Hypo Bank were being refused a EUR 35 Billion bailout by German banks although it appeared that the German government were stepping partly into the financial breach with a line of credit from their central bank, a cool £40 billion of liquidity. This was for a company whose share price plummeted from E15 to E3 in the last two days of the month. The credit crunch that I was mulling over at the start of the year was rapidly descending into full scale financial meltdown with governments all over the world having to throw a financial lifeboat at, or even part nationalising, ailing financial institutions. To predict the future at present you would need to be Mystic Meg, certainly not an economist. St Paul's Apartments may turn into an unfinished, over scale, brutalist shell. A monument to the failed age of over-leveraged capitalism. The options seemed to be narrowing by the day.

As I write work continues on St Paul's Apartments, the cladding for the first of its residential floors is being attached although whether it is near the specification first offered up to prospective buyers is another thing. The brown system built apartment fronts, think caravan panels, have not only ruffled the feathers of those in the city that have been carefully charting this building's progress but have raised the hackles of the Sheffield City Council's planning department. Word is that they are going to put up four floors of cladding and see how it looks.

If the council planners, or rather the councillors in a planning committee, pull the plug on this design it is hard to see what future the building will have. A whole raft of questions must be sailing across the desk of Sheffield's new Chief Executive. This is going to be bloody difficult to talk up.

The first question is whether there is the money to finish this project and if so from where? Exactly who owns it now? In the labyrinthine world of real estate finance it is always a bit complex to address such a proposition at the best of times, at the worst of times the answer to this question could be anybody's guess. In fact does anybody own it at present? Who is making the decisions? Even if a line of liquidity can be discovered that will enable the building to be finished there remains the thought that some judicious cutting of corners to get the cost down will be required resulting in an elegant skyscraper being a shadow of it potential glory. A reality that the city may just have to live with.

Then it is worth thinking about who is going to buy the flats when they are finished. Prices were steep; some say 10-15% over the odds to begin with. I had enquired about a two bed room, west facing flat on floor 27. It would have relieved me of £245,000. This was over two years back when the site, once the home of the circular registry office 'The Wedding Cake', was but a cleared piece of land hemmed in by hoardings shouting out the imminent arrival of high rise living. Potential buyers could secure a flat with a 10% deposit. Such an 'off-plan' approach works well for speculators in a booming market. I had heard stories of people who back in 2002 had brought off plan on the Ward's Brewery redevelopment at the bottom of Ecclesall Road. By the time they had to pay the 90% balance they had sold on the flat making as much as 50% on the deal. A lot of money for very little outlay even if only half the story were true. Property speculation must have seemed like taking candy from a kid in those days.

Now if the tower is completed it must be considered how many of those depositors, covering about 60% of the finished flats, will forgo their 10% if the real value of the property falls below that which they are paying. What will the 27th floor flat be worth, £200,000, £190,000? Again it is anybody's guess at present. There is a point when you cut your losses and run. Mind you even if they want to go ahead with the purchase what hurdles will they have to jump over in order to get financing, mortgages are like rocking horse shit at present. Then there are interest rates. The margins of buy to let investors would be severely tested if they rose to a level that even the most ambitious rental income would not cover. With an impending recession this might not be a problem, rates are more likely to fall, especially if consumer spending stalls. Somebody, maybe a lot of people, is going to take a big hit on this. It seems doubtful that anybody will build a project like it in Sheffield for a very long time.

A final thing to ponder is whether the development is going to be known as St Paul's Apartments, a name that is meant to reflect the church that stood on the site of the adjacent Peace Gardens until its demolition in 1948. I suspect on completion a new name will be coined by the populace like the Swiss Re tower in London becoming simply known as the Gherkin. The multi-storey car park next to St Paul's, although unfinished, is already attracting the moniker of 'the cheese grater' on account of its angular, sharp edged cladding.

Yet my major concern with St Paul's Apartments is the building itself. Whilst it may be fantastic to gaze out from your 27th floor eyrie as the city twinkles beneath your feet with the sun setting across Hallam Moor, everybody else in the city is going to spend the rest of their life having to look at the bloody thing, an address that a few hundred, mainly wealthy transient people, call home. This is a building that is seriously in your face. Everywhere you go in the city it is there. Dominant with its yellow jacket shielding the setting concrete of the new floors being added to its shell. Floor 24 and counting. It is now the tallest building in Sheffield, surpassing the 'Arts Tower' of The University of Sheffield which stands at 78 metres and 20 floors.

The comparison is interesting as the 'Arts Tower' has gradually become a much loved feature of the Sheffield skyline. Built between 1961 and 1965 - good skyscrapers take time - this is Sheffield's homage to Mies van der Rohe, the great 60s steel and glass architect of American skyscrapers. It is elegant and simple, sitting as it does on a dominant promontory perched above the city centre. Having never visited New York I cannot confirm that it is a quarter scale copy of the

1958 Seagrams Building, one of van der Rohe's signature buildings, as it is claimed. In the mid 1960s it was the best architectural statement of dynamic modernism that was created in Sheffield, it wasn't just a stump of concrete. In 1993 it was given the protection of grade 2 listing from English Heritage.

A consequence of being a listed building is that when you decide to spend £15 million refurbishing and recladding a building, as the University of Sheffield announced this month, it will basically look the same at the end of its makeover. They will however get a reduction in the building's carbon footprint from 8kg/m2/per year to 5kg/m2/per year. Sometime in the future somebody will lay explosive charges under this building. It will be Tinsley cooling towers all over again. But time, corrosion and land values will see this building fall. This will not be in my lifetime.

It is bizarre but the same fate obviously awaits St Paul's Apartments, sometime in the dim and distant future. It may be much sooner if it remains unloved and unfinished. We do not build forever, especially if, as I suspect, this is a building that will not inspire the same affection in Sheffielders as the 'Arts Tower'.

Perhaps it is fitting that the culmination of the credit fuelled housing boom will leave as its legacy on the city such a large monument to spiralling avarice. Yet such smug self satisfaction about the demise of uber-captialism is of no benefit to the city. The building stands, unfinished, higher than anything in the city. The skyline is changed as dramatically by its presence as it was diminished by the loss of the Tinsley cooling towers. If it reaches its proposed 32 floors there will barely be a place in the city that will not glimpse its towering ambition. It could be the architectural stamp on the new 21st century city centre, the sum part of the whole of the Heart of the City Project,

The Sevenstone Retail quarter (also put on ice this month as financial credit dried up) and the myriad of other projects that have left the city skyline littered with high-rise cranes for the past couple of years may become a memory as a building boom, perhaps only rivalled by that of the 1890s, when so much of what passes for grand Victoriana in the city centre was built, comes to a staggering halt.

St Paul's Apartments had a rival for tallest building in Sheffield. Velocity Tower, a curvy glass tube apartment block that sits at the city end of Ecclesall Road. It is pretty much the considered opinion of the online skyscraper aficionados of Sheffield that this is the superior contender. It has been sitting idle and life-less at 22 floors for most of the year whilst the planning department and the local developers haggle over its completion. In this it mirrors the Arts Tower, which also started off smaller and then through committee, compromise and haggle ended up taller. At the beginning of September the Council granted the developers of Velocity Tower permission to go and add another 8 floors and a 14 floor adjacent block. Velocity had wanted to go to 36 floors. Bravado and then some given the current economic climate. The city council's decision is intriguing, just another 8 floors at Velocity and St Paul's Apartments remain the tallest building in the city. It had crossed my mind that the kudos of being tallest was important for St Paul's Apartments to be finished and more importantly sold, 8 floors rather than 14 was strategic.

This is a shame as the Velocity Tower has some architectural merit. It is sleek and thin. Glass rather than concrete dominates. Its curves glitter in the setting sun and it sits at one of the most awkward to fill spaces in the city centre. The 'designer' apartments will be able to look upon one of the city's most busy round-abouts for evening entertainment and the residents might reminisce about the commute to the suburbs. A quick dash through the urban underpass at their feet will take them to Waitrose, their corner shop.

It is a point of some speculation as to what is going to be the fate of this building. Velocity Tower has a business model very different from most of the city centre residential developments. Velocity proposes to rent the apartments itself rather than sell on. This means that it will not raise a large amount of capital to pay off its development cost in the short term but rather will accrue a long term income through rental. Are banks going to tolerate this approach as they gag to recapitalise as quick as possible. Only the owners of the Sheffield based developers Velocity know and they sure as hell aren't telling me. I suspect that they are at that moment in their business careers that Sir Alex Ferguson, manager of Manchester United, calls 'the squeaky bum' time. I hope they pull it off; they have genuinely tried to contribute something to the cityscape.

How do I keep up to date with the hurly-burley of change in Sheffield city centre? Well, although I gaze over it every morning as I leave the house, I probably only get 'into town' a couple times a week and one of those is getting a bus home from work after dropping down into the city on the tram from Crystal Peaks. I rely on the experts, whoever they are: Lewis Skinner, Adam Blade, Take Me Higher, Muddy Coffee, Arepeegee, jt123, skyfitsboy and particularly Hella Good, the photographic chronicler of a changing city. They all hang out at the 'Sheffield Metro Area' blog of Skyscrappercity.com. This site is a one stop shop for all things construction. You can marvel, scream or just gawp at the troposphere kissing skyline of Dubai, check out the latest bankrupt building project or simply banter with people who not only love their city but are, given their high level of insider information, actually building the city. Who is Hella Good?

I also poke around asking awkward questions to people who have every right to tell me to 'get stuffed'.

It is a challenge to the 'British' way of life this city centre high rise living. Unlike many of our European neighbours the middle classes have always gravitated towards the suburbs. To some extent the essence of Britain is suburbia. A house isn't a home without a garden. The British personality is a little semi-detached. Anthropologist Professor Kate Fox of Oxford University talks about our 'social dis-ease', that slightly uneasy reserve that runs through so many of our social interactions. We seem to need space to escape, a castle to defend, a nod to our ingrained rural idyll. Not easy in one of the most densely packed countrys in the world.

Sprawling suburbs were a gift from the 20th century to our cities, spreading into the surrounding countryside first prompted by trains and trams, then from the 1930s the car. Our cities were increasingly designed to ease the passage of cars, from one urban function to another. We live here, work there, shop in that area and go to school on the other side of the city. The 1990s saw the rise of suburban shopping, Meadowhall, Crystal Peaks, Hillsborough Barracks, suburban leisure and suburban work. By 1992 Sheffield city centre was declining by the day as the middle class drove to the free car parks that surrounded the new suburban consumer sheds to express their burgeoning wealth. Sheffield city centre had become a strip of charity shops, boarded up frontages and a few doughty big time retailers like Marks and Spencer. By 1993 a third of all shop units in Sheffield city centre were unlet. Footfall was down, profits were down, and civic pride was down. In the U.S. this phenomenon was known as the 'doughnut effect'; when downtown became rundown and life migrated to the suburbs.

It was a concern that Sheffield would replicate the 'doughnut effect' that led to Sheffield Council instigating the 'Heart of the City' project in the mid 1990s. It will have taken 15 years before all the elements of this city centre revamp are in place. The instantly popular Winter Gardens, The Millennium Galleries, a much reviled set of office blocks, a 4* hotel, the 'cheese grater' that futuristic cube of angular metal cladding that hides a car park and finally the 32 floors of St Paul's Apartments. To some extent this is a greater outcome than was initially proposed and for that the booming economy of the last decade must take responsibility.

It is however the growth in city centre living that has been the most dramatic change. No more the litter strewn streets of early evening desolation. A living, eating, socialising community had arisen out of the developer's bottom line and the exhortations for an 'urban renaissance' that had followed the groundbreaking 1999 report from Lord Richard Rogers's Urban Task Force. This document set out in 300 pages a vision for the 21st century city that set out "the importance of developing a higher quality urban product by creating compact urban developments". In the introduction Richard Rogers, architect of the Millennium Dome, The Swiss Re Building and Heathrow Terminal 5, states;

> **"How can we improve the quality of both our towns and countryside while at the same time providing homes for almost 4 million additional households in England over a 25 year period?"**

On the second weekend of September I took the opportunity to consider the possibilities of this aspiration first hand by looking at two attempts to re-populate the city centre whilst improving the quality of the built environment for everybody. It was the annual

'Heritage Open Day' and I used it to check out two of the more interesting city centre housing developments. Butcher Works and Park Hill. The contrast between the two is immense.

I began on the Thursday afternoon; a mad dash after a lecture, trying to catch the end of a presentation hosted by Urban Splash and its partners Sheffield Council and Parkway Housing Association at the Broad Street Community Centre about their bold, and as so many Sheffield folk would say, possibly mistaken, attempt to breathe new life into Park Hill flats. Urban Splash, a Manchester based developer with a proven track record of innovation and chancing their arm, had already upped sticks and left by the time I arrived but I hung around for an hour watching a PowerPoint presentation and flicking through a set of press cuttings from Park Hill's opening in 1959. I was struck by the opening ceremony when the Lord Mayor, Harold Lambert, turned up to hand over the keys to the first lucky couple, Mr and Mrs Fred Jackson. The husband had gone to work. Taking the time off for such a momentous occasion was not an option for a working man at that time.

Unfortunately no tour of the stripped out building was possible although two separate camera crews hovered, interviewing breathless council officers and lining up shots to capture the buildings scale and modernity.

Transforming Park Hill is a monumental task. £100's of millions of private money primed by £10's of millions of public money is being set in train. The approach is, unsurprisingly, stage by stage given that Park Hill is the largest listed building in Britain. This listing a point of some controversy.

In the full council meeting of October 5th 2005 the current council leader Paul Scriven set out his and the Liberal Democrat position on Park Hill with an extensive motion. In it he "calls on the present administration to recognise demolition and redevelopment as the only acceptable option for Park Hill and begin the process to de-list and demolish the site." This was part of a 'Not in my name' campaign aimed at removing Park Hill from the skyline, a move that gathered support when the building was featured in the BBC series 'Demolition' in December 2005.

This campaign found a willing cheerleader in Lynsey Hanley, who in her 2007 book "Estates: An Intimate History" observes that such 'slums in the sky' had an impact that "seemed to divide and rule over, and to make faceless, the people who lived there". This may be the case but the declining quality of life that appeared to afflict the tenants of Park Hill, particularly in the 1980s, had its roots in poverty and fundamental changes in society such as rising consumerism, increasing individualism and expanding crime. The building itself was not wholly to blame. Sure it is big, brutalist and bold. Yet Park Hill's flats command the same views that St Paul's Apartments would like to charge a premium for. The size of the flats is more generous than most of the new city centre apartments. It is a mere matter of a few hundred metres from the railway station, one of the best sports centres in the country and a major university. Location it has in spades. And it's unique.

The 'Architectural Review' of December 1961 describes Park Hill thus;

> **"Park Hill seems to represent one of those rare occasions when the intention to create a certain kind of architecture happens to encounter a programme and a site that can be hardly be dealt with in any other way, and the result has**

> **the clarity that only arises when aesthetic programme and functional opportunity meet and are instantly fused."**

I'm not sure I'd wax so lyrical about Park Hill, a fortnight previous to this famous review The Sheffield Telegraph reported that "gang battles flared up at the flats" with the playgrounds being full of "hooligans" and "love-making in the lifts"- of course such 'deviant' behaviour didn't really exist at this time in the 1960s, the 'golden age' of Daily Mail fantasies. Whatever the roots of Park Hill's decline there can be no doubt that, historically, it is one of the most important buildings in the city. The attempt to re-vision it for the 21st century is audacious, fraught with difficulties and deeply unpopular with many in the city. I hope it succeeds.

Butcher Works has been one of my favourite buildings in Sheffield for a long time. I first stumbled upon it in the early 1980s when it was hard to work out what went on in the fortress like confines of the 1820s tool makers works. Its position on Arundel Street, right in the heart of the city, was a clear indicator of times gone. Film companies regularly used it as a location to shoot Dickensian drama. All they had to do was remove a few telephone wires, add a bit of smog and it was the 1850s all over again.

I took the opportunity to have a poke around Butcher Works the following Saturday. What I hadn't realised was that in renovating this gem into city centre flats and craft workshops a number of historic features were left in situ. A complete grinding room on the top floor, a one man smelting and forging works tucked into a space barely bigger than a toilet and an original toilet that served the grime encrusted and lung function compromised grinders. A flat here was like living in a museum. This was a building that continued to represent the industrial urbanism that had driven Sheffield into life.

Around the courtyard the distinctive smells of a silversmith, pewter moulder, bespoke joiner and a jeweller integrated the residential with the industrial for the modern age. Richard Rogers would undoubtedly say 'that's how to do it.'

The following weekend I reacquainted myself with the rural idyll that has proved so illusory to the majority of us in this predominantly urban society. With Elbow on the car CD exhorting us to throw open our curtains to a beautiful day, the mist was just lifting out of the valleys as we sped south from Sheffield under a clear blue sky. We were on our way to what has become in very short time one of the cultural highlights of the North, The Sotheby's 'Beyond Limits' selling exhibition laid out in the gardens of Chatsworth House.

This is only the 3rd year that the Duke of Devonshire, a director of the world famous auction house Sotheby's, has combined his day job with his back garden. It is a rare treat and on a peerless autumnal day where the only blemishes in the sky are the streaks of jets, something of staggering beauty.

Of course we are spoiled. Not for us the 'the endless M1 that you have to endure' which so depressed Germaine Greer when she ventured out of her southern comfort zone to visit the Yorkshire Sculpture Park in December 2007. We have on our doorstop, well a quick jaunt towards Leeds and a cracking place to meet up with West Yorkshire friends for a Sunday stroll, one of the most rural of art galleries to be sauntered through. Thanks to the Y.S.P. at West Bretton we are conversant in Andy Goldsworthy, Gormley, Hepworth and Henry Moore. Smearing cow shit on a gallery window to obscure the view across the rolling fields, well what could be more....err natural?

The cherry on an already plump cake of contemporary sculpture is the 'Beyond Limits' show. It has taught me that Damien Hirst isn't just an entrepreneurial chancer but an artist of real merit, that Mark Quinn is an acquired taste, which like sherry has not tickled my palate and that George Condo's reflective Miles Davis sculpture may look tired and unimaginative in a gallery but in the clipped beech hedge pool garden of Chatsworth it is capable of ambushing negative preconceptions about modern art. We approached the gardens with an expectant gait.

The sun had brought out a bumper crowd, the gardens were thronged, many languages chattered and picnicking families chowed down whilst gazing at work that even if they sold their every possession they still would not be able to afford.

Of course it is not simply the art. You could have set the pieces in the anodyne white walls of a gallery and many of them you would have passed without a glance. Yet set in a garden that can rightly claim to be one of the greatest in a nation rammed to the hilt with great gardens, some of the pieces come alive. Planet by Marc Quinn improbably sits at the end of the great southern lawn. An alabaster white baby boy whose penis excites comment from not only my own children but just about all children under the age of ten. At the other end of the great lake Robert Indiana's 'American Love' strikes a surreal pose through which to view the frontage of one of England's most stately of homes. Every year at least one piece captivates me and this year an untitled piece by 85 year old American abstract artist Beverley Pepper works for me in every way possible. Its simplicity is enhanced by its orientation which sets a clear transect towards one of the most regal monkey puzzle trees outside of Chile. Place really does matter.

'Home' Chapter 9: September

I harbour a fantasy to wander the gardens of Chatsworth alone, to lie disturbed by only dragonflies next to the trout filled pools that sit underneath Joseph Paxton's monumental rock garden. Do the Devonshire clan afford themselves such pleasures? I guess that it is some progress, almost as monumental as some of the sculptures, that ordinary folk can lose themselves in the greatest of all back gardens without an irate, patrician gamekeeper howling 'get 'orf my masters land'.

Obviously the running of an estate as grand as Chatsworth doesn't come cheap. This, after all, was an estate that was able, in 2004, to line the whole route from the great house to the church altar in the neighbouring estate village of Edensor with starched and respectful staff on the occasion of the last duke's death; Andrew, the 11th duke since 1640. Family roots of such an historic aristocratic family go beyond 1640 to Sir John Cavendish who, not for the reason of hailing from Suffolk, found himself on the wrong end of a pikestaff in the Peasants Revolt of 1381. However an ambitious family was not to be thwarted and it is alleged that the dissolution of the monasteries by Henry VIII gave Sir William Cavendish, Sir John's grandson, the financial wherewithal to buy the estate of Chatsworth in 1694. His marriage to Derbyshire aristocrat Bess of Hardwick had drawn him north in the first place. Aristocracy was carved out of blood, land and power.

The consequence of such fortunate financial acumen back in the 17th century is an estate of such palatial proportions that American visitors gawp in awe. Even after thirty plus visits I can still gasp. I've been about a bit and I'm struggling to think of a better, greater, more tamed example of the English rural idyll. Grand but intimate, private but public. The highlights are a fountain that soars into the sky at such a rate that its phallocentric allusions are barely concealed,

Edensor, a confection of houses that belong in a fairy tale and a towered folly that peers down on all that lies below it in the Derwent valley. Trees of antiquity that will continue to soar into the Derbyshire sky long after your children have been buried, climate change permitting.

And land, lots of land, farms, grouse moors, grazing and woodland. The Chatsworth estate is huge slice of economic life in north Derbyshire and we, the taxpaying citizenry, support it with our 'gift aid' admissions fascinated as we are by a life so grand our forebears could only imagine treading across the carpet like lawns that frame the cascade tumbling down from the wooded slopes to the Cavendish family home. For a few weeks only one of the world's great art galleries. For the rest of the year the world's greatest back garden.

I've been fortunate and adventurous enough to lurch my way across much of what was painted pink in the atlases of colonialism, trading posts that grew into cities as a result of the efforts of merchants of raw materials upon which empire was built. Wherever the British went they set out gardens, parks, tree lined roads. Indian cities are testimony to this. Chatsworth is the model. The rural estate where nature is decorously brought to heel. This is 'the' British folk memory and it is why selling city centre living to middle class masses is an uphill task.

October

I hadn't been in to town for over a week when I got a less than welcome opportunity on the last day of September. I was on strike. I know it sounds almost quaint today but I'm a public sector worker so this approach to pay negotiations had not completely disappeared with the miners. I took my children to school so didn't make the picket line, my colleagues get to work real early, it would have been all done and dusted by nine o'clock and I never much cared for the hurly burly antagonism of the picket line. Still I wouldn't have minded a pay rise; it had been a couple of years now. Did you know that FE lecturers get paid about £3,000 a year less than school teachers for basically the same job? Actually do you care? Probably not. The city did not grind to a halt as a result of our strike. It garnered a brief piece on BBC Look North. Our status as the 'Cinderella service' of education remained undimmed.

Not for us the resolve of workers at Keetons, the Sheffield engineering factory who on the 31st December 1994 ended an eight and half year strike. When on the 2nd July 1986 the 38 members of the engineering union went on strike they were dismissed. Over 3000 days later, of the 38 one had died, three were ill, and twenty had found other jobs or reached retirement age. Now that is what you call intransigent bloody mindedness. These people are true Yorkshire role models. For years I wandered past their seemingly endless picket set up outside the Town Hall. On occasion small change found its way into their sticker strewn collecting buckets. They became part of the scenery. I wonder what the survivors make of it now, nearly 14 years on?

Keeton's were the ultimate expression of a long standing propensity of Sheffield folk to organise and agitate for the interests of labour. Historian David Hey identifies strikes in 1777-file trades, 1787-table knife makers, 1790-scissor trade and the 1796 spring knife trade strikes as heralding "a new era in industrial relations". The 1866 'great file makers' strike was particularly notable for its violence with gunpowder explosions, shootings and murder. These 'outrages', as Leng the Tory editor of the Sheffield Telegraph at the time dubbed them, led to the 1867 Royal Commission of Inquiry into Labour disputes. Surprisingly one outcome was the legalisation of unions (1871) and Sheffield embraced this opportunity with more enthusiasm than most.

The 1912 national miners' strike, a bitter six week affair paved the way for the idea, if not the reality, of a national minimum wage for miners. The national steel strike of 1981 achieved little but a great deal of police overtime in Sheffield and of course the legendary miners' strike of 1984/85 is a major piece of the city's social history. Kicking off at Cortonwood colliery, just over the hill from Wentworth Woodhouse, on 5th March 1984, the Miner's Strike stretched on for almost year. It was bitter and painful. I was arrested hitch-hiking on the M1 for wearing a 'coal not dole' badge and was slapped and shoved to the ground by bored 'southern' coppers, a mere sideshow compared to the pitched violence of Orgreave. This strike divided families, the city and the country.

The provocateur of the miners' strike, Margaret Thatcher, only visited the city once, a year before it kicked off. On 28th April 1983 it took a thousand police to protect her from the howling mob that laid siege to The Cutlers Hall opposite the cathedral where she addressed the assembled business multitudes of the city.

Today Cortonwood is a retail park, Orgreave a business park and the strike a memory of lingering bitterness. It is hard to imagine that there will not be more than one party in Sheffield when the demise of Lady Thatcher is reported however the revellery will probably not be as intense as that enjoyed by the Catalan Republican city of Barcelona on the death of Spanish fascist dictator Franco in 1975.

All that remains in Sheffield of the once proud National Union of Mineworkers is their, as yet unfinished, and soon to be demolished headquarters, a folly both financially and architecturally. It has sat unused and unloved next to one of Sheffield's favourite buildings, The City Hall, for far too long. A great improvement is expected when at the start of next year work begins on an office block to accommodate staff of the department of Children, Schools and Families and its more grown up sibling the Department of Innovation, Universities and Skills relocating from the red brick ziggurat at Moorfoot, another soon to be lost landmark.

Being a middle class bunch of lecturers, albeit some pretty hard up ones in some cases, if the academic staff of Sheffield College, went on all out strike we'd probably last a week or two and then we'd go back to work to meet up with some pretty pissed off students. Still I got to go into town and may get some more opportunities in the future if we haven't dragged management to the negotiating table crying 'mercy, call it off'. I'm not holding my breath.

I went in search of Sheaf Graphics. They were housed in Beehive Works on Milton Street. This block, built between 1850 and 1864 is possibly the best remaining, broadly undeveloped, example of Sheffield's cutlery industry of the mid 19th century. It sits, unmolested by development, in Milton Street, a quiet corner at the edge of the city centre. It is a mish-mash of additions creating a jumble of housing and industry, cheek by jowl, much as the majority of the city centre would have been back in the late 19th century. The terraced houses, with their sash windows oddly thrown open to the scudding rain still suggested occupancy. The backyard of Beehive Works still housed Sheffield's last working grinder, Brian.

Entering this central yard to ask directions was a flashback in time, the three men sheltering under a brick arch who advised me of what bell to ring drew deeply on their cigarettes. Sheaf Graphics was upstairs in a smart open plan office, art prints adorning its brick walls. The new and the old chivvied along within spitting distance of each other.

When I left Beehive Works I wandered through the city centre, a wet Tuesday lunchtime, but it was animated and thronged. The university students were back. Some, clutching A to Z maps with a look of faint concern, were clearly new to the city, others strode more confidently, lap top bag to hand. The average age of the city had fallen by a good ten years. After the slumbers of the summer a riot of youth had descended upon the city.

Of course such upheavals do not pass without some hurly burly. The last edition of The Sheffield Telegraph in September carried the banner headline “Student Fury”. This was a bit of a hardy perennial. Since I had washed up in Sheffield, as a student, the annual bacchanalian rituals of thousands of newly arrived undergraduates to the city had caused consternation to the prim amongst the populace. I guess most people were secretly relieved at their arrival; it was a shot of adrenalin to the city. Autumn is the most hedonistic exuberant time in the city, the revels of the students spilling over into the wider population.

This year's story was the same as last year's story. Rowdy, drunken, 'over-exuberance' rattled the windows of many a suburban street. Traffic bollards found themselves on cars, signs were removed to adorn student bedrooms and vomit flecked the pavements. The Sheffield Telegraph reported residents claims in those areas of the city in which students tended to live that they were being 'hounded out by rowdy behaviour'.

Of course this year's revellery is probably but a poor comparison to the legendary 'Pyjama Jump'; a night of excess and sex that spilled down the hill from the University of Sheffield into the clubs and bars of West Street. This was standard fare for our prurient tabloids, A 'redtop' once printing a picture of students having sex on a pool table in a 'shock horror, how disgusting but we know you will be mildly titillated by it' story. It was also part of the reason the University of Sheffield brought this 'charitable' event to a close in 1996. There really was a limit to the amount of nightie clad hairy legs that the city could stand, it was the ultimate stag and hen rolled into one. I never went, It all sounded a bit much. I sort of preferred to get stoned listening to Talking Heads and discussing energy policy than lurch lusciously down West Street. Let's face facts students have a long and inglorious history of behaving badly, in all sorts of ways.

To be honest I wouldn't choose to live in a student dominated area of the city now. The endless churn of neighbours and the lack of a settled community would be less preferable to my area of families and small town dynasties. I'm older, more parochial and quite like garden centres and D.I.Y. I have an allotment. Yet I have lived in such areas and it's not the end of the world. They settle down once they have to do some work, mostly.

This year, the University of Sheffield, stung into action by front page headlines, sent out a letter to their students reminding them to be orderly citizens. In reality a mere nine students had their collars felt by the long arm of the law for disruptive behaviour in the neighbourhoods of Broomhill and Endcliffe, the heart of student land. Retailers and fast food outlets on the other hand were making a collective sigh of relief as trade shot up. It is estimated that the student spend in the city in pubs, clubs, shops and restaurants is around £120 million a year. Taking out four months, when the undergraduates go home to get their washing done and take out some time to get their livers to regenerate, that stacks up to approximately £300 per student, per month. A lot of that is front loaded in October and the glut of bands, club nights, comedy and culture that is fed by this spend reaches a level of giddying choice at this time of year.

Casting my eyes across the listings guide of the Sheffield Telegraph provides me with a myriad of opportunities to enlighten, invigorate, laugh, bop or even to debase myself. The penultimate week of the month sees Queen, Bryan Adams, Katie Melua and Hot Chip lead the list of music's big hitters. A further 100 acts were also playing in town that week including the possibly unmissable, but sadly missed, King Mojo's Psychedelic Beatnik Phenomenon featuring Elephants on Acid. Then there is jazz, a further sixteen gigs, folk, twelve, the Moscow Philharmonic Orchestra, free Chopin recitals in the cathedral, an evening of flamenco and the gypsy violin sounds of Russian fiddlers Koshka.

Maybe you fancy going on to a club, well The Leadmill, DQ, Dulo, The Forum, Corporation, Plug, Nylon, The Casbah, The Raynor Bar, Cubana, Sanctuary, Penelopes, The Harley and Red House should cover most tastes on a Friday night. Perhaps a laugh, the 'Grin Up North' comedy festival stretched across 18 days this month. Once that had tittered its last the 'Off the Shelf' festival of reading and writing declaims its first stanza. Next month it's a documentary film festival oh and a folk music festival. Can you keep up?

Good job there is something decent on television. It's too exhausting to go out. I'll leave it to those bright young things.

What cannot be denied is that higher education is big business in Sheffield. Some 55,000 students attend the two universities, which between them employ a little over 10,000 staff of whom 3,500 are academics. In terms of employment that puts both universities on a par with a very large steelworks. There are probably as many people working in education as in manufacturing within the city. Turnover at Sheffield Hallam University in 2007-08 was £160 million, the University of Sheffield will significantly surpass that figure as it draws down more research funding although less students. We have probably gone far beyond the point where the net economic impact of the universities on the city and immediate environs is £500m a year. These things are difficult to calculate accurately.

What it is possible to be far more confident about is the centrality of a university to a city region in this global age. Ten years ago to the month I spent two weeks researching a chapter of a geography textbook in Bangalore, the six million strong state capital of the Indian state of Karnataka. Why most people have heard of this city is its information technology industry which at the lower end brings unsolicited phone calls into your home and at the top end is developing ideas for things you didn't even realise you needed. How did Banaglore travel from impoverished ex-raj city at the time of national independence in 1947 to global hub of every major player in IT? Well a few factors were in place already like a nicely laid out city, a decent climate and a smart ambitious populace. Yet without the prestigious India Institute of Science - founded by J.N. Tata historic patriarch of the Tata clan who now own a big slice of the local steel industry with Stocksbridge and Rotherham's Corus - and the newer Bangalore University this city would not have developed such a forward thinking and innovative population.

As Sheffield has a lower than national average rate of A level achievement for its population it relies on first attracting people into the city to study and then seducing them to stay. Analysing the destination of leavers from higher education forms for 2007 graduates of the University of Sheffield reveals that 31.9% were either working, studying or signing on in the city six months after graduation. This figure is almost certainly higher for Sheffield Hallam University as it draws on more local students in the first place. I have written references for literally hundreds of local students who successfully gained a place at Hallam, the University of Sheffield significantly less.

The theory is that universities are engines of growth and dynamism for a local economy. Clearly in Banaglore this has happened, Cambridge, UK and Boston, USA, have also seen massive benefits from their prestigious higher education alumna sticking around to reinvent science and technology within 'eureka' yelling distance of their undergraduate quad. Does this happen in Sheffield?

The symbiotic relationship between Sheffield's universities and the rest of the city go beyond the economic. Both universities are an assertive part of the city's built environment and as I have already suggested the youth and vitality they attract drives the music, art, literature and hedonism that sweeps through the city in October. It is a form of cultural collusion between the working class roots of the city, with its pragmatically hedonistic tip, and the learned middle class interlopers. As an interloper and a southerner to boot I can state without a shadow of a doubt that the last twenty years has seen Sheffield become much more welcoming to difference and diversity. The sharpness of the division between gown and town was palpable back in the early 1980s. Estuarine English was commented on, derided and a potential affliction, today cultural diversity is much more the norm, Fargate is a linguistic soup, who knows what is being spoken and by whom. Last week at the bus stop I had arguing eastern Europeans, a gaggle of Punjabi tongues and what sounded like, to my untutored ear, Japanese. All on their way into town. The universities have a huge part to play in all of this.

The significantly large full cost fees paid by foreign students, at The University of Sheffield £9,920 for a degree in Geography, £13,050 for Chemistry, help cover the cost of a university building boom that has gifted the city it's best conceived and most interesting new buildings of recent years. The University of Sheffield has steadily been colonising the streets between its lofty Weston Park base and the city centre. On Saturday 18th I took the opportunity afforded to me by my children being engrossed in the Lauren Child exhibition at Weston Park Museum to spend a couple of hours strolling around these new developments with my architecture obsessed brother - this is a man who the following weekend paid nearly £100 to go on an architecture fieldtrip visiting sites of interest on the M1, Newport Pagnall services being a highlight!

Ian expertly negotiates my game of guess when this building was built. We start with Firth Court, the only building with vaguely Oxbridge airs (1905), with its solid Accrington redbrick Tudor castle pretensions. We move on via the skeleton of a python in a case by the door of the Animal Science Department to The Arts Tower (1965 but officially opened by the Queen Mum a few days before England's '66 World Cup victory- yes it is that old). We are disappointed that the continuous paternoster lift, for which the building is rightly revered, is not working so we loiter around chatting to the porters about the soon to be commenced revamp of this the University of Sheffield's most distinctive addition to the city skyline. Passing the Dainton Building, (Chemistry, 1953), we then cross over the ring road to admire the awarding winning, copper green hues of the Information Commons (2007). A library in all but name and awarded the accolade of best new building in Yorkshire 2008 by RIBA. This is faced by the new Biosciences complex (2008) which we tag the Biba building, on account of its bold colour lines in descending shades of brown and blue. Slipping around the corner into Leavygreave Road we catch a draft of the heady scent from the Henderson's Relish factory. Student 'exuberance' had possibly taken its toll here as the wooden sign board that sat on the gable end of this down at heel Victorian premises had been half taken down on the night of 30th September. As Managing director Dr Kenneth Freeman explained;

> **"We have had reports that two young men and a woman were on the roof, then later seen carrying something large and flat down Glossop Road. I believe they must be students intent on playing a prank or with the intention of taking home a souvenir of their stay in Sheffield. But this is a very important sign to us, everyone in Sheffield knows it."**

The good doctor, alchemist of Sheffield's piquant relish offered to leave a few bottles of Henderson's on the doorstep for anybody bringing the sign back. No joy yet.

Across the road from Henderson's is the site of one of my greatest contributions to the city, the Victorian Jessop's Hospital for Women (1878). This place will always have a special place in my heart as my eldest daughter was born here in 1999. Then it was easy to see why the much longed for move to a new shiny maternity hospital further up the hill was yearned for. Ironically the 'red light' district sat outside its front door - arguing prostitutes keeping my partner awake three floors above street level. The fixtures and fittings were from another age but fortunately the medical care was not. I spent a week tiptoeing around the 'Special Care Baby Unit'. Megan's birth place is now a building site, awaiting a new addition to the surrounding Victoriana. Fittingly the History Department of the University is earmarked to move in. This looks like a boldly adventurous addition to the university's portfolio and with yet another influx of 'tired and emotional undergrads'. Henderson's had better bolt their new sign to their wall, after all they are part of the fixtures and fittings of the city as well. Long may the University of Sheffield not offer to buy their site.

Across the road from the old Jessop's is Gell Street, its confines concealing an unmissable recent addition to the cityscape. The Soundhouse (2008). This undulating sculptural box is covered with a rubber membrane pinned to its structure with bright shiny bolts. It is, Ian suggested, the ultimate S and M club, alas in reality it is a Department of Music rehearsal room. It is hard to work out how it will age because you have never seen a building quite like it; will they have to re-rubber it twenty, fifty years down the line? We spent 5 minutes jumping up to touch the rubber clad walls before my phone rang to summon us back to the land of harmless children's entertainment that is 'Charlie and Lola'.

Playful, irreverent architecture seems to be mainly found in public commissions. The underlying merit of much of the private sector additions to the city centre has been profoundly depressing. Driven by accountants not architects there is a much heard view that the poor build quality of some of the new city centre residential blocks is so bad that we are actively building the slums of the future. It would probably involve expensive litigation if I named and shamed the guilty parties but suffice to say there is some right crap being built in Sheffield city centre at present. I suspect some of it will last less time than even Broomhall flats (1968-1988 may their rubble be more useful for hardcore under a motorway)

I had the opportunity to be gently provocative about this view a few days later when I met up with Paul Cocker, a director of Blundells, the largest estate agency in the city. Paul has probably set foot in more houses in Sheffield than anybody. He has been valuing property in just about every city street for 30 years, his knowledge is encyclopaedic and his manner avuncular and relaxed considering we are in a property market freefall at present.

Paul is a proud local with family roots in the city's small tools trade and a 60s upbringing within an artisan's household. How he became the city's leading estate agent after leaving school at 16 and qualifying in the further education sector is no mystery on meeting him, personable he has in spades.

Paul confided that he wasn't always overwhelmed by the quality of city centre apartments being put up. He revealed that only between 10-15% of the apartments in the city centre were owner occupied - a figure much lower than Leeds. The rest had been sucked up by buy to let speculators. For these people, financial returns were the key consideration, not floor space, architectural merit or community. EU data suggests that new UK housing is the smallest in floor space terms in the whole continent.

I had discovered for myself that the rental market for such property in the city remained buoyant when I experimented trying to rent a flat a few months back. Sorry to those estate agents whose time I wasted, remember me, recently divorced man eyeing up his options whilst the solicitors were carving up the marital home? It wasn't simply a case of turning up to a look at a range of properties, demand was high. The backsliding housing market had resulted in a lot of young professionals just about to make the jump into bricks and mortar sitting tight in rental property. Paul confirmed that renting was now the hottest estate agent meal ticket in town. More surprisingly he thought a fair amount of these rentals were to students and academics on short contracts.

“There was”, Paul said, “no real sense of community, no families, no young children and the population was transient and quite often foreign”. This was a community that leaned on the universities to sustain them. There isn't any formal academic research into the impact of city centre living in Sheffield, the nearest relevant study is in Leeds. Here Geographer Dr Rachael Unsworth has been following the residential redevelopment of the city centre since 2003. Sure there are some significant differences between Leeds and Sheffield. The average price of a Leeds city centre flat in March 2007 was £175,000, in Sheffield £121,000, however average monthly wages In Leeds at that time were £2,274 gross, in Sheffield lower at £2,066. Clearly Sheffield is a more affordable city centre to live in. Put another way wages in Sheffield are 91% of those in Leeds, but housing costs 69% of our cocky northern neighbour. Rents are lower in Sheffield too. This may be important in explaining the poor build quality, “a lack of imagination in the internal planning and layout of many flats”, as Paul Cocker diplomatically expressed it. Simply put Sheffield hasn't had the money in the private sector to build with style and panache, margins had been tighter, now they were non-existent.

There is though, much that can be quite reasonably extrapolated from the Leeds study to Sheffield, particularly the occupier survey, which short on waiting for the results of the 2011 census to be released in 2013, might be the best idea of who is living in these city centre apartments. Some selected highlights are that only 2% of households have any children, 46% are single person occupancy, 61% are 30 or under, it is a broadly 50/50 gender mix and 51% describe themselves as single. The report goes on to state;

> **"Top reasons given for renting are flexibility, an expected short stay and not being able to afford to buy. The proportion of rental properties versus owner occupied is unchanged since 2005 (56 per cent rented and 44 per cent owner occupied). Eighty per cent of rented apartments are furnished properties acquired through a letting company."**

What is intriguing is that 60% of respondents expect to move out of the city centre in two years. Some because they are students - a low 10% of respondents but perhaps this is accounted for by the possibility that students are more likely to be amongst those who didn't return the survey form - but most expected to move to semi-detached and detached houses in the suburbs, having children being the most commonly cited reason for such a move.

What these city dwellers complained about wasn't the noise but the lack of food shops (49%), a lack of parking (24%) and a lack of green space (23%). 7% could find nothing to complain about at all, ah those pre credit crunch days.

Now it may be that Sheffield's city centre housing market shares few of these Leeds attributes, certainly the general feeling is that students make up substantially more than 10% of occupiers in Sheffield, yet no comparable study has been done in the city bar a

Sheffield City Council commissioned report by property consultants DTZ in 2006. This report was meant to inform future planning decisions. It pointed out that "the vast majority of the resident population are aged under 40 years old, are single or couple households, typically renting from the private sector with some owner occupation." It also set out the wide range of disadvantages to city living;

> **"A view that too much of the new residential developments look the same; The poor quality of internal specifications and layouts in new developments; The need to provide apartments with larger floor areas; Growing concerns around the affordability of apartments; An evening economy that promotes noise, anti-social behaviour and feelings of poor safety; A poor quality streetscape and problems with traffic and parking."**

That such concerns existed within the city council hadn't led to a noticeable increase in the quality of such projects. This was a bit of a worry. There were some good additions, mainly refurbishments of existing industrial buildings. Cornish Place at Kelham Island, the 1822 factory of cutlery manufacturer James Dixon, was, Paul Cocker and I agreed, the first and probably the best example of urban living apartments in the city. Spacious, elegant, classical and.... oh! Errr... Victorian! It would be pretty unfair to damn all the new build residential units in the city. Some, in the very heart of the city are very popular, Victoria Plaza on West Street, Velocity Tower has got it's 'wow factor' and even the brooding monolithic, sub Parisian La Defense, West One has got its fans- I am not one of them. Many of the very central new apartments at the lower end of specification spectrum and thus cheaper were now being colonised by students from Sheffield Hallam University.

'Home' Chapter 10: October

Over the past few years Sheffield Hallam University has been consolidating itself on two major sites. Leafy Collegiate Crescent abutting Ecclesall Road and the City Campus which sits around the unmissable hulk of the 12 storey Owen Building. This is a building, or rather a collection of interconnected buildings that is architecturally striking inside but rather mundane if a little intimidating on the outside, from certain angles it reminds me of a huge cruise liner edging its way through the city centre. The highest platform of the buzzing atrium leads into a set offices that accommodate Sheffield Hallam University's top brass. At the end of the month I found myself sat waiting in this stylish eyrie of an ante room for John Palmer, Director of Communications and Public Affairs for S.H.U. His office is far from flash, it is workmanlike with a Sheffield United scarf on the shelf above his desk and a Love 2 Be in Sheffield poster on the wall. John lives in Warwickshire.

John has a straight forward job he has to tell the story of how Sheffield Hallam has become one of the country's fastest developing universities. From the reasonably humble beginnings of the Sheffield School of Design founded in Victoria Street in 1843 and the 1905 City of Sheffield Training College for teachers in Collegiate Crescent, Sheffield Hallam, given its charter in 1992, has become one of the largest higher education institutions in the country. He ran through the data, 16,124 undergraduates, 4,300 post graduates and another 10,000 students on a multitude of other courses. The second largest provider of nurse training in the country. He was particularly proud that recently Sheffield Hallam was voted the best UK university to study at by foreign students; that is 3,204 foreign, fee paying students at present, a particularly large number from India. Somebody needs to be smiling about the declining £ on foreign exchange markets and these people are they.

'Home' Chapter 10: October

I wanted to understand the impact that higher education had on Sheffield. John suggested a few figures to play around with. 4,000 direct employees but a figure closer to 10,000 if you factored in all the people working for local firms working with and supplying the university with goods and services. The wage bill alone for Sheffield Hallam was close to £140 million. The 30,000 students were probably spending at least £300 million in the city each year, accommodation topping their bills but a fair amount on food, drink and dancing, oh and books I hope.

There is no doubt that Sheffield Hallam has a different pitch to its bigger, wiser - if we are counting Nobel prize awards - certainly older and more famous sibling up the hill, The University of Sheffield. John suggested that Sheffield Hallam was a 'selling university' the University of Sheffield a 'buying university'. It's all those grades and the inevitable hierarchical intellectual pyramid that is higher education. I had always felt this difference. First when encountering those University of Sheffield super confident ex private school students with armfuls of arcane knowledge whilst a lowly aspirational working class student of 'the Poly' in the early 1980s.

More recently in trying to forge links from an F.E. institution for broadly working class 'Access' students with a few, but not all, of the University of Sheffield's academic departments. Once, when in 1993, I was being interviewed for a place to read for a part-time PhD at the University of Sheffield the academic surveying my C.V. said "Yes, I see you have got your MA from Sheffield Hallam University, you do realise that '*we*' are a 5 star research university?" I got the message and didn't bother with six years of hard graft to make me more employable /intellectual /egotistical. Hindsight suggests this was probably a mistake.

John Palmer described the difference as Sheffield Hallam "being concerned with problem solving research whilst the University of Sheffield had more 'blue sky' research". Most of S.H.U.'s research commissions came from the government, although a major interdisciplinary research project was being funded by the food industry. This concerned how to keep food fresher and to make packaging more sustainable. Not headline grabbing research but something that would affect all our lives. Pragmatic problem solving stuff but no Nobel awards.

The impact that S.H.U. has on the built environment is starting to rival that of the University of Sheffield. John observed;

> **"We do our best to get involved in the fabric of the city, what we build needs to reflect the city. After all it is our name."**

The best example of this is architect Nigel Coates's innovative Student Union Building. Not originally built for Sheffield Hallam but to host the National Centre for Popular Music, a creative manager's view of popular culture. I'm sure it sounded a great idea at the pitching meeting and to be fair if it had been built in London it would be packed with backpack adorned, adolescent, language class students from Japan at this very moment in time. Not so in Sheffield. I only went once, for an hour. I'm not sure that staring at the rock and roll artefacts is my thing; I'd rather listen to music or play it. Most people in a city, that when it came to music was more famed for making it than consuming it, tended to agree. It shut. I imagine the artefacts of the 'age of rock' are now nailed to the walls of Hard Rock Cafes the world over.

The shiny 'kettledrum quadraphenia' of Coates's off the wall design is, in my view, the best example of post-modern architecture in the city, if only they'd give it a good polish every now and then.

All around the Owen Building, heart of Sheffield Hallam, the quality of the built environment had leapt in recent years. The demise of the Psalter Lane Art Department and its relocation into the new Furnival Buildings, opposite the strikingly imaginative reworking of 19th century Sterling Works by Freemans College, is a great piece of integrated urban design. It has even incorporated the original road pattern within the building. Spinning off from Sheffield Hallam is the soon to be opened 'Digital Campus' on what was the site of the old city centre swimming pool. This is a good example of the intellectual multiplier effect a good university can bring, a newly signed up tenant being Bunnyfoot, a research consultancy working for Microsoft, the BBC and several government departments. The company cites “the need to work amongst like-minded creative people” as the reason “to be part of the city's digital campus”.

Unlike the University of Sheffield, Sheffield Hallam does not rent much of its own student accommodation. Instead that recent phenomenon the private sector student flat provider has blossomed all over this part of the city. It is this transient population that injects the animation and energy into the city streets as the clocks leap back into evening dark. And why do they come to this once decaying industrial city?

“Sheffield is perceived as quite a 'cool' city with its continuing music scene.” suggested John Palmer. Acknowledging this debt Sheffield Hallam was awarding an honorary doctorate to local musician Richard Hawley next month, an accolade Richard had earned as both an evangelist for the city and an internationally acclaimed recording artist.

I'm not entirely sure why I chose Sheffield all those years ago. Was it 'cool'? No. Was it 'happening'? No. Was it the only place that would accept me after my stumblingly feeble attempt at A levels, I think that was it. I often mutter to my students that I am ideally placed to teach them A levels, I know all about how to fail them. An excess of rock and roll being one of them. Thank goodness a welcoming city and a 'selling university' took pity on me. I owe them both.

November

C; it started with a chord in C, the sound of the suburbs. If only it was that simple. This is just the 1978 pop punk song by The Members, 'The Sound of the Suburbs', which tells of a lad strumming his guitar in his bedroom. Sheffield pop artist Pete McKee summed the scene up in his painting 'A Good Education'. An image of a teenager perched on his bed, with his Velvet Underground poster pinned to the wall whilst getting his fingers around a tentative chord, probably a C, on his first guitar.

I had been wondering. Could a city ever have a sound? Something so distinct and culturally resonating that from the first half a dozen bars, a place, an identity, a city sweeps into your mind. Does the Mersey really have a beat? Can you trip hop to Bristol or wallow in grunge on the streets of Seattle? Clearly songs can evoke places and times. The Clash made sure that you heard that 'London' was 'Calling' in the early 1980s and the last couple of years have seen Sheffield's Arctic Monkeys plaster their *vignette's* of estate life from Hunters Bar to San Francisco. Lead singer Alex Turner's flat vowels and sharp wit following in a tradition of creative song smiths from the city. But can we call it the sound of the city? In the case of the Arctic Monkeys it is not simply about place but the zeitgeist, the moment. This is probably true for most new music because very little of it continues unchanged over time. It's an evolution from generation to generation.

Yet geography does have a part to play. In the middle of November Chris Searle, the radical educationalist, who, in the 1980s was head teacher at Earl Marshall School in Firvale and who now counts being the jazz correspondent of the communist daily paper The Morning

Star amongst his activities, brought out a book entitled "Forward Groove: Jazz and the Real World from Louis Armstrong to Gilad Atzmon". In the book Chris, who continues to live in Sheffield after a career spanning several continents, pays homage to the city of New Orleans, U.S.A, where, when not battening down and bailing out before and after hurricanes, the local sound, a distinctive form of jazz, can be found floating out of the bars on famous Bourbon Street - a re-creation of which was once implausibly proposed as an extension to Meadowhall shopping centre. Chris accounts for this sound, with its unshakeable connections to the 'Big Easy', by observing that in New Orleans; "black people going back to slavery and Africa, playing on European instruments made music from the Caribbean fused with influences that have come down the Mississippi River - French, Spanish, Christian - ..... Creating a music so hybrid as to defy precedent". Clearly place was of supreme importance to creating something almost unique, a city with its own sound.

When local academic E. D. Mackerness addressed the historical development of music within Sheffield in his 1974 book "Somewhere Further North: a History of Music in Sheffield" and later in 1993, within the aspiringly definitive, multi-authored, "The History of The City of Sheffield", he approached his task with a set of class blinkers that suggest that his grasp on local culture was not all that wide ranging. His is an account that is rooted in orchestral, choral and a dash of 'lighter' brass and military music. The music halls of the poor, the hymns and folk traditions of the pubs and the rise of 'popular music' out of post-war Americana are absent. It has virtually nothing to do with the city and is the sound of middle class gentility. In summing up his 1993 history Mackerness makes some concessions;

'Home' Chapter 11: November

"Some young musicians are equally at home in the classical and popular idioms; jazz and rock groups are numerous, and in the sphere of barber-shop vocalization Sheffield holds many records.....There is even now a sizeable public for middlebrow music as heard in working men's clubs and similar places of resort."

Is that barber-shop records in the sense of hard to find recordings languishing in an as yet undiscovered secret section of 'Rare and Racy'? Or is it in the sense of the most melodious five part harmony? Are there, were there, competitions for this sort of thing?

I am vaguely aware that classical music concerts in Sheffield are perhaps more common than I suspect. I walk past Calow Classics on Abbeydale Road a fair number of times in the week. This is a one stop shop for all things Beethoven and beyond. It always has a fair number of 'gigs' advertised. This month Ecclesall Church hosts a programme from the Sheffield Sinfonia. It isn't however what springs to mind when you start thinking about Sheffield and music.

For me that is Joe Cocker, Jarvis Cocker, Def Leppard, Cabaret Voltaire, The Human League, ABC, Heaven 17, The Arctic Monkeys, Moloko, The Comsat Angels, Pulp and The Long Pigs. It's also about places; The Mojo Club, The Limit, The Leadmill, The Boardwalk, City Hall, The Roxy in a multitude of incarnations, shut down factories with the locks cracked and a sound system installed, reggae at the Everyone Centre and jazz in the Polish Club, a folk sing-along in Fagins. All of these musicians and places but really there is no Sheffield sound, just a hydra headed creativity that makes the city one of Britain's leading music cities. Similar sized cities in Europe have but a fraction of Sheffield's musical repute. Go on name me a band from Frankfurt, Turin or Valencia. Tell me about the ground breaking music coming out of Lille and Copenhagen.

It is only since the sixties that an idea of a sound emanating from a place went around the world. It is the mass culture of global communication that came with radio and television that ironically created a feeling for local identity that went beyond the local. An idea of a place that was intimately connected with a particular music. Something that could be imagined beyond the crackling airwaves. The rock and roll that grew out of Memphis, country and western from Nashville and the Californian dreaming of psychedelia. Even a fly blown cattle town in the Texas Panhandle, not much bigger than Chesterfield, Amarillo, gets exhorted globally courtesy of Conisborough crooner Tony Christie. More of him later.

British towns and cities somehow seem to lack the romance of far flung America. Nobody has enquired as to the way to Wakefield, although apparently some people do belong to Glasgow town. As for Sheffield, is there a song that is a recognisable paean to the city? Perhaps Pulp's 'Sheffield Sex City' which starts with singer Jarvis Cocker incanting districts of the city starting with Intake and ending at Broomhill before suggestively touring the city of his mind, district smut.

> **"cos the city's out to get me if I won't sleep with her this evening**
> **Though her buildings are impressive and her cul-de-sacs amazing**
> **She's had too many lovers and I know you're out there waiting"**

Maybe not, I'm not sure it quite crosses the generation gap. Sordid is not quite the thing when considering a hymn to home. Coles Corner by Richard Hawley might be more on message. First my 81 year old mother-in-law is a fan; even my Grime and EMO loving General Studies class thought it was pretty cool in a "sort of Frank Sinatra way." It also ticks two Sheffield boxes, it is achingly romantic - and this is a romantic city as Jarvis on a slightly earthier tip is apt to dwell upon - and it has a melancholy that sings of a hundred thousand slate roofs on a wet Sunday afternoon. Coles Corner is a place of local myth, the long gone department store at the bottom of Fargate, a venue for trysts over many generations.

On the 10th November an attempt at pulling together some of the disparate strands of Sheffield music was released to the world. 'Made in Sheffield' an album by 65 year old Tony Christie, a minor star of the 1970s who, amongst other relatively low key accomplishments, had once attempted to represent Britain at the Eurovision Song Contest in 1976 - 'Save Your Kisses for Me by Brotherhood of Man in case your wondering what usurped Tony. Tony was the archetypal northern working man's club act except he probably saw himself as more cruises and conferences than a slot in between the prize draw and the Abba covers act. He began his rehabilitation into a rather more contemporary idiom when Sheffield musical mavericks 'All Seeing Eye' got him to sing the Jarvis Cocker penned single 'Walk like a Panther' which made it to number 10 in the January 1999 charts.

It was Lancastrian comic Peter Kay who really threw Tony Christie back into the spotlight when his comic reinterpretation of what had been Tony's signature song, 'Show Me the way to Amarillo', spent 7 weeks at number 1 in 2005. Yet it has taken the vision of Richard Hawley, the musician's musician of modern Sheffield, to realise the depth of talent that Tony had been hiding under his ballad-lite bushel.

The 'Made in Sheffield Album' is a big deal. Its launch was part of the BBC Electric Proms - oddly on the ferry that plied across the Mersey.

Creative Sheffield, the quango that is charged with the responsibility of promoting the city stuck its hand in its pocket to fund an invite only gig at the City Hall - I wasn't on their list of the good and great. Finally a documentary of the album being made was put together by the auteur of The Clash, Don Letts, and this premiered at The Showroom Cinema's documentary film festival on the 12th November. Invite only as well.

In fact it didn't look possible that I could find some sort of perspective to dwell upon all this activity to launch a piece of music that so proudly asserted its roots in the city of Sheffield. It might be considered the first concerted attempt to make a statement about a sound for the city. If it is, the sound is romantic and melancholic. Lush and plaintive. Not flash, understated, cutely observed.

Tony Christie's publicist ignored my e-mail and calls. I'm probably not persistent enough to be a journalist I give up easy. I tried a different angle.

One weekday evening right at the end of October I was chilling in front of the TV. During the adverts I'd wandered into the kitchen to poor another glass of wine. I was chortling over a Paul Merton TV documentary where he had just visited Shillong, the state capital of Assam and self styled rock and roll capital of India. Grizzled old leather glad rockers were singing about chillin' in Shillong, bandanas, flying V's and all. The phone rang, it was Richard Hawley. Uh huh, OK stay cool!

I'd e-mailed Richard's manager a week previously to see if I could get an hour of Richard's time to talk to him about Sheffield. Really he is the closest thing to the bard of Sheffield around at present, usurping his good mate Jarvis Cocker when he decamped to live in Paris a fair few years back. Richard isn't the sound of the city. No, Richard is more about writing modern folk music for a people in a place. As he told me “I've been around the world 14 times but kiss the ground when I get back to Sheffield.” Lucky old us; actually lucky old world that he gets out so much. The man's a star, of sorts, albeit one resolutely swimming upstream and trying to duck out of the glare of the spotlights. A very Sheffield sort of star, a muscian who values graft and craft more than celebrity. I'm amazed he can spare me the time after all who the chuff am I?

Trying to regain my composure Richard gave me a quick rundown of his week ahead to see where we could squeeze in a meet. Between performing with Elbow - this year's rightful winners of the Mercury Prize - and being in the studio recording a new album we settled on a midweek drink at the pub. I had a fag straight after I put the phone down.

In my e-mail to persuade Richard, or rather his manager, Graham Wrench, that I wasn't just another one of an increasingly long line of journalists beating their path to Richard's fretboard, I mentioned that I was a mate of John Pedder. John and his irrepressible missus Bronwen sell antiques but before that they toured the world peddling Sheffield made music , John in the 'gorgeous' Babybird and Bronwen kicking the shit out of the drums for one of Sheffield's greatest also ran's Speedy (nee Blammo). John and Richard went way back when. They lived in the council tenements on Hawley Street in the 1980s, they were part of the original city centre gad-abouts, The Limit Club was but a short stagger for them. A lengthy cast of Sheffield 'faces' passed through these flats at that time including Pete McKee, the pop art chronicler of working class Sheffield that Richard Hawley is mining musically.

'Home' Chapter 11: November

I meet up with Richard in Fagins on Broad Lane, an old street that climbs up past the Irish crofts of St Vincent's, the industrial inner city north of the city centre. It is a boundary road leading up towards the University of Sheffield. As we stand outside smoking we are surrounded by cranes and newly built blocks; of flats I guess. A BMW garage abuts the bottom of the road; a wrought iron sewer gas lamp sits across the way. This is fast changing Sheffield. But Richard is resolutely old school, "Jurassic Labour" he claims. From his quiff, black strides, big glasses, tabs and pints Richard could be a throw back to his dad, or his uncle, or grandfather. Musicians all. The Hawley's are like an industrial version of griots, the dynastic musicians who trudge across the margins of the south Sahara. Richard's uncle, Frank White, "greater than Clapton" some have muttered, is still gigging his rocking blues, he is playing up the road at Trippets later this month and can still kick it.

Fagin's still retains just about every virtue of a classic boozer, nothing about it has been touched by a 'chain'- although ironically it is part of a pub chain - it is resolutely Barbara and Tom's place. A good life of Guinness and Abbeydale Moonshine, a room full of folk musicians singing round and an unchanging ambiance. The swooping painting of a Spitfire that Richard used on the inside cover of his last album 'Lady's Bridge' hangs from the wall. It even has a diminutive snug that Richard and I settle in.

Now it would be great to impart some significant insights from the tortured soul of a great artist, but really I guess we just got pissed and talked all sorts of nonsense. I rolled out of another, much later shutting, pub in the early morning and poured myself into a taxi. In between we had a go at trying to get to grips with the influence of the city on Richard and his music. I knew I should have kept taking notes after the third pint.

'Home' Chapter 11: November

There can be no doubt that Richard is a true son of the city, Sheffield Hallam University are going to make that civically plain later this month with an honorary degree. Born in the late 1960s on Scott Road, Pitsmoor with a progression through, Firshill Primary and Firth Park Schools Richard was raised to rock and roll. In his mid teens he toured in Europe during the school summer holidays in a family band. When he finally hit the mean streets of, well Hawley Street, he was already a boy with a reputation. "He just wanted to play with anybody, always coming down to your level rather than expecting you to go up to his" was how John Pedder, an early musical spar put it.

Treebound Story was his first band, I never saw them, heard they were pretty good mind. Yet it was the Long Pigs, who really launched Richard into a world where he could actually make a living out of being a musician - believe me a task much harder than the bright lights and fast living of rock and roll might suggest. The Long Pigs 'rawked', well that's what they probably said in America when they found themselves touring stadiums with U2. They were that close to the big time. They split after 2 albums under circumstances that still appear to rankle with Richard.

Not to worry there is always that other gigging Sheffield band, Pulp, to stand in the backline with. You see a lot of hotel rooms and very little of your family living like this. Finally Richard's dad and a few others suggested he might want to step out of the shadows and try getting his larynx around a few of his own tunes. The rest is history; 4 albums, one nominated for the Mercury Music Prize, sold out gigs where ever he goes, including The Royal Albert Hall and of course Sheffield City Hall. Now he was back in the studio, plotting yet another album with a Sheffield themed title, after 'Late Night Final '(the cry of the Sheffield Star sellers back in the day), 'Low Edges' (a

60s council estate on the southern edge of the city), the impossibly lush 'Coles Corner' and finally Lady's Bridge (the crossing from which the city grew). I suggested to Richard a few titles that I'd thought up with my eldest daughter- Salmon Pastures, Tongue Gutter, Nether Edge, Hawley Street, Frog Walk- Richard smiled wainly and moved on.

Richard also didn't think that Sheffield had any particular kind of sound. It has, in recent decades, been a music scene that had been characterised by "a succession of maverick individuals "rather than movements. However he did make a number of interesting observations;

> **"The estates of houses, all the same, street after street and the conformity of working class life created a desire amongst some to strive for something more individual, to be different."**

Richard went on to talk about the idea that it didn't really matter what type of music people produced, there was no definitive city sound, what mattered was that people were hungry, eager to play. "I just wanted to make records". That craft was important, being able to play. Ah craft, I was well short of that, when I looked at my notes through bleary eyes the next morning, I couldn't believe what gibberish I'd written - we'd chewed the cud for nearly four hours, I should have had a scoop, an insight, instead I had a hangover and a vague memory of a thoroughly entertaining evening.

We had talked about the changing city, the old rehearsal rooms in derelict factories, like Cabaret Voltaire's Western Works, an old industrial building, a spit from the Henderson's relish factory which has now disappeared under the University of Sheffield's continuing expansion. Richard waxed lyrical about 'Yellow Arch' studios which he used as his recording base. His record label had offered him anywhere in the world to record, but he preferred to commute across the city to an ex Victorian factory that a decade previous had been turned into the most basic of rehearsal and recording spaces. In its early days I once went to a party there, it was a bit of a dive. Today it was a serious space, a grown up recording studio, the base for a loose collective of musicians who had grown up together in Sheffield. Richard extolled "its sound", in his case a lush, symphonic, Johnny Cash meets Sun Records sort of thing. Romantic and melancholic. Andy Cook, who has nursed a dream in putting together Yellow Arch, is a rather accomplished drummer who has played just about everywhere with everyone.

Andy Cook's musical sidekick and collaborator is Colin Elliot who is also Richard Hawley's musical right hand man. Such is Sheffield. It is rather intimate and parochial, a place full of social inter-connections and wheels within wheels. Since the late 1970s a complex 'family tree' that would have challenged even the most assiduous of archivists like Peter Frame had evolved in the city. Who had played with whom? One of the reasons that this progression was so extensive was that it appeared that the Sheffield way was to spend years playing pubs to two men and a dog, rehearsing in unheated Victorian warehouses and producing a sizeable back catalogue of ideas before any sort of a sniff of commercial success came your way. How long had Pulp hung around The Limit Club before they became the hottest act in town - everybody's town - in 1995. In fact 22 years separate Pulp's first and last gigs, both in Rotherham. The Arctic Monkeys by comparison had virtually been rocketed towards global fame with a mere 28 months separating their first gig at The Grapes pub on Trippet Lane in 2003 and their first single - 'I Bet You Look Good on the Dance Floor'- making it to number one. Indecent haste by Sheffield standards.

What the Arctic Monkeys shared with so many other Sheffield musicians was the continuation of a tradition of 'social realism' in lyrics. Scattered with references to the city, its places and its people. Tales of taxis to High Green via Hillsborough, working girls on the street in Neepsend and estate culture where 'tracky bottoms stuck into socks' are matched with 'knackered Converse'. On Tony Christie's 'Made in Sheffield' a plaintive ballard entitled 'Paradise Square', the cobble-stoned Georgian square tucked behind the cathedral, evokes a more personal city. My favourite musical geographic reference in Sheffield is 'Jervis Lumb,' the stream that runs down through Norfolk Park, which Sheffield's wailing bluesman, Andy Weaver, turned into a character for one of his sharply observed tunes. Andy's only been gigging a couple of decades so he should expect to break it into the big time in oh about ten years hence.

A couple of days after meeting up with Richard Hawley I found myself in an even more unexpected liaison. Peter Stringfellow, whose London nightclub and high life antics are a staple of the 'Hello' celebrity culture, paid a brief and rare return to his home city to launch his co-authored book 'Pop Art of Sheffield: King Mojo and Beyond'. It was a Monday night in Trippets Wine Bar and I went out of fascination rather than pleasure. Much to my surprise I had a thoroughly entertaining evening.

What Peter was part of was a trimvirate, including Dave Manvell and Paul Norton, who had produced a 99 page book focused on the Pop Art of the Mojo Club and Sheffield in general.

Peter Stringfellow can rightly claim a major place in the historical development of musical Sheffield. He was the entrepreneur who grasped the swinging sixties and brought them to dowdy, workmanlike Sheffield. His club, King Mojo, which opened in 1964 at the Victorian double bayed detached house that was 555 Barnsley Road, became the first window on the world in Sheffield for the rapidly evolving 60s phenomenon the teenager.

Stringfellow had already made a splash in the city when he had put on an up and coming band called The Beatles at the Azena Ballroom on White Lane, Gleadless Top, on the 12th February 1963. The venue remains; today it is a Somerfield supermarket with Supertram whizzing by it. The Mojo was something else. It must have been the hottest ticket in town; a darkened, art strewn space where the energy of beer and speed could be worked off to the unfolding talents of the sixties. This was at heart a 'Northern Soul Club'. It was a forerunner of the legendary Wigan Casino, one of those places where a musical identity was formed, where culture, however unwittingly, was forged.

I still find it difficult to comprehend that on the 8th January 1967 King Mojo's played host to the Jimi Hendrix Experience. Peter recounted the story.

> **"Somebody had tipped off the police that this black guy from America was coming and he had got some drugs. At that time Sheffield didn't have a drug squad so they sent around the Fire Brigade. The Senior Fire Officer came into the dressing room where Jimi was staring wildly into a mirror and enquired 'now then, has tha' got any drugs'. Jimi denied it and as the Fire Officer left, wishing him a good evening, Hendrix lit up a massive spliff and said 'I'm ready for the stage' ".**

Peter went on reeling off anecdote after anecdote of a "gentle time" when the only drugs "where your mum's slimming pills" and "everything was not done for money but fun". At that point some wag in the audience shouted "can tha' have my money back then". He knew he was back on home turf.

I supped champagne - my how times move on - and loitered with one of the new wave of Sheffield club entrepreneurs, Ralph Razor, in the queue to get my copy of the book signed. Ralph had some particularly sharp white winkle pickers on and an in depth knowledge of Pete Stringfellow's contribution to Sheffield club culture. It felt like Ralph, in his late twenties, was picking up the cultural baton from his older be-tanned and be-jewelled mentor. I promised him I'd check out his club Razor Stiletto sometime. I was home by ten; it was a Monday night after all. Ralph went onto host a video DJ evening at the Forum. Youth, it's the time of your life, as Peter quite clearly remembered.

I was further reminded of the importance of art in the promotion of popular culture when I ended up researching the films of Eve Wood, the celluloid chronicler of the Sheffield Music scene. Eve's classic is called 'Made in Sheffield'- it's that same old theme again – and is about the 'birth of electronic pop' in the city. Its visual tag line is a guitar being flung from a walkway in Park Hill flats. This poster for this film is blue-tacked to the side of the filing cabinet that sits behind my left shoulder in my office at home. Eve is about to release a follow up entitled 'The Beat is the Law' that should see the light of day in 2009. In time these films will become hugely significant artefacts of social commentary. At present, to raise money for the development of the film, Eve is selling artwork from Martin Bedford, a gangling hippie who produced some fantastic iconic posters for gigs at The Leadmill, as well as once being landlord of my local pub,

The Broadfield. He was also involved in the agit-pop art collective 'The Loft'. Martin's posters are a direct connection to the world of The Leadmill.

For me The Leadmill is music in Sheffield, like many people of my late baby boomer generation I virtually lived there during the 1980s. From jazz on Sunday lunchtime to riotous nights of musical hedonism The Leadmill is the space in which so many of the most memorable music moments I've encountered were played out. The building had form, as the venue of the Esquire Club in the 1960s but it was in 1980 that it was launched with the support of the city council as an arts venue. By the end of the decade it was acknowledged by 'The New Musical Express' as the best music venue in the country.

Before the area was gentrified the Leadmill stood across the road from the central bus garage, the vents of which, on a cold evening, blew voluminous clouds of steam into the street, creating an atmosphere of expectation for the queuing punters forcing their way towards the old wrought iron football turnstiles that led into the building. Tour buses were parked up outside and touts loitered at the end of the street. It was an exciting space. Virtually the whole musical diaspora of the last three decades have at one time or another graced the compact stage and the slum like changing rooms housed in the cellar. Nothing could be further away from the glamour of popular culture. I once stood on the stairs leading down to the cellar discussing giving up smoking with Joe Strummer. What I didn't realise was that this was the penultimate gig for Joe, a colossus of British music - one of his first gigs was also in Sheffield at Snig Hill's Black Swan, aka The Mucky Duck - the Boardwalk today. Within a month he was dead of a massive heart attack and I still hadn't, unlike Joe, given up smoking.

For local bands a headline gig at the Leadmill is a rite of passage on the rocky road to success. It goes something like this; stumbling over melodies at the school disco (re: Def Leppard at Westfield Comprehensive in 1978), a support slot at The Grapes, top of the bill at the Boardwalk, then the Leadmill and finally an evening laying the ghosts of Barry Noble's Top Rank in the company of two thousand clutched plastic pints of Carling in the Academy. From then on it's a life of stadiums, merchandise and artistic doom. I've only been once to the Sheffield Arena to see a gig and that was Neil Kinnock's ill-starred 1992 performance, 'alrighhht'. I have no intention of sitting down in my tour t shirt with my popcorn to see rock and roll, soul, funk or anything that essentially is built to make you move.

I know that The Leadmill has been the starting point of a myriad of relationships and marriages. Everybody has their iconic moments in time, sweat dripping off the roof in a fuggy micro-climate of exertion. Massive Attack, Norman Cook, Hugh Masakela, Courtney Pine, Lee Scratch Perry, Tackhead, L.T.J. Bukem, Julian Cope and Nusrat Fatah Ali Khan are particular favourites of mine; seared into my memory. It remains my favourite place to see a band especially after my first visit, a few weeks back, to Plug, the functional upstart to the Leadmill, to check out Sheffield's partly adopted son the reggaefied hip hop rapper Roots Manuva. There are no ghosts in the rafters of Plug. Clean lines and an efficient bar does not a rock and roll venue make. I want scuzz. I want a sound system that can level small buildings - well probably not these days. I like a bit of history.

Actually some of my most memorable musical moments have been in the anodyne environs of The University of Sheffield's Octagon Hall, which has functionality stamped all over it. Yet with two thousand people in and bass bins that can rearrange your internal organs whilst making, literally, the hairs on your body stand on end, the Octagon can produce magic and ringing in the ears.

Having a young family I had for a number of years pretty much given up going out to gigs. I had dipped my toe in at the start of the year by catching up with the Human League at the Academy. Apart from their seminal remix album 'Love and Dancing' I had never quite got the point of their electro pop. When I arrived in Sheffield in 1982, 'Dare', their 'triple platinum album' - how many sales is that, lots - was but a year after release. Their synth driven melodies were becoming synonymous with Sheffield. Personally it passed me by but it made me feel that I was living in a place where things were happening, culture was being created. My home town, Leighton Buzzard, Bedfordshire, could boast only the Barron Knights and Kajagoogoo as musical heritage. It was a little sad to reflect that in 2008 The Human League were basically a covers band of themselves. The packed house loved it, nostalgia sells. Such evenings will keep them in sequins for a while longer, although I think it is only fair to say that the stand-out track on Tony Christie's 'Made In Sheffield' album is a cover of the Human League track 'Louise'.

Regardless of the fact that it was fast approaching one of my busiest times at work, and when I mean busy I mean stupid amounts of work, 55 hours a week just to make sure I didn't drop too many of the multitude of balls that I was throwing into the air, I attempted to 'live it large' in the last week of November by catching up on music Sheffield.

The plan was the opening of Pete McKee's latest exhibition at the Bowery Bar just off Devonshire Green, on Monday night, Jarvis Cocker on Tuesday night, Nick Cave and The Bad Seeds on Thursday and the S.A.D.A.C.C.A. centre for an old school reggae evening on the Friday. Saturday night Ovaltine and a Vicks vapour rub. If you've got the energy, cash and inclination the city is a great playground of the senses.

I started badly blowing out Pete McKee in order to spend an evening marking student coursework. His latest show is entitled 22 Views of Sheffield and it is as an affectionate portrayal of Sheffield life as you are likely to see. It is a mish-mash of dog racing, the hole in the road fish tank, 'Praise or Grumble' on the radio, kids in the Peace Gardens and the queue at the Leadmill, a Sheffield I've lived. As much as I'd like to splash £2000 on his latest works, and really I would, he is the real deal, Patrick Heron meets Andy Capp, Pete's prices are now a bit out of my financial league. I think it'll have to be a print. His genre, a cartoon-esque depiction of Sheffield life was beginning to usurp the work of Joe Scarborough as Sheffield's favourite artist. Joe specialised in distorted Sheffield cityscapes and like Pete he had a special focus on the people of the city. I doubt whether either artist would translate much outside of the confines of the city. It was hard to see London fashionista's with Pete's 'Upstairs at the Hallamshire' hanging next to their Rothko prints. It really is a Sheffield thing, maybe Jarvis will take one back to Paris.

Tuesday I approached with more resolve, Rolling home from work I checked out the Academy for Jarvis Cocker tickets fully expecting it to be sold out. No about 50 tickets would be returned; I booked my place without having to resort to a pleading phone call to Simon Stafford, Jarvis's virtuoso keyboard player, ex Long Pig and Joe Strummer sidekick and distant mate from way back when.

Jarvis had promised a gig, a lecture, a disco. He was never one to tread water. Regardless of his 'turncoat' ways Jarvis Cocker has defined Sheffield in popular culture more globally than any musician, perhaps ever. His scurrilous words of wisdom are pinned to the walls of Sheffield alongside a Poet Laureate. He has literally made his mark. He lives in Paris now. I suspect that he will keep coming back, the city is in his DNA, he can never really leave unlike his namesake Joe Cocker holed up in his isolated American ranch.

Jarvis made his name chronicling the working class culture of Sheffield, he is sharp, quick witted, a sociologist of his roots. Apparently he is a reserved, self effacing sort of guy, I've no idea, apart from seeing him in Pulp a few times in their developing career, once sitting at a table next to him in the Forum, and a brush past him at a Garden Street rave at the height of his global fame in 1995 I've never met him. His music however defines him. I had high expectations.

Damn right he played no Pulp numbers. He strode onto the stage looking like a 1970s Geography teacher, beard included and proceeded to illustrate the ideas for his songs with slide projections he controlled with a remote zapper. A 1960s artist's render of the yet to be built 'Top Rank' – in which the gig was proceeding -, the now defunct children's slide in Endcliffe Park and Supertram. The band wrestled their way through some potential new classics, Caucasian Blues, Big Stuff and Girls Like It Too. Throwing shapes and leaping around like a man possessed Jarvis made me feel decrepit, being as we are the same age - I'd have required paramedic assistance if I had performed a couple of numbers at this pace. The audience response was a little muted - I suspect many yearned for the old hits as provided by The Human League earlier in the year. On the way back from the bar I bumped into a musically mesmerised Richard Hawley, I stumbled some sort of greeting, he called me love. I didn't stay for the disco, as Jarvis said from the stage, "It was midweek and we'd got things to do".

Next up Nick Cave and The Bad Seeds. Thursday, back at the Academy. Nick Cave has nothing at all to do with Sheffield other than being here. It cost an eye watering £32.50. When a wag hollered out to the Caveman "What do you think of Sheffield?" He replied "Very nice, I think I might buy a holiday home here". With a door take in the region of £65,000, he could easily afford to. If he did I wondered if he would take his kids in search of Jarvis's mythical park slide, now replaced by a shiny new playground in Endcliffe Park. On reflection I actually think Jarvis was referring to the slide at Forge Dam playground which the last time my children fell off the climbing frame there it was still up and sliding.

To be fair £32.50 may be steep but it sold out in a couple of days and touts were asking much more outside. Hardly surprising, The Bad Seeds are one of the most bewitching of bands and Nick Cave a performer of such intensity that it is hard to take your eyes off him. The audience was predominantly over 30 and white, 100% white. Richard Hawley loitered in the same spot as Tuesday, I trust he'd gone home in between.

Friday was always going to be a struggle; it had been beyond a decade since I'd gone out more than twice in the week. If you were made of sterner stuff and had deeper pockets than me you could relentlessly fill your nights with an unending menu of cultural tittle-tattle. I threw in the towel.

That Friday I had planned to hook up with friends and head on down to the S.A.D.A.C.C.A. centre on The Wicker. This place, the cultural hub of Sheffield's small Afro-Caribbean diaspora - long standing but no more than 1.5% of the population - is host to all sorts of events but I've only ever been to the last Friday in the month reggae revival night, and then only a couple of times over the years. What I'd forgotten and what my spar, Donald, reminded me of as we discussed it over the phone on Thursday evening was this wasn't the sort of thing that got going until midnight. He was knackered after a long week haranguing students and I wasn't keen enough to budge him. It was as Donald described it "a proper Caribbean night out, a big night out". We bailed out, these things you have to be right up for, no half measures.

The reason I had wanted to go down to the S.A.D.A.C.C.A. was to get a handle on the fact that the sound of Sheffield wasn't simply a bunch of white working class youth, this was a multi-cultural, multi-faceted city. There were a multitude of musical beats to follow. I wondered why the city had never unearthed a great black musician? I wanted to remind myself that bubbling under the glossy hype of popular culture all sorts of realities could be found in the byways and bars of the city. Even the churches twinkled to string quartets and gay choirs sung carols in the Winter Gardens. Sound was all around. Trouble was I was knackered and I needed to write some student references or somebody's hopes and dreams of university might be stalled. Another night, another tune.

The last weekend of the month a fog settled over the city and my brain. A month of trying to get a grip of a musical city. The reality was this was a mammoth task, a full time job, and I had one of those already. However a few ideas had coalesced in my mind.

I'll stick my neck out here but if music is your thing, really any kind of music - actually probably not country and western or opera - then Sheffield could "fill up your senses" unlike few provincial cities in the world. Sure London, New York, Paris and Berlin are in a different league. They have no 'sound' either but a cacophony of diversity and development beyond compare. But the few musicians and bands from Sheffield that have stuck their heads above the parochial parapet of the city and gone global have created a discernable musical identity. A distinct accent, a love of the off-beat, an ability to innovate and surprise. Sheffield is the sort of place that creates culture not simply consumes it; music is but one facet of that. If this culture has a theme it is more likely to be one of the intellectual working class crossed with a desire to break away from conformity, oh and add a dash of hedonism. What does that sound like? Nothing in particular but an attuned ear would be able to sense its roots. An attuned eye, that of Pete McKee, sees it all clearly; there they are, sitting around the glass crammed single table of Fagin's snug, from left to right, Alex Turner, Jarvis Cocker, Tony Christie, Phil Oakey and Richard Hawley, 'Legends in Their Lunchtime'. A mythical musical moment in time.

December

December can be an exhausting month. I have more work than I know what to do with and a flurry of places to be, things to do, people to see. You set off for work in the cold dark before dawn, spend all day under fluorescent strip lights and then leave way past dusk. The windows of the bus are obscured by dirt as sodium blurs the hunched journey home. And then there is Christmas and all of a sudden you're meant to be having a great time. The kids are fast approaching hyper-ventilating meltdown. I'm sure there is stuff to do, like cards to Australia and panto tickets to buy, that if I don't pull my finger out will not get done.

If life sometimes appeared to me as if it was lurching uncontrollably from one tricky deadline to another it was a complete breeze compared to the life of Alistair Darling, The Chancellor of the Exchequer. He'd have gone grey if he wasn't already as white as a ghost, around his neck the albatross called the British economy and the hopes and concerns of 62 million people. I guess he'll try to 'get away from it all' this Christmas, Tierra del Fuego, Easter Island, maybe Mars might be far enough.

Gordon Brown's longest period of sustained economic growth for the British economy was now a distant memory. The country was already in recession, house prices continued to tumble, repossessions were soaring, the pound plummeting towards parity with the Vietnamese Dong and bankruptcy spreading virulently through over-leveraged business like an economic plague. The spectre of mass unemployment hung over the forthcoming year. Still not to worry Gordon could not only save the banks but by sacrificing 'prudence' at the altar of Keynesian profligacy he might even save the economy. The solution? We were going to spend our way to economic recovery. A national sport was about to become your patriotic duty. Shopping.

Shopping was not my area of expertise. That is unless it involved wine, records or second-hand books. However with a 2.5% reduction in V.A.T. and with, on the 4th of the month, the Bank of England base rate falling to 2%, the lowest it had been since 1951, a time when the government was still trying to kick start the economy out of the post-war doldrums, it seemed almost churlish not to shop. Of course the paradox was that after the years of Brownite Scottish financial reticence it was now the done thing to get into debt. Bizarrely I had a couple of debt counselling agencies ring me up unsolicited in the first week of the month. Maybe they were being prescient.

Shopping wasn't really Sheffield's area of expertise either. The city centre of Sheffield trailed in 33rd in the 2007 Experian British retail league table with an estimated spend that year of about £703 million. Meadowhall Shopping centre came in 27th with its 2007 spend estimated at £839 million. Combined it was a different story, and then the city came in 3rd nationally with only Glasgow Central (£1.87 billion) and London's West End (£4.86 billion) above it. To be fair if you add Manchester Central to the Trafford Centre then Sheffield is left trailing in its wake by nearly £700million. However, unlike Manchester, the dual locality of shopping in Sheffield had dissipated its retail cache. There is no Harvey Nichols's, that barometer store of affluent consumption, as Leeds and Manchester were apt to point out. The reputation of Nottingham, with its twin city centre indoor shopping malls, imposing central square and Lace Market; Manchester with everything from Affleck's Palace to the revamped post IRA Arundel Centre and Leeds with its Victorian covered arcades and high rise swagger all surpassed that which could be offered by their dowdy northern neighbour. If I was honest I'd say all three had better, more impressive, more retail friendly city centres than Sheffield. Not that I was particularly bothered by this personally, I wasn't a committed shopper. I had my well worn path of favourites which I was periodically drawn towards as needs must. My favourite area to idly window-shop wasn't even in the city centre but the cluster of small shops in Sharrowvale Road and Ecclesall Road. Chesterfield market on a Thursday wasn't bad either, always quirkily interesting.

Through the 1980s and early 1990s retailing declined in Sheffield city centre at a dramatic rate. It slipped 20 places in the national league table of retailing. Meadowhall's arrival in the city in 1990 heralded not only the transition of the Lower Don Valley but led to the city-centre plummeting towards rock bottom. In 1993-94, the halcyon years of John Major's Conservative government, Sheffield city-centre became a decaying mix of stalwart national retailers like John Lewis, Top Shop and Marks and Spencer, everything a pound shops, charity shops and boarded up units. From the increasingly grey markets, up the High Street, along Fargate, past the drinkers in the old Peace Gardens, down the Moor, the city's linear shopping experience became increasingly denuded. Something had to be done. A heart had to be put back into the city. That was the plan.

I've been trying to recall exactly when it was that a full meeting of Sheffield District Labour Party was held in grand chambers within the Town Hall with a single item on the agenda – Sheffield: The Heart of the City Project. 1994-95? Paul Bloomfield would know, he chaired the meeting. I had an onerous task that evening. It was in the summer. I recollect the light pouring in the mullioned windows. As the District Labour Party representative of Heeley Ward Labour Party it fell to me to reflect my mandate's wishes and argue against the Heart of the City project. I had my reservations. The Ward had felt the deal was over advantageous to developers and that Sheffield City Council should hold control over this extremely valuable city centre site, at that time dominated by the 'eggbox', the 'new' council offices. Caution was the new watch word after the financial liabilities incurred by the council in the hosting of the 1991 World Student Games - an occasion when Sheffield astronaut Helen Sharman metaphorically re-enacted the financial fallout of the event by tripping over the red carpet on her way to light the flame. I did something that I didn't think I'd do and spoke against the revamping of Sheffield City Centre and then voted in favour of it. It took some explaining at the next ward meeting but basically our arguments were a bit crap all things considered. It was not like we were offering up some alternative plan.

The financial figure being touted at that time basically boiled down to about £120 million of investment, mainly private sector capital with central and European government regeneration funds (about £41 million of the total). The council's contribution was the land.

We got the Peace Gardens first, with its revitalised memorial to Sheffield radical, Samuel Holberry, squirty fountains, artisanal sculptural walls and planting with pizzazz. A hit. Next up knock down the 'eggbox' after decanting most of the council's staff into the newly finished Howden House down the road. Following on after the bulldozers had levelled the 'eggbox' was the construction of the Winter Gardens and Millennium Galleries. A soaring piece of architecture which would not look out of place in any global city. Iconic and an even bigger hit. Then the 4 star hotel and the DLA Piper Office Block; emphatically not a hint. For months, it seemed like years, the letters page of The Star and The Telegraph raged at the rank functionalism of the DLA Piper offices and the hiding away of the Winter Garden's curves. This was the pay off, you don't get something for nothing, and a squat modern office block and a hotel was an object lesson in the observation that normally buildings and spaces in the public realm are better designed and often more carefully constructed than most things the private sector offers up. At least it appears that way in Sheffield. If only they had built the hotel before the Winter Gardens we could have been spared acres of invective in newsprint.

Then a hiatus of a few years when - with the removal of the 'Wedding Cake', the old registry of hatches, matches and dispatches - came the final chapter of the Heart of the City project. The 'cheese grater' car park and the on, off and on again 32 storey St Paul's Apartments, (although I prefer the moniker 'Hesketh Tower' in honour of Liberal Democrat chair of planning Cllr John Hesketh whose 'expert' opinions on planning and design are now helping to reshape the city).

What relevance has this to shopping? Well it is a combination of this 'flagship' project, further spin-off projects like the revamping of Fargate, an overall upturn in economic fortunes of the city and a refocusing on the overall city centre environment that has hauled Sheffield out of the retail abyss. True Norwich, Croydon, Aberdeen, Bromley and Milton Keynes all still have bigger shopping centres - that is more retail floor space and a higher turnover - than Sheffield. But then none of them has got Meadowhall parked 3 miles north-east of them. Understanding Meadowhall is the key to understanding the changing face of shopping in Sheffield and what the city centre has become and what potentially it may become.

The seeds of Meadowhall were sown way back in 1986 when two

Yorkshire entrepreneurs, Eddie Healey and Paul Sykes teamed up to transform the derelict site of the demolished Hadfields steelworks abutting the M1 flyover. At the time the sites crushed rubble dereliction made it the perfect backdrop for the Sheffield shot post-nuclear holocaust film 'Threads' shown on BBC TV in 1984. But Healey (son of a DIY shop owner from Hull) and Sykes (who made his first fortune selling second hand bus parts to the Far East from Barnsley – junk for junks) had a vision. They were the poster boys of Margaret Thatcher's entrepreneurial revolution. After spending £400 million of mainly borrowed money and 4 years developing it they opened Meadowhall to the unsuspecting public in September 1990. It was a new age, the assertive statement of the rise of consumer capitalism. It blew Sheffield away, both in terms of Meadowhall being an immediate hit and it blew away the city centre. In its wake followed the ascendancy of the suburbanised car city of Sheffield, with fringe shopping, working and living, a deregulated public transport system and new connecting roads by the mile. Within two years of Meadowhall opening city centre trade had fallen by a fifth. By 1994 nearly ½ million people a week were visiting Meadowhall. To some degree everything that has happened since 1990 in the city centre is a response to Meadowhall.

In 1999 Eddie and Paul cashed in their chips when British Land, Britain's second largest real estate investor, bought it in a deal where they took on the companies leverage, sorry we should call it debt as they did back then, some £470millon, and sold the rest on for a cool £700 million give or take the odd bit of small change. Nice work boys, they remain a couple of the richest people in Yorkshire. Recently Eddie Healey celebrated his 70th birthday at The Dorchester Hotel, London, with 300 guests and a one hour performance by 'Girls Aloud', an estimated £400,000 was blown on it all. Has there ever been a better realisation of that old Yorkshire exhortation "Where tha's muck tha's brass"?

British Land, however, has fallen upon less auspicious times. Their share price has fallen from 1714p in December 2006 to 534p at present (17/12/08) and cash is required to pay off their bankers. In the second week of the month the 'Financial Times' reported that the company were touting around for a buyer for half of Meadowhall. Some £700 million and falling at present - 50% was worth about £850millon this time last year. An unnamed Abu Dhabi sovereign wealth fund was said to be interested through a London based 'opportunity fund'. According to that font of all knowledge, dodgy and otherwise, Wikipedia - it's OK I checked out their source, Morgan Stanley, and they are never known to be wrong are they? - The sovereign wealth fund of Abu Dhabi - a state owned investment fund - is worth around $875 billion. Meadowhall would be a medium sized investment for them and a great piece of horizontal integration; with every litre of petrol used to take the good consumers of Sheffield to Meadowhall the more able Abu Dhabi investors would be better able to buy up the other half of the shopping centre.

I must confess that I probably only go to Meadowhall a couple of times a year at most, its cinema tends not to show sub titled French intellectual soft-core porn, its restaurants are resoundingly chains - a few decent ones mind - its shops so multitudinous and stuffed full of abundance it is dizzying. I've really no call to go and its 6 miles away, and I've got to drive. Really it is not my thing. It's the sort of place that people who think Singapore is a good holiday destination like to go to.

However for the purposes of research I decided to go to Meadowhall on the penultimate Saturday before Christmas; at lunch time, whilst it was teeming down with rain. If it wasn't going to be heaving then, well, Alistair Darling would really have a challenge on his hands.

The car-park was just at that teetering point where a reasonably short trawl of the unending lanes eventually revealed a space. A few less goings and a few more comings would have pushed it closer to grid lock. The overspill car parks were not yet opened. A hundred metres across the wet and windy tarmac and the cloying warmth of 'Next' enveloped me. Now Meadowhall is easy, it's just like the City Centre, linear. You start at one end on the ground floor and come back on the upper floor, squares, domes, bronze steelworkers and cookie stalls litter your route. And beige, I'd forgotten how much beige and marble, shiny clean, litter free marble. It was warm, it was dry, and it was anywhere.

It was also packed, although not heaving packed it was packed enough to rattle through a stream of apologies as I bumped into people, trod on toes and collided with bags full of stuff. People were unfailingly polite, nobody tried to get me to sign a lifetime direct debit to support Oxfam, get me to sign a petition, answer a questionnaire or persuade me to repent my sins. It was multi-cultural and it was predominantly a female space. I calculated approximately 3:1 women to men during an unscientific ten minute pedestrian survey I took whilst eating an M &S sandwich outside HMV - a potentially more male part of Meadowhall you might have thought. Groups of teenagers gawped their way down the aisles of their aspirations, one group was obviously on a birthday trip decked out in sashes and more make-up than you would have thought humanly possible. I didn't really know what to do. I guess a bit of Christmas shopping then, so..... Waterstones.

I'm not entirely surprised that Waterstones, Britain's hegemonic 'high street' bookseller, is, in the city centre of Sheffield, more commodious, better stocked and more knowledgably staffed. It is one of the few 'high street' businesses that probably still do more business on the 'high street'. Its Meadowhall neighbour, M & S, is of extensive proportions stocked with more socks than you can shake a foot at and a food store you fairly have to beat your way down the aisles to reach your free-range egg and cress sandwich. I felt safe in Waterstones.

Everywhere there are 'sales', even closing down 'everything must go sales.' Stuff seems cheap, but what would I know, I don't buy a lot of stuff. Certainly a couple days after this visit the Sheffield Star reported a 4% increase in visitors to Meadowhall over the year. And it was far, far busier than Sheffield city centre that day. Even though a continental market, a big wheel, fairground rides, carols and lights were on offer in the city centre as well as shopping. It was teeming down with rain, need I say more. No competition I guess.

I'm always a little amused that the centre-piece of Meadowhall, The Oasis - the food, cinema and cute little specialist shop area of the centre - is partially modelled on a Mediterranean town centre, some have suggested Marbella in Spain. That is an outdoor, warm, sun dappled Mediterranean town square with the tables all set out around - in Meadowhall's case a big screen - in the case of Marbella a somnolent moon, or blazing sun hanging in the sky. It is curious how we are drawn to the vibrant chaos of towns like Sienna, St Tropez, Barcelona, Palma and Venice with their narrow lanes, animated street life and well worn urbanism when we are in the sun but in the rain nothing beats a good air conditioning system and a beige roof.

Later in the week a thread set off in the Sheffield Forum website which started with the assertion 'Meadowhall much better than

Town Centre'. Blogger 'Lestat' backed up her confident opinion with a host of reasons;

> **"Free parking,**
> **No beggars and litter,**
> **Not so many studentified students and illegal immigrants,**
> **More quality shops,**
> **Easier access to and from the complex,**
> **Not half as many chavs (in the town centre - this also applies to United fans),**
> **All in all a better shopping experience."**

We were edging towards a similar territory to the anti-Britain rants on the BBC website that had initially prompted this book – such is the bullish certainties engendered by Internet anonymity. Free parking was a clear plus - although there have been sustainable mutterings that the government might consider taxing parking at out of town shopping centres, that's an idea that has probably been quietly shelved in recent months. Three reasons however refer to her fellow shoppers, what they shouldn't be. Students, illegal immigrants and chavs. One can't help wondering how 'Lestat' identifies illegal immigrants in the city centre, it is not as if they have a yellow star sewn onto their clothes. Maybe she wishes they did. However indirectly, 'Lestat's' arguments do come to the heart of the key difference between Meadowhall and the city centre. The former is private space, where the visitor has to conform to a set of external rules. You are granted permission to be on these 'streets' and this can easily be taken away from you. The latter is public space, your space. Sure there are rules. City centre ambassadors patrol to smooth the multitude of social interactions that arrive every day. The police are present. C.C.T.V. cameras monitor. Yet nobody can ban you without bloody good reason and a court order with teeth. Huge, surging demonstrations can throng the streets, beggars, buskers, chuggers, market researchers, inquisitive students doing GCSE studies, religious fundamentalists, religious non-fundamentalists, gangs of teenagers, gaggles of foreign language students, all of them can ask, question and generally bother you. Great. That's life! 'Lestat' prefers a consumer bubble.

The city centre isn't simply about shopping; it has a far greater sense of purpose. It is the city of Sheffield in a way Meadowhall will never be. One day Meadowhall will be pulled down, three, four decades into the future and in its place, a reedbed sewage farm and vineyards will rise. Of course not you say, just like they would have said if I had suggested in 1960 that on the site of the Hadfields East Hecla steelworks one of Britain's largest shopping centres would be built. “Don't be daft soft lad.”

On the drive home from Meadowhall I called in at Patrick Joaun's Brightside Lane wine store The Bon Vin. I don't go often but the incorrigibly French Patrick always has an avuncular welcome. He offers me a sherry, cognac, red, white, mince pies and 600 wines to choose from. We get chatting about last year when the River Don rose up and his warehouse was flooded. Thousands of bottles were lost, dumped at a big warehouse somewhere over Rotherham way. It was where businesses took their out of date, contaminated, unsaleable stock. Palates of every imaginable goody. A Meadowhall of trash. I think of those perfectly serviceable bottles of Burgundy protected by their cork that ended up being poured down the metaphorical sink. I buy a bottle of the red stuff for Christmas Day. It was still raining as I cruised through a sparsely populated city centre. Perhaps everybody is sheltering in Woolworths.

Woolworths was the first purpose built store to be constructed on the bombed out Moor some eight years after the end of the war in 1953. The company's current imminent demise was a result of Woolworths's bankers refusing to lend it any more money to buy stock, the problem being its suppliers all of a sudden wanted to be paid in cash, on the button. 30,000 staff and 800 shops in UK were about to go. A buyer couldn't be found, even for just a £1. The demise of this store, a staple on every high street, an integral part of my growing up, was a profound shock to the nation. Between the ages of 5 and 14 it was just about my favourite shop, selling everything I needed, pick and mix, Airfix kits, cheap footballs and colouring felts. I even bought my first single there, 'Rubber Bullets' by 10CC, in May 1973.

The following, and the last Saturday, before Christmas I went into the city centre, an early nine o'clock start. Our first port of call was Woolworths. The shelves were emptying fast; in fact the shelves were for sale. I commiserated with a member of staff, he was nonplussed, he'd got another job and anyway the pay was crap, Tesco's paid better. My daughters availed themselves of the pick and mix and I bought a couple of world map posters for work, down from £3.99 to 20p. It was a sad, dishevelled store and it sat in a dishevelled part of town, The Moor. Demolition of part of the Moor and a couple more 'everything must go' closing down sales gave the drizzle drenched pedestrian street an air of the 80s recession. As we scurried up the hill we passed the empty shop unit that contained within its window the artist's impressions of the shiny new retail quarter, 'Sevenstone', that has been proposed, granted planning permission and whose imminent development has blighted a whole section of the city centre as businesses relocate before the arrival of the bulldozers for the rescheduled start of construction at the end of 2009. Sevenstone will be transformative; a visit to Liverpool to see their similar redevelopment 'One' makes that plain. Yet it is worth considering how the city centre has arrived at the cusp of this proposed makeover.

It wasn't until the mid 19th century that Sheffield city centre started to take on the form that it does today. The medieval streets were far from grand and a programme of road widening was required. This was centred on the High Street, connecting the markets in the old castle area to the grand edifices of power up the hill, the parish church and Cutlers Hall. The greatest changes, some of which remain with us today, came in the 1890s when the local born Flockton and Hadfield architectural clans set in stone their Tudor Gothic visions of late Victoriana. By this time shopping had already taken on clear class divisions in the city. The markets were one area of town. These included Norfolk Market on Haymarket, built in 1851 in a 'Tuscan' style with central marble fountains and tragically demolished in 1959 to make way for a slice of municipal modernism the, and soon to be replaced again, current markets. There was also the open air Sheaf Market known as Rag n' Tag. These were the haunts of Sheffield's stoical industrial working class; the markets and the end of terrace general corner shop, not open all hours.

The growing middle class had Coles and Walsh's department stores up the hill and other more refined establishments like the first ever Thorntons chocolate shop (1911) clustered around Fargate and the High Street. Already shopping polarised the town. Refinement spread uphill along Division Street towards Broomhall and an alternative working class area snaked downhill from Pinstone Street along The Moor. Often the same shops had branches on The Moor and in the Market Area; people didn't actively choose to walk from one end to the other and back, 3km of linear shopping streets, 6km in total. Remember until the 1980s hardly anybody drove into the city centre.

That this pattern carried on for many years is clear. In 1996, a group of Sociologists led by Professor Ian Taylor of Salford University set out to compare Manchester and Sheffield in their study of 'the emergence of the post-modern metropole' entitled 'A Tale of Two Cities'. Chapter 5 is entitled "Shop 'til you drop' - The 'Nice Shops' and the Markets in Manchester and Sheffield". Their qualitative inter-actionist approach to research means the book is full of talk about the difference between the markets and department stores, with class being the defining perspective. "Across the road from Rackham's (now T J Hughes) and down, it really is appalling. That part of town is finished completely" suggests one middle class lady. A local policeman emphasises the point by stating;

> **"They travel into town by bus. Rough, working class, honest upstanding people who use the markets. It's the poorer people who use the markets...you get pushed and shoved about a bit at the market, they don't say please and thank you."**

They might have to travel a bit further in the future as one of the gaping holes created on The Moor this year are being set aside for the development of a new 57,000 sq feet indoor market hall, to be completed during 2009. This will be a significant geographical rebalancing of retailing within the city centre, something attempted by Earl Fitzwilliam way back in the 1850s when he launched a short-lived penny market on the site of the old Ecclesall Market on what is now The Moor. It is with some confidence that I do not expect to see the Meadowhall blogger 'Lestat' crossing the threshold of the new markets unless her store cards have had their credit crunched.

'Home' Chapter 12: December

The evolving pattern of retailing in Sheffield owes part of its history to Hitler. The city centre took a hammering in the Second World War, The Moor was pretty much levelled and The High Street and Markets were battered about. Very little money existed to redevelop the city centre until the 1960s when a rhapsody in concrete smothered Sheffield in a utilitarian modernism. Castle Market (1960), Atkinsons on The Moor (1963) Coles moving to Barkers Pool (1963) and Debenhams (1967). Middle or working class it didn't matter both got some shocking 60s architecture. However this was a bit of a golden age for shopping. The 'white heat of technology' unleashed not only deeper pockets for most but an array of new consumables to peruse.

I'm always struck that so many reminisce about how they could leave their houses unlocked in the 'good old days' of slum terraces without fear of crime. Frankly they had nothing worth nicking unless a mangle could fetch a good price down the boozer. Now we had 'stuff', consumer durables. Acquisitive crime grew steadily from this point. We were moving into a society where we were increasingly defined by what we bought and from where. Shopping had become a leisure activity for not just the upper classes but for all classes. Even the poor could join in because relatively speaking they were nowhere near as poor as they used to be and 'stuff' got progressively cheaper and cheaper. Remember when most people used to rent their TV or the price of the first mobile phone you saw. The steady decline of the proportion of household income spent on food since the 1950s is clear evidence of this trend.

On my first visit to Sheffield on July 12th 1969 my father caught this moment, the white heat of new shopping, with his Super 8 camera. What did he film? The fish tank in the 'Hole in the Road', no really. The new Roxy nightclub, Park Hill flats and the family loitering outside the shops in Fargate. We were camping in Oakes Park; it was just about the furthest we'd ever travelled in our Morris Traveller up to then. In a couple of years he drove it all the way to Yugoslavia, so he'd obviously got a taste for utilitarianism, mind you he was an atheist Marxist engineer so it was only to be expected. For him Sheffield probably suggested the beginning of some sort of socialist utopia he could only dream about in Luton.

By the time I properly arrived in Sheffield in 1982 the shopping patterns of the sixties had been consolidated. Fargate was the centre of things; the markets provided me with cheap food and the department stores a glimpse of the middle class ease that was beyond my grant but was my aspiration. My favourite shops were 'Bring it all Back Home' a rambling museum of exotic travel that sprawled over many floors at the Sheffield University end of West Street, a sort of hippie department store. Then there was 'Rare and Racy' on Devonshire Green, whose knowledge, contained within its unchanging ordered chaos, educated me as much as the Polytechnic library.

I called in 'Rare and Racy' - “We sell previously enjoyed artefacts that will delight your eyes and ears” - after finishing shopping with the kids for their mum's Christmas present. On the stereo as I walked in was a pre-release copy of a new Cabaret Voltaire remix album. In Sheffield I'd say that was cool. I wasn't cool enough to recognise it I had to ask. Joe Mhlongo and Alan Capes, who had grown up with the shop from its inception in 1969, were busying themselves with sifting, sorting and cataloguing a bewildering array of stock. Where do you begin? After much idle gawping I bought a 1926 copy of Edward Carpenter's 'Towards Democracy' and a 1967 signed copy of H Keeble Hawson's, 'Sheffield the Growth of a City 1893-1926'. It was a pleasure to hand over the money. I toyed with the idea of buying a 1940 photograph of a bomb disposal team trying to clear Devonshire

Street. The gutted bomb damaged buildings on the south side of the street are testament to why it is now a faintly Gaudiesque open space, Devonshire Green.

I knew that Rare and Racy struggled, a couple of years ago 30 local bands contributed to a couple of benefit gigs to see them through a particularly sticky patch. This is the measure of the place, a true Sheffield institution. Would anybody do that for Woolworths?

I'd never really sat down and chatted to Joe and Alan before, just small talk, I wasn't really sure what to ask them, what's your favourite book? I wandered why they did it; next year was their 40th anniversary? Alan succinctly put it.

> **"We take about £200 a week each from the business, we are not in this for the money. Basically it is to keep out of the mainstream lifestyle. I'm not interested in the straight world."**

You couldn't fault their integrity, they had played a long game, through thick and thin. I was thrilled that they could still amaze after all these years, Alan went on; "A student came in the other day and he said I've walked past this shop a load of times and I've finally come in and it's the best shop I've ever been in."

I was fascinated who had been through their doors after all these years, well all the usuals, that is probably every vaguely creative person in the city over the last 4 decades who had the wit to read the odd book. Why Richard Hawley was in only the other day. They had particularly fond recollections of the 'Carry On' film actor Bernard Breslaw and apparently Jools Holland was notably enthusiastic. Actually I got the impression they thought it was a pretty dumb question, they really didn't give a shit who came through the door as long as people came through the door.

What of the future? They were no whippersnappers and this was a labour of love. “One day at a time” said Joe, “What else would I do”. We discussed whether Sun Ra played Oldham Arts Centre or Wigan back in the late 80s and talked about old 78 jazz records - a stack of which I inherited from my dad. I mentioned 'Bringing it all Back Home' as being one of my other favourite shops and Joe said Peter Benyon, who owned it, now had the shop next door to them, 'The Natural Bed Company'. I popped in for a chat. I asked Peter what led to the demise of 'Bring it all Back Home' in 1987. “Well we woke up one day and everybody was wearing black”, was his cryptic response. Peter had experienced both sides of the divide. He set up shop in Meadowhall in the early days, one of a number of local independent retailers to do so. It wasn't a success; he is now back in town, trying to be a part of “a critical mass of interesting local shops”. A fellow traveller in that endeavour was Stuart McAdie, owner of 'Fusion', retailer of all things surf punk and beyond in the shop right at the back of The Forum, the catalyst development that set in train the city council designating its environs as 'The Devonshire Green Quarter'.

These were tough times to be selling youth culture. However what Stuart and Peter had foreseen was the rise of Internet shopping. They both had a significant presence online and sold far more widely than just Sheffield as a result. Increasingly this was an important part of their business survival. A presence in the high street was diminishing in importance. A cartoon earlier in the month within The Sunday Observer Magazine summed it up. “November, go to the shops to see what to buy for Christmas, December, order off the Internet because it's cheaper, January, complain at the demise of high street shops”. Stuart thought that “bricks and mortar retail still mattered, if only to show people what they could buy”.

It wasn't entirely surprising but those tireless commercial data crunchers Experian had a division that studied shopping patterns on the Internet, 'Hitwise'. At the end of November they revealed;

> **"that more shoppers than ever are abandoning the high street for the Internet this Christmas, with many of the fastest growing retailers online familiar high street names."**

'Hitwise' measure the visits to online retail sites and then translates that into the assumption that it equates to sales. Maybe. Top of the Pops, so to speak, was Amazon with Play.com in 3rd but up there in the top five were those tried and tested 'high street' brands Argos, Tesco and Marks and Spencer. It is intriguing to consider whether Michael Marks, a Jewish refugee from Poland, who set up a stall in Leeds city markets in 1884 and who expanded down to Sheffield to become the centrepiece stall in the Norfolk Market Hall in 1897 would recognise the world of commerce today. M & S promised discounts of up to 90% in its post-Christmas sale and retailers were starting to fall like dominoes, Zavvi, the high street DVD and CD retailer on Christmas Eve. Nick Hood, a partner at insolvency specialists Begbies Traynor was reported as commenting;

> **"There will be hundreds of smaller retailers going bust and up to 15 national and regional chains, including one or two that will really make your eyes water....which will leave big holes in the high street."**

Such trends only compounded the concerns about the viability, or even possibility, of Sheffield city centre's all singing, all dancing 'New Retail Quarter', Sevenstone, ever being started. It was firmly on hold. The latest statement by leader of the council, Paul Scriven, about

Sevenstone appeared upbeat;

> **"The new retail development will make Sheffield a premier retail and leisure city. No-one is standing still waiting for the end of 2009 to come, Sevenstone is moving forward. Hammerson and the City Council are firmly committed to delivering this scheme to transform Sheffield's retail offer."**

I'd probably say exactly the same if I was in his shoes. However he probably has a bright young spark in his corporate planning unit who is tracking the viability of Hammerson as a developer. The Guardian on the 27th December reported that Hammerson currently had "16% of its equity on loan to hedge funds, all of them believed to be shorting its shares to profit from further falls in values". In this revelation the core of modern capitalism is exposed. Hammerson's share value had more than halved in value over the past year, the value of its property portfolio has plummeted. Speculative hedge funds sniffing a profit borrowed shares from Hammerson, for a fee, to sell them on in order to drive the share price down. Then they could buy them back for less, give them back to Hammerson and pocket a profit on the demise of the company. The bit I do not get is why, even for a fee, would Hammerson think that this was in their share holder's interest, many of them private pension plan investors? No doubt much of the profit such speculation generated would be off-shored out of the reach of the tax man. You can be sure, absolutely sure, that those who gain most from a recession are the rich. If you have got liquidity when prices are falling you can end up very asset rich in a desperate fire sale. The same Guardian article also observed that sovereign wealth funds and 'vulture funds' emanating from "China and the Middle East" were poised to enter the market at the bottom. Globalisation will be the name of the game in 2009 more so than ever, Britain's assets may be about to head 'east' in the revenge of the colonialised and patronised over a bloated, complacent ex-Imperial power. The development of Sevenstone brings sharply into focus the question of whether a new economy can really be sustained simply by consumer capitalism, especially if the vast majority of what we consume is produced abroad. Where is the wealth, how is the wealth going to be generated that will enable us to buy this stuff?

Sounds grim but will it result in Sevenstone not being built? Probably not, after all this is all a money merry-go-round and nothing is better at driving that than shopping centres. They are the fulcrum of consumer capitalism. But it will not be built yet and maybe nothing like is currently on the drawing board. We have entered unprecedented times and the dark clouds of recession that I reflected on whilst wandering the cranes of reconstruction on the 1st January threaten to become a deluge of depression. Predicting the future seems like a mugs game.

I do not doubt that Sheffield will still be a good place to live, relatively speaking, in fifty years time. Beyond that it's anybody's guess with a predicted average temperature rise of between 3C and 6C to adapt to. In that fifty years Sheffield has the opportunity to set out on a journey to re-invent urban living in the 21st century. It has a lot of advantages over many other urban areas. Beyond its initial spurt into the industrial revolution, built upon water-power and coal, Sheffield has exhibited no natural geographic advantages beyond its native wit for innovation and craft. As a city it has rarely shouted its wares wide and far. Survival will depend upon that wit and wisdom, not geography, and the ability of the city to project something desirable onto a global stage.

Our population will grow – believe me Britain will still be one of the most agreeable countries in the world to live in the future, its maritime temperate climate probably fending off the most extreme impacts of climate change – its population will be older, much older. Population density, especially urban population density will have to be higher if we wish to maintain any sense of rurality, and anyhow we may need every bit of agricultural land we've got in a few decades time as we try to feed another 3 billion mouths. We certainly will be more diverse, more global, but we will also be struggling to be heard in a global cacophony of economic assertion, from Bangalore to Bogota. If we are to be pre-eminent at anything, as Orwell asserted was the natural inclination of Sheffield folk, may I suggest that it should be radical change.

Nothing gave me more pleasure over Christmas than reading David Price's 2008 published "Sheffield Troublemakers: Rebels and Radicals in Sheffield History". It reminded me that beyond the ability to 'rise above it all' on the hills ringing the city, Sheffield also has been at forefront of just about every radical change in society that has been enacted over the past 200 years. The extension of the franchise, socialism, feminism, even anarchism. The rise of municipal welfarism, social housing and more recently a radical public transport policy that was torpedoed by Thatcherism. Sheffield's social heart was, and remains, conviviality, graft and craft. Communitarian, but a little socially conservative.

Now, more than ever, seemed to be the time to re-invigorate that tradition of radical thought that had brought us this far. Whatever radical might mean in the early 21st century. Was that a paternalistic state that could coercively save us from ourselves, if only the electorate could be persuaded to sign up for 'jam tomorrow rather than jam today'? Or perhaps it is a decentralised, local, voluntary liberty that would succeed by appealing to our better nature over and above our more craven nature? One of the consequences of the economic recession was going to be a great deal more politics, hopefully radical politics.

Does it all make me want to up sticks and leave? Most certainly not. Neither Britain nor Sheffield. Home is where your heart is, for better or worse. It is shaped and infused with the substance of the place in which you live. It is built upon its past but with a vision for the future. It is culture passed on, amended and added to as time edges by. The geography of a city is an expression of that culture over time.

The penultimate evening of the year we sign off 2008 as a family. An early pizza at 'B B's', Antonio and Jill's longstanding family Italian restaurant on Division Street – my kids absolute favourite place to eat - and then off through the sparkling light filled streets to 'pantoland' at the Lyceum Theatre; 'Aladdin'. Nothing quite sums up time and place within a traditional context quite as well as a good pantomime. Although the roots of pantomime are complex the form we think of as traditional is about 140 years old. You know, "song, dance, buffoonery, slapstick, cross-dressing, in-jokes, audience participation, and mild sexual innuendo". Well Aladdin ticked all those boxes and set itself in the present - the Emperor of China was credit-crunched- and in its place – references to all sorts of areas in the city including a suggestion that visitors from 'tha Wybourn' might marvel at electricity and carpets. Pinning the whole thing together was Bobby Knutt, that is "local legend Bobby Knutt" as the posters proclaimed, whose broad local accent may have required sub-titles if this version of Aladdin had been performed in America. The packed out crowd howled, heckled and laughed until tears ran down cheeks. It was sentimental, occasionally a touch lewd - after all the Genie was based upon 'Barry White', the 'sea-lion of lurve' - and lurched off script with shambolic ease.

'Home' Chapter 12: December

Life has a great ability 'to go off script'; the best laid plans and all that. That had really been my personal story of this tale of Sheffield in 2008. I started with a vague plan and then stumbled about off script from the moment Jack died. In that I'm sure that many of my ex-students might say this is not unlike one of my lectures.

The story of Sheffield over this year has been equally calamitous. The long boom and subsequent transformation of the city was grinding to a shuddering halt. Old certainties were being challenged. However this was the world over. Suddenly so many lifestyle bolt-holes didn't seem quite as secure as home. The Spanish housing market was crashing faster than Britain's. The entire EU was in recession. Even China was experiencing a reduction in its rate of growth, the U.S.A. was possibly about to discover that 'no I can't' might be more appropriate for Barack's bright new age. The confidence of my preface had drained away. A new age was upon us, a new story for the city was about to unfold. 2008 was history. With friends coming around in a few minutes to help celebrate the New Year there is no time for further reflection beyond Sheffield, what an extraordinary place to live an ordinary life, I hope it can remain so.

Now, a glass of wine I think.